Terry Philpot

C000041494

Beside
the Seaside

Brighton's places and its people

The famous and infamous associated
with Brighton – where they were born,
lived, educated, stayed or died

Beside the Seaside

Brighton's places and its people

Terry Philpot

Beside the Seaside: Brighton's places and its people

Terry Philpot

First published in Great Britain in 2015 by Step Beach Press Ltd Brighton

A CIP catalogue record for this title is available from the British Library.

ISBN 978-1-908779-43-4

Picture credits: © Terry Philpot, Gary Williams, John Lee

Typeset in Brighton, UK by Step Beach Press Ltd

Printed and bound by Spinnaker Print, Southampton

Step Beach Press Ltd, 28 Osborne Villas, Hove, East Sussex BN3 2RE
www.stepbeachpress.co.uk

To Richard Masterson, friend and proud Texan,
in thanks for all these years of lively correspondence,
discussion and kindnesses

The author

Terry Philpot is a writer and journalist, whose work has appeared in *The Guardian*, *The Times* and *The Independent*. He is a regular writer and reviewer for *The Tablet*. He has won several awards for journalism, including Editor of the Year. He is the author or editor of 18 books, from adoption to sex offending. His last book is *31 London Cemeteries to Visit Before You Die* (Step Beach Press, 2013). He is a trustee of three charities.

Contents

Foreword

Keith Waterhouse's famous alleged one liner about Brighton being a place that 'looks as though it is helping the police with their enquiries' always evokes a smile and in conversation invariably leads to stories of excess and revelry gone wrong. However, it does contain a gem of enlightenment. Reading the entries in this book you cannot help but be struck by the thought that people often move to Brighton for pleasure and in search of a good time.

Many risk takers have also sought to exploit its good name, but left their mark. Take Magnus Volk, who all but bankrupted himself inventing the electric railway and his splendid sea train the famous 'Daddy Longlegs'. But what a legacy he left us. So, too, David Mocatta, Rowland Hill and John Saxby who between them brought the railway to Brighton which began the transformation of our city and its fortunes in the first half of the 19th century.

But I also love a place that attracts the radicals like Prince Kropotkin and the reactionary like Prince Metternich, that can play host to future kings and queens like 'Prinny' and Victoria but have the tolerance and vision to welcome the Byngs and the Rattigans, the Constables and Sickerts of our world. Where else, other than Rottingdean, I wonder, could capture the interest of both Rudyard Kipling and Edward Burne-Jones as a backdrop to their creativity and inspiration?

Memorial plaques celebrating the life, times, achievements and contribution that people make have the potential to leave perhaps a skewed perception of a place. This book, with its 'warts and all' approach, avoids that pitfall because it is about more than plaques but many other buildings where its subjects were born, educated, lived, stayed or died. It celebrates its fair share of princes, the rich, famous and infamous, the murderers and and musicians but also tells us much about the people who have enriched its life, given something back and made it the attractive place it now is.

Our modern city, fashioned by visionaries like Herbert Carden and Lewis Cohen, celebrated by actors like Flora Robson, artists like Aubrey Beardsley and jesters like Max Miller brings to its people – from all walks of life – a stunning and rich history and legacy to tempt and entertain us. I predict this wonderful volume will strengthen interest in the special place that is our City by the Sea. I foresee walks around these sacred spots reaching far into the future as awareness of its diverse political, cultural and ethical history grows – *Beside the Seaside*. Enjoy, and beyond that enquire.

Lord Bassam of Brighton
Opposition Chief Whip, House of Lords

Acknowledgements

This book would most certainly not have been possible without the staff of the British Library, whom I have to thank once again. More locally, the staff of The Keep, the archives of East Sussex and Brighton and Hove (formerly at the Brighton History Centre, Brighton Museum and Art Gallery). Both were efficient and very helpful.

There are also a number of people who deserve individual mention:

Jill Armstrong, director of development, marketing and communication, Brighton and Hove High School, gave me an informative tour around the school, which, as The Temple, was once home to Thomas Kemp.

Stephen Baldwin threw light on the confusion over the location of John Wisden's birthplace, while Sr Bianca of the International Centre of Newman Friends at Littlemore, Oxfordshire, assisted with some clarifications about the cardinal. David Beevers, keeper of the Royal Pavilion, was kind enough to take me along the (now closed) tunnel that joins the palace with the Dome, as well as talking about various aspects of the building's history. Dr Anthony Biswell, director of the Anthony Burgess Foundation, supplied me with the hitherto elusive Hove address of Anthony Burgess, which had not been available to him at the time when he wrote *The Real Life of Anthony Burgess* (Picador, 2005). Sheila Bransfield kindly filled me in on the exact addresses of Edward Bransfield. She also alerted me to the fact that Fabian von Bellingshausen may not have beaten her ancestor to Antarctica.

Fr Robert Fayers, then of St Paul's Church, informed me of the fate of 'Belvedere', once home of the Rev Arthur Wagner (flats now stand on the site).

Mark Gillingham, archivist of the Past and Present Association of the Brighton Hove and Sussex Sixth Form College, assisted with information about EJ Marshall. Roy Greenslade gave me several leads about some of the former inhabitants of Arundel Terrace, while Rose Collis, local historian, told me that Ronald Searle lived there.

Mike Hill, author of *The Works of Graham Greene: A Readers' Bibliography and Guide* (Continuum, 2012), was very helpful in pointing to information which gave me specific locations of where Greene stayed in Brighton. He also put me in touch with the author's daughter, Caroline Bourget, who informed me about her father's stays at the Royal Albion to seek the 'tranquility', which she remembered from her teenage years. Another Greene scholar, Yan Christensen, secretary of the Graham Greene Birthplace Trust, was also extremely helpful in tracking down the author's Brighton movements. Robert Hill-Snook, gardens manager at the Royal Pavilion, explained the history of the gardens, when we met by chance.

Judith Hodson, archivist of Varndean School, supplied information about the history of the school, where Paul Scofield was a pupil, while alerting me to the fact that Evelyn Laye and Helena Normanton had also been educated there in its days as York Place School.

Dr Kalyan Kundu of the Tagore Centre, London, offered information about Rabindrath Tagore in Hove, including a translated extract from a letter by Tagore about how he had foreseen his new home.

Candida Lacey told me the exact date when her friend Kay Dick moved to Brighton and she was also very helpful in reading, with the expert eye of a publisher, that particular entry.

Dr Alex May, research editor of the *Dictionary of National Biography*, kindly traced the birthplaces of David Garnett and Chesney Allen (which allowed me to correct a much-repeated error that had claimed that Allen was actually born in Brighton), and gave me a specific address for AE Coppard. He also alerted me to the fact that Eddie Whaley lived in Brighton, supplied information about him and also told me that Jacqueline Nearne had been born in the town. Selma Montford, honorary secretary of the Brighton Society, supplied me with information about the buildings of Thomas Simpson, while her colleague Ninka Willcock, trustee of the society and a local and family historian, added to that information and generously read Simpson's entry.

Dr Derek Oakensen, collections curator of the Old Police Cells Museum, alerted me to the fact that Henry Solomon's appointment as chief officer of police is frequently wrongly given as 1838, but also that his office was not situated where the museum now is, which was, indeed, a former police station, but elsewhere in the basement of the Town Hall. However, he also gave me valuable information about policing at that time and, not least, told me about Solomon's successor, Thomas Hayter Chase, the entry for whom is based on Dr Oakensen's PhD thesis, extracts of which he generously sent me.

Robert Philpot drew my attention to Margaret Bondfield's connection with Hove, which, in turn, led me to learn about the remarkable Martindales, *mère et filles*.

Dave Sharp of the parish of St Nicholas & St Andrew, Portslade, offered Fr Enraght's exact address in Russell Square and also checked the entry for accuracy. Jackie Sullivan, archivist of Roedean School, clarified the various homes of the school until it moved, in 1898 and 1899, to its present site. Howard Spencer provided me with the otherwise elusive details of all Fred Perry's addresses in Rottingdean. I am grateful to the Henry Salt Archive for the addresses of where he lived in Brighton.

Heather Roberts, archives assistant at the Co-operative Archives, helped regarding details about George Jacob Holyoake.

Roger Watson, curator of the Fox Talbot Museum, Lacock, Wiltshire, offered information about William Fox Talbot's time in Rottingdean, while Valerie Whittle, former chairman of the Rottingdean Preservation Society, was very helpful regarding some points about former residents and properties in the village.

Geoffrey Whitfield kindly went back to Dora Bryan's home in Crescent Place to remind himself of the exact address in order to tell me. Arthur Wynn pinpointed the precise address in Brunswick Square of Lord Alfred Douglas's first home in Brighton.

I cannot let pass my great thanks to Paul Lantsbury and his staff at the elegant Kemp Town House. They were perfect hosts during my stays in Brighton. This was also the ideal place to stay for associated reasons: it has served as an hotel or lodging house, more or less without break, since 1864 (when founded as 'Mary Pearson's hotel & guesthouse'), and so staying there encourages a real sense of the spirit of the old, as well as the new Brighton, which I hope also animates this book.

Introduction

Is Brighton shaped by the people who have been born in the city or have chosen to live there or visit it, or is there something about its ambience that attracts an unusually large number of the famous and infamous – from comedians to revolutionaries, writers to social reformers, actors to inventors and politicians to painters? It is an impossible question to answer, but the city's fame (or notoriety, depending which aspect you focus upon) means that after London Brighton has more commemorative plaques and tablets on its buildings than any other British city or town. Thus it far outpaces the Roman city of York, the medieval seats of learning of Oxford and Cambridge, the old royal residence of Edinburgh, the great industrial cities of Manchester, Glasgow, and Birmingham, and the great ports of Bristol and Liverpool – all of which boast more than their fair share of literary, artistic, historical, political, manufacturing, scientific, musical and other associations. Thus, this book is about the buildings – houses, hotels, schools and other places associated with the famous and infamous, the obscure but interesting, the noteworthy and the discreditable.

However, if this book drew attention only to those associated with Brighton's formally commemorated buildings, it would tell only part of the story of the city's inhabitants. The plaques, however, do deserve attention.

Plaques and commemorative tablets in Brighton

Commemorative plaques – 'memorial tablets' – were first suggested in 1863 by William Ewart Gladstone, when Chancellor of the Exchequer, and in 1867 the (later Royal) Society of Arts erected the first one: a brown ceramic plaque on the birthplace of Lord Byron at Holles Street, London. The house was demolished in 1889 and a plaque was restored in 2012 by Westminster City Council on the site, which is now that of the John Lewis store. (The earliest surviving plaque is that for Napoleon III in King Street, St James's, also put up in 1867.)

Brighton has a variety of commemorative markers: ceramic blue plaques, ones of local design in a variety of stones, grey slate circular ones, and others with styles decided by those who have erected them. But the original commemorative tablets have a particular distinction. They were first commissioned by Brighton Borough Council in 1924 (and the first erected in 1925) from Eric Gill, sculptor and craftsman, a son of the town, who lived and worked in nearby Ditchling. Gill's tablets are particularly noteworthy due to the dolphins and coral sprigs that surmount them.

The town's commemorative plaques and tablets have been placed by a variety of organisations, including at least one group of residents, the local authority, the Regency Society, the British Music Hall Society, the British Film Institute and others.

The climate has, sadly, dealt roughly with some of them: the sea air and weather have obscured some of the Portland and Hoptonwood stone tablets. Others have been painted over by house owners. The slate roundel to Sir Edwin Landseer in Regency Square is so weathered as to be barely readable, as is that to Thomas Kemp on the wall of his former home, The Temple in Montpelier Road. The inscription on the tablet on the Duke of Fife's Fife House, Lewes Crescent, to commemorate both the Duke and the 6th Duke of Devonshire, has been had obliterated and what remains is painted over; Aubrey Beardsley's tablet in Buckingham Road (placed around the corner in West Hill Place) can be read but has also been painted over. Where I have discovered errors on plaques, I have pointed this out.

This is a book which it is intended will be read and enjoyed even by those not in a position to visit the places mentioned. But I do hope that it will enable many readers to seek out hidden places, as well as well-known ones, and learn more of the famous and infamous, as well as the obscure but interesting, throwing light on a variety of fascinating lives as well as the areas where the buildings are, or were, situated.

This is not a history of Brighton but maybe something of its history emerges through the lives of its most notable inhabitants and the buildings associated with them. In walking around – which is, surely, the only way to appreciate anywhere – I hope that the reader will learn, as I have, even more about the unique and beguiling place that is Brighton.

Terry Philpot
Surrey, January 2015

A note on entries and addresses

Choosing whom to include and exclude

I have concentrated on those who were born, lived or were educated in Brighton or who visited often, or stayed there for some appreciable time. However, it would be foolish to claim that my list is exhaustive. (I have excluded living people who have some association with the city.)

But that said, the local historian Antony Dale indicates the problem of whom to include and whom to leave out, when he writes: 'During the 60 years between 1820 and 1880, in fact, nearly every great literary and political figure of the day visited Brighton at least once and more often many times.' Dale's book *Fashionable Brighton*, being concerned with that period, thus takes no account of the decades before then or the years since. I am pleased, however, to have included the home of the writer of those words, who made such a significant contribution to the city.

The choice, then, has not been an easy one. I have not included the many people who were distinguished only by wealth or title or who held some minor government office. In the past, many titled and wealthy, but otherwise unremarkable, people came for the season and also just for a few days due to the comparative proximity to London. Neither have I included the many High Court judges, military personnel or other leading professionals, whose lives were not of sufficient interest for inclusion.

Due to lack of space I have also not included most MPs who have represented the constituencies that cover Brighton. Many are now forgotten and have left little mark. However, they have included Henry Fawcett, blind MP, minister under WE Gladstone and a defender of Darwin, as well as Julian Amery, a minister under Harold Macmillan but also a newspaper correspondent during the Spanish Civil War and war-time military service liaison officer to the Albanian Resistance Movement. However, I do make an exception for Sir Charles Thomas-Stanford, who bequeathed his home, Preston Manor, to the town.

There are well-known people whom I have omitted also because their stay was so brief that it cannot justify substantial association with Brighton. One, for example, is Sir Robert Peel, the future prime minister, who stayed at 24 Brunswick Terrace in August 1828 for a month. Benjamin Disraeli also visited. Another visitor was Lord Brougham, Peel's contemporary, who took 16 Brunswick Terrace for his wife for the season in 1833, when he was Lord Chancellor, and came himself for a few days at least twice during that time and was back the following year.

Lloyd George enjoyed the Brighton air and in the 1890s even suggested to his wife that they move to the town. But his visits were not as extensive or as well documented as those of his predecessor WE Gladstone. Henry James also came, staying at Lewes Crescent, while another writer, DH Lawrence, cycled a couple of times from Croydon and stayed at lodgings in Rottingdean. It is said that the singer Dusty Springfield used to visit her parents in Hove.

In more modern times, the Emperor Haile Selassie spent a small (but, as far as I can discover, save for a few photographs, undocumented) part of his exile during 1936 to 1941 living at Woodingdean House (now the site of Ovingdean Close). (Most of this time he spent in Bath and stayed a short period at a hotel in Worthing and in Wimbledon.)

However, one notable exception among those who made brief stays is the Earl of Cardigan, who led the Charge of the Light Brigade, and is included because of what happened during his short stay, and the consequences.

There are other kinds of brief stay. Alas, Sir Felix Booth, whose eponymous family gin distillery has contributed so much to Brighton's conviviality, died suddenly when staying at the Royal York Hotel in 1850. Another brief 'stay' was that of the occultist Aleister Crowley, who seems to have had no connection with Brighton but he was cremated in the town (though his ashes are now reported to be lost), having died in Hastings.

Another person with a tenuous, if very permanent, connection is Sir George Everest, surveyor-general of India, who gave his name to the world's highest mountain. He died at his home in London but is buried in the churchyard of St Andrew's Church, Hove, although seems to have had no connection with Brighton. The mystery is all the more intriguing because he is interred in the same grave as two of his children who died in early childhood. Also in the churchyard is Everest's sister, Lucetta Mary, and Thomas Wing, his father-in-law.

Thomas Hughes, author of *Tom Brown's School Days*, is buried in Woodvale Cemetery but only because he died at the Royal Crescent Hotel, 101, Marine Parade, en route to France in 1896. Another person using the town as a way of reaching France (but managing to leave alive) was William Wordsworth who, while here in 1791, called on Mrs Charlotte Smith, whose *Elegiac Sonnets* he admired. One hundred and forty years earlier a similarly fleeting (if more urgently impelled) presence was King Charles II, who escaped to France, via what was then the village of Shoreham, during the English Civil War.

There are others, too, where information is so sketchy as not to justify an entry. For example, Charles and Mary Lamb holidayed here in 1817 'in sight of the sea'. Again, Somerset Maugham came occasionally, but all I could glean from the words of his biographer, Selina Hastings, about his need to leave his busy London social life in order to write was: 'Sometimes he would run down to Brighton for a few days and put up at the Metropole . . .', as well as the fact that he would occasionally stay with his friend and fellow writer Edward Knoblock (who is included) at the latter's home in Clifton Terrace. (Maugham's nephew Robin, another resident and also a writer, left a sharper footprint to justify inclusion.)

If I could not locate exact addresses – that is, finding the number or name of a building, rather than just a street name – I have had to exclude the subject. For example, William Wilberforce, the parliamentarian and abolitionist, stayed in the town – and dined at the Royal Pavilion – but his letters give his address only as 'Brighton'.

Likewise, it would have been good to have included the once well-known actor Arthur Treacher who was born in Brighton, but whose birthplace I could not find. Other well-known people are said to have lived in the town but I could find no confirmation of this.

There is one important exception to these omissions through lack of this kind of definite information. I could not omit Tom Sayers, English bare knuckle champion boxer, who we know was born in Titchborne Street, but we do not know the exact address because the tenements were unnumbered. He is commemorated by a plaque in nearby 78–89 North Street.

The entries

Where possible, I have written about the subjects' lives in Brighton rather than other aspects of their life. Their time in the city may have coincided with the time when they were famous (for example, Sir Laurence Olivier, the actor), or they may have achieved fame much later in life (for example, Sir Edward Marshall Hall, the great lawyer), or may have lived in the town when their best days were past (for example, Lord Alfred Douglas, poet and lover of Oscar Wilde). Max Miller is a rarity in retaining a life-long connection.

Where there is insufficient information about the Brighton aspect of subjects' lives, I have written a short general biographical note.

Some entries contain other significant and specific local addresses (that is, a building, as opposed to a street, which can be identified), which are not shown at the top of the entry, but are given in bold type in the text. Burial places (but not those of cremation) are also identified in this way. Also in bold type are some other notable people who are not given an entry, as well as others who have been given one and whose names are followed by '(*qv*)'.

I have added 🅿 after the addresses with a plaque or commemorative marker.

Brighton, for the purposes of the book, of course, includes the area covered by the city council – thus, also Hove, Rottingdean and elsewhere – rather than only the historic limits of the town.

Addresses

I have done my best to verify the numbering and re-numbering of buildings and to note changes of use.

I have also attempted, as best I could, to ascertain whether buildings are still standing, and the vast majority, maybe remarkably, are. Available information is not always reliable, even using electronic sources, and there is no up-to-date listing of commemorative plaques.

There has been much building over the years and Regency buildings have given way to Victorian ones, and those, in their turn, to ones of more recent date. However, as in so many towns, one can often view the upper floors of the original buildings by looking above the plate glass windows and revolving doors. East Street, with its fashionable shops, is a good example of somewhere where much of the original remains one storey up. Even Western Road, replete with small shops, occasional outlets, charity shops, a few chain stores, banks and buildings societies, still has a remarkable number of frontages that Thackeray and Dickens would have seen.

All addresses are given as street names if in Brighton, and with place names after street names if they fall outside the generally assumed boundary of Brighton city limits.

The **entries**

Richard Addinsell (1904–1977)

COMPOSER

5 Chichester Terrace

Born in London, Addinsell gave up his legal studies when he became interested in music. He left the Royal Academy of Music after only two terms, without a qualification.

He wrote for the West End stage, but is noted most for his film music, including *A Tale of Two Cities*, *Blithe Spirit*, *Goodbye Mr Chips* and *The Prince and The Showgirl*. His best known composition is 'The Warsaw Concerto', written for the 1941 film, *Dangerous Moonlight*. It has been recorded more than 100 times and has sold more than 3,000,000 copies.

He came to this house in 1960 and lived here for many years with the courtier, **Victor Stiebel**, who died in 1976.

William Harrison Ainsworth (1805–1882)

NOVELIST

38 Brunswick Terrace, Hove
6 Brunswick Square, Hove
5 Arundel Terrace

Ainsworth, the author of 43 novels and now all but forgotten, had visited Brighton in 1827. In August 1845 he came to live at Brunswick Terrace and a year later at Brunswick Square. But by the time he came to settle in Arundel Terrace in 1853 his situation was not as it had been.

He had been an enormously successful novelist, who was particularly known for writing 'criminal romances', novels about well-known criminals (in *Rookwood* he invented the fictional journey of Dick Turpin's ride from London to York). But his eponymous novel about Jack Sheppard was much criticised for glorifying criminals (a criticism also made of other so-called 'Newgate novels' by other authors) and this seems to have shaken him because he gave up that genre for less fashionable historical romances.

Ainsworth had dashing good looks – 'witty, elegant and tastefully dandyish', writes Simon Callow. At his London home he entertained, among others, **William Makepeace Thackeray** (*qv*) (although a 'Newgate' critic) and **Charles Dickens** (*qv*). Ainsworth introduced Dickens to John Forster, his future biographer, George Cruikshank, his first illustrator, and John Macrone, his first publisher. But the friendship between the two novelists waned in later years, as did Ainsworth's popularity.

By the time he moved to Brighton, he was becoming more and more reclusive. However, through the Brighton years he owned and edited *Bentley's Miscellany* (from 1845 to 1870), which he had bought for £17,000. (At an earlier date, he had taken over the editorship from Dickens.) Nor did his situation stop him writing: *Star Chamber, The Flitch of Bacon, Spendthrift, The Life and Adventures of Mervyn Clitheroe*, and *Ovingdean Grange, a Tale of the South Downs* were among the 12 novels written in Arundel Terrace.

But he was continuing to write for less money and he left his prestigious publisher, Chapman and Hall, when they offered less generous terms, for a less well-known one, and while with them his sales declined steadily.

He married his second wife, Sarah Wells, in 1866 (he had separated from his first wife, with whom he had three children, in 1835) and the next year, when their daughter was born, they moved to Tunbridge Wells, and then to Reigate, where he died.

Elizabeth Allan (1910–1990)

ACTOR
7 Arundel Terrace
Courtenay Tye, Courtenay Terrace, Hove

Born in Skegness, Allan began as an MGM starlet and appeared in many films including *A Tale of Two Cities, David Copperfield*, and *The Heart of the Matter*. She was also a panel member on television's *What's My Line?* and had her own TV series in 1954, *The Adventures of Annabel*.

ELIZABETH
ALLAN
1910–1990
film and stage star
lived here

She lived in Brighton with her husband **William (Wilfred) O'Bryen**, to whom she was married for 37 years. He was a theatrical agent, representing Allan, and later a senior film executive.

Chesney Allen (1893–1982)

COMEDIAN
21 Park Crescent Place

Most reference works incorrectly say that Allen was born in Brighton – in fact, he was born in Battersea – but he did live at this address as a child. He started off as a solicitor's clerk but made his debut theatrical appearance at 18, beginning in straight acting and later turning to music hall comedy. He served on the Western Front in the First World War and met his future stage partner, Bud Flanagan, for the first time in Flanders. The highly successful and long-lasting partnership of Flanagan and Allen began in 1926, and led to films, television and recordings. They were also members of the Crazy Gang. The duo, known for their gentle cross-talk humour and sentimental songs like 'Underneath the arches', 'We're going to hang out our washing on the Siegfried Line', 'Umbrella man' and 'Run, rabbit, run', ceased in 1945 when Allen retired through ill health. He made occasional stage appearances with the Gang thereafter, but acted mainly as their agent and business manager.

Henry Allingham (1896–2009)

LONGEST-LIVED VETERAN OF THE FIRST WORLD WAR
AND BRITAIN'S OLDEST MAN EVER

St Dunstan's Centre, Greenways, Ovingdean

Henry Allingham had moved from his home town of Eastbourne in 2006, a month before his 110th birthday, to live at St Dunstan's, where he died aged 113 years and 42 days. In those three years he remained active – he published a book of memoirs, *Kitchener's Last Volunteer*, made more than 60 public appearances in Britain and abroad between his 110th and 111th birthdays, and was made an honorary freeman of the city of Brighton and Hove in 2009.

Born in London, Allingham died the oldest verified man in the world, the oldest British man of all time, the oldest ever surviving member of the British Armed Forces and oldest survivor of the First World War. He was also the last survivor of the Battle of Jutland and the last surviving member of both the Royal Air Force and the Royal Naval Air Service (with which he served on the Western Front).

Hundreds lined the route and gathered outside the church for his funeral, with full military honours, on 30 July 2009 at St Nicholas' Church, Church Street. His coffin was carried by three RAF airmen and three Royal Navy seamen. The Queen was represented by the Duchess of Gloucester, and a vice-admiral and air vice-marshal were in attendance. There was a fly past of five replica First World War aircraft, while British and French buglers played *The Last Post* and *Reveille*. A bell was tolled 113 times. Allingham was cremated at Woodvale Crematorium.

William Waldorf Astor, later lst Viscount Astor (1848–1919)

NEWSPAPER PROPRIETOR AND PROPERTY OWNER

Western House, 155 Kings Road (now site of Embassy Court)

Born in New York City, Astor, who was the owner of Hever Castle, Kent, the Gothic Mansion, 2 Temple Place, London, and at one time also of Cliveden House, Buckinghamshire, died at this address on 18 October 1919.

Early in life he served in the New York state senate as a Republican and was also a US minister to Italy. He built the Waldorf Hotel in New York, which later became the Waldorf Astoria Hotel, and built the Waldorf Hotel in London. When his financier father died in 1890 he left Astor a legacy said to be $100,000,000. That year Astor took his family to London: his wife Mary (Mamie) Dahlgren, their two surviving sons (Waldorf Astor, later second Viscount Astor, and John Jacob Astor, later Baron Astor of Hever), and a daughter. In 1899 Astor became a naturalised British citizen.

His early ventures into newspaper ownership in the UK led him to buy the *Observer* in 1911.

The *Oxford Dictionary of National Biography* states: 'Astor was a shy, austere and, by all accounts, unlovable man. He despised his native country and said so in print.'

Augusta Sophia (1768–1840)

DAUGHTER OF GEORGE III

North Gate House, Church Street

The princess was the sixth child and second daughter of George III and his wife Queen Charlotte. The queen was distant but the king was emotionally attached to his daughters. Augusta Sophia never married, despite pleading with her brother, the Prince Regent, later **George IV** (*qv*), to waive the Royal Marriage Act to permit her to marry, albeit secretly, an English officer named Sir Brent Spencer with whom she had been in love for years. He never did.

Her other brother **William IV** (*qv*) gave her this rather ugly, three-storey house in 1830. Two years later it was refaced with oriental windows and decorations to match the style of the new North Gate, to which it now stands adjacent.

It is the last house of what was once a terrace of nine, known as Marlborough Row. They were erected in about 1774. Numbers 1–4 were demolished in 1820 and numbers 5–7 in 1821, while number 9 was a small blacksmith's shop whose owner refused to sell out. When the land was needed for the widening of Church Street it was compulsorily purchased.

Augusta Sophia would always come with the court to Brighton during each of William's years on the throne, when he and **Queen Adelaide** would stay.

Hermione Baddeley (1906–1986)

ACTOR

5 Arundel Terrace

This apartment was a holiday home for the character actor from 1958 to 1961. While known for her roles in *Passport to Pimlico, Belles of St Trinians, David Copperfield* and the two minutes, 20 seconds Oscar-nominated role in *Room at the Top*, she will always be associated with the role of the blowsy Ida in the film of *Brighton Rock*.

Enid Bagnold (1889–1981)

NOVELIST AND PLAYWRIGHT

North End House (now Aubrey House), The Green, Rottingdean Ⓟ

Enid Bagnold, author of *National Velvet* and *The Chalk Garden*, wrote of Rottingdean: 'Here we keep what we've got, to defend, to consolidate, to put one's tongue out at Brighton.' And she did – for 53 years.

She and her husband, **Sir Roderick Jones** (1878–1962), principal proprietor of Reuters news agency, were introduced to North End House by **Sir George Lewis**, a prominent lawyer, who lived with his wife in **The Grange** (now the local museum and art gallery) across The Green. Jones bought the house in1923 for £3,000 and added a new wing. The house had once belonged to the painter **Sir Edward Burne-Jones** (*qv*) and later another painter **Sir William Nicholson** (*qv*), who designed the entrance hall with orange and black squared linoleum.

Within months of the purchase Jones bought a seaside boarding house called Gothic House, which was physically attached to the house and made this a part of the new property. The room at the top of the spiral staircase of what had been Gothic House was given over as his wife's Tower Room, where she could write. (In recent years the house has been returned to its original state of three separate properties.) The couple maintained houses in London during their years here: at 24 Berkeley Square, 113 Eaton Square and 96 Cheyne Walk. They owned a Rolls Royce, a Dodge and a Buick.

Bagnold loved bathing in the sea and often walked down Rottingdean High Street in her costume, even when heavily pregnant (the couple had four children). The house's garden is said to have inspired *The Chalk Garden* and the family in *National Velvet* is said to be based on the family of the local butcher, the Hilders. Velvet and her sisters are modelled on the Hilder children and the horse-riding daughters of General Asquith who rented **The Elms**, once home of **Rudyard Kipling** (*qv*), each summer. But the Hilders were not best pleased, claiming that they were caricatured. In particular, Mrs Hilder was incensed to find herself portrayed as Mrs Brown, a bossy, overweight matron.

National Velvet was illustrated by Bagnold's daughter Laurian. Bagnold was paid $40,000 in 1935 by Paramount Pictures for the film rights and in 1944 the film made Elizabeth Taylor a star.

Anne Sebba, Bagnold's biographer, writes: 'North End House was a strange, cluttered place, with none of the grandeur of a "country house", but an undeniable atmosphere. The artefacts collected were not merely *from* her past, they *were* her past.'

There were large weekend parties, with guests such as the diarist and Conservative politician Chips Channon, the society hostess **Lady Diana Cooper** and the actor Charles Laughton. Bagnold, though, hated the preparations and would often buy 36 Sunday newspapers so that guests might occupy themselves for longer in silence in the mornings.

Dale Cottage, which the Joneses also owned next to North End House, was lent to **Cecil Beaton** and his mother during the Second World War for what Bagnold called some of 'Dr Rottingdean's ozone cure'. In war time the Joneses made The Elms, which they also owned, available for use as a hospital. In her widowhood Bagnold gave it to her daughter, Laurian. During the War, Bagnold also became a smallholder, using a three and a half acre area behind North End House, where she kept a miscellaneous collection of animals. She badgered both the town clerk of Brighton and Air Marshal Lord Trenchard, who by then held no official position, about what she perceived as her village's vulnerability to invasion. However, as late as 1938 she had been extolling 'Hitler's new type of democracy' in *The Sunday Times*.

The Joneses never fully integrated into village life and she was wary of the 'half-acid, half-affectionate nature of the village gossip'. However, in much later life she became patron of local societies such as those for preservation and drama. But in widowhood – Sir Roderick died in 1962 – although she was plagued by loneliness she failed to elicit the sympathy of her neighbours who thought that she and Jones had been stand-offish.

In 1972 Bagnold objected to the plans to build an extension of two lavatories and two changing rooms for the 11th century St Margaret's Church, which stood across The Green from North End House. 'It's the lack of respect for the past, for antiquity that I mind', she wrote to the vicar. 'Fifty years you've been here', Canon Ivor Walters replied, 'and you've never given a penny to the church'.

She moved to a flat in London in 1980, the house being too large for an elderly woman and her nurse. It was also in a bad state of repair and too far for friends to visit, and she had none locally. A two-day auction of her belongings raised £72,321.

Maurice Baring (1874–1945)

NOVELIST AND POET

Half Way House, Steyning Road, Rottingdean (now site of Highbury House care home)

Maurice Baring, as his friend **Lady Diana Cooper** said, 'felt himself a Croesus' when the death in 1929 of his brother, John, Lord Revelstoke, head of the eponymous family banking firm, freed him of some of his financial worries. He bought this house in 1928 and also rented, for a nominal sum from another brother, Cecil, a house in London's Cheyne Row.

Both houses reflected the styles of his past: olive branches on William Morris wallpaper; waters colours of France and Italy; and photographs of Sarah Bernhardt, famous beauties, and others he had known in his journeys in Russia, Denmark and France. There were stacks of books, theatrical programmes, letters, menus and sketches everywhere, along with white and blue bowls of potpourri. In the garden there were pinks and pansies. Lady Diana privately thought it 'awful'.

Above the main room was his private chapel – Baring was a renowned Catholic convert – with Stations of the Cross executed by his niece Daphne. While a French critic found that the house had 'un raffinement d'un autre âge, et ce luxe discret que les anglais confort', Baring's own room was sparse – there was no more than a wooden table and a camp bed – and cold.

A near neighbour **Enid Bagnold** (*qv*) found him 'so alarmingly shy that he made me tongue-tied' when they had dinner together. And while she said 'I couldn't do it again; I didn't', she did because she would see him almost every night for years. However, although he never married, one biographer refers to 'a succession of aesthetically lovely young women with whom Maurice populated his life and, later, his house at Rottingdean'.

While Baring wrote more than 60 books, including poems, essays, historical non-fiction and novels, only two date from the Rottingdean years. For all the new friendships locally and the visits of older friends, like the composer and suffragette **Ethel Smyth**, and the writer **GK Chesterton**, much of this time was overshadowed by Parkinson's disease. By the outbreak of war Baring was bedridden, 'enduring', as Lady Diana Cooper, who affectionately nicknamed him Mumble, observed on her weekly visits, 'with saintly fortitude a long and merciless overthrow'. His constant companion was Dempsey, a bright blue budgerigar, which sat on his head and shoulder. But, on at least one occasion when he and Lady Diana met both 'felt so gay, sipping sherry and nibbling chocolates and arguing about the Pope', she wrote.

The noise of air raid warnings became more than Baring could endure and he left for an island in the Highlands of Scotland, thinking the move temporary, but he died there in 1945, having suffered constant pain. His Rottingdean house was destroyed by enemy action.

Dame Henrietta Barnett (1851–1936)

SOCIAL REFORMER
45 Wish Road, Hove

Dame Henrietta and her husband, **Canon Samuel Barnett**, were active in the East End of London where they were responsible for the creation of Toynbee Hall, the Whitechapel Art Gallery and the Children's Holiday Fund. She also conceived the idea of Hampstead Garden Suburb and helped protect Hampstead Heath from development.

The Hove house was a holiday home and Barnett once said that her heart was uplifted every time she came to the coast by train and saw the Downs approaching. She spent her last years here, and she and her husband are buried in the churchyard of **St Helen's Church**, Hangleton Way, Hove.

Ada Ellen Bayly (1857–1903)

NOVELIST (WRITING AS EDNA LYALL)
5 Montpelier Villas

Bayly was born in this house on 25 March, 1857, the youngest of four children of a barrister. At an early age, she lost both her parents and she spent her youth with an uncle in Surrey and then attended boarding schools in Brighton.

She never married and spent much of her life living with her two married sisters and brother, a clergyman in Herefordshire. She published her first (unsuccessful) novel in 1879, but went on to write another 18 novels. *The Golden Days* is said to have been the last book to have been read by the critic John Ruskin. She died in Eastbourne.

Aubrey Beardsley (1872–1898)

ARTIST AND ILLUSTRATOR
31 (then 12) Buckingham Road **(around the corner in West Hill Place)**
21 Lower Rock Gardens

One of the leaders of the Aesthetic movement and associate of Oscar Wilde and James McNeill Whistler, Beardsley was born in the top front room of this corner house, on 21 August 1872. This was his maternal grandparents' home, where his mother, Ellen, his father Vincent, and one-year-old sister Mabel, later to become a well-known actor and friend of WB Yeats, were forced to live due to their impecunious position. (His father, listed as 'a gentleman', had inherited a fortune, which he lost.) The house was substantial, then ivy-covered and rather drab, under the strict supervision of Ellen's father, the retired Surgeon-General William Pitt, scion of a respectable local family. Other residents were Ellen's mother, Susan, and two unmarried sisters, Mary and Florence, along with a maid-of-all-work. The Pitts had opposed the marriage – Vincent was a man with no money and no trade – and there was considerable tension between the parties.

It was, though, a comfortable home and Ellen was a talented creator of silhouettes, a pianist and a noted local beauty, known, due to her slender figure, as 'the bottomless Pitt'.

Beardsley's juvenile art does not include Brighton subjects but he knew the town well, and liked the Chain Pier on which he would walk when he had lines to learn at school. His biographer Matthew Sturgis writes: 'The eccentricity of the piers, the elegance of the Regency terraces, the rococo excesses of the Pavilion, the tawdry glamour of the sea-front: all these came to play a part in his art...'

In 1874 Vincent found work in London and moved his family there. In 1879 Beardsley was sent to board at a prep school at Hurstpierpoint, Sussex, but came back home in 1880. When his father lost his job in 1884 and Ellen was ill, the children were despatched to live with their wealthy 70-year-old eccentric great aunt, Sarah Pitt, in Lower Rock Gardens. Here they suffered, according to another biographer, Stanley Weintraub, 'hardly more than custodial care, and [a life which] sometimes resembled something out of the more grotesque pages in Dickens'. They were awakened at daybreak and went to bed in darkness. There were no toys and one book. Their great outing was to church – Miss Pitt's main interest – which was a mile-long uphill hike to the Church of the Annunciation in Washington Street.

However, there was respite: in November Beardsley became a day boy at Brighton Grammar School and in January became a boarder. At first miserable, his years here became some of his happiest of his life. He was indifferent to lessons but was a good performer, a voracious reader, and a keen artist. He and his best friend at school, **Charles (CB) Cochran** (*qv*), would go to the Royal Pavilion for play and pantomime matinees and, on one occasion, appeared in a play by Beardsley. In 1888 Beardsley left school – and Brighton – to become a temporary office clerk in London.

In the summer of 1891 he took two weeks' holiday in Brighton from the office, staying with his great aunt. He and his old school friend and fellow artist, **GF Scotson-Clark**, who was living and working nearby, drew, sketched, and painted. They 'built castles in the air', they said, one of which was to open a shop in London's Bond Street to sell original black-and-white drawings and 'little Impressionist landscapes'. They would sit in the house's drawing room 'occasionally taking a draught from a flagon of Australian Burgundy *à la* Balzac'.

Arnold Bennett (1867–1931)

NOVELIST

Royal York Hotel (now a Youth Hostel), Old Steine

Bennett's association with Brighton is best known for the fact that he partly located *Hilda Lessways* in the town. However, while he started the novel on 6 January 1911 and finished the 100,000 words on 14 June the same year, he wrote none of it in Brighton.

That honour falls to his earlier and superior novel, *Clayhanger*, of which

he wrote all the first part and much of the second part in January to March 1910 when he and his first wife, Marguerite, were staying at the Royal York Hotel (called 'The Royal Sussex' in the book). This stay was the first time that Bennett, to his pride, was recognised by a hotel manager. When he gave Bennett his card, the manager exclaimed: 'My God! Is it you?' The same day his diary records: 'Our first stroll along the front impressed me very favourably, yesterday afternoon. But I am obsessed by the thought that all this comfort, luxury, ostentation, snobbishness and correctness, is founded on a vast injustice to the artisan class. I can never get away from this. The furs, autos, fine food, attendants and diamond rings in this hotel only impress it on me more.'

Brighton was 'full of wealthy imperative persons dashing about in furs and cars'. It was election time and, he wrote, 'I could spit in the face of the arrogant and unmerciful Brighton, sporting its damned Tory colours'. He saw the town as a 'symbol of a system that is built on the grinding of the faces of the poor'. He noted in his diary that 'in various ways Brighton seems to be what London was. Its architecture is old Belgravia and Tyburnian [sic]'. He visited the pier, the Aquarium and Black Rock, rolled around laughing in the seats at the Hippodrome, walked to Hove, met a friend, sketched, saw plays, attended concerts and read.

Edna Best (1900–1974)

ACTOR

Redcliff, Pembroke Crescent, Hove
2 St Albyns (now Kingsway Hotel), Hove

Best, daughter of a well-off stockbroker, lived at these addresses as a child. Her first professional stage appearance was when she was 17, and she entered films in 1921. She was also the ladies' swimming champion of Sussex.

Her films included the original version of Alfred Hitchcock's *The Man Who Knew Too Much*, *Intermezzo: A Love Story*, and *Swiss Family Robinson*. She also appeared on television, and in 1957 she received an Emmy Award for her part in Noel Coward's *This Happy Breed*. She was inducted into the Hollywood Walk of Fame.

Robert Bevan (1865–1925)

ARTIST

17 Brunswick Square, Hove 🅿

This was the house of Bevan's grandfather, Edward Polhill, 'gentleman, landowner and mortgagee', who served on the commission that owned and governed the Brunswick Estate. Bevan's parents, Laura and Richard Bevan – he was a banker, but not with the family bank, which became Barclays, and a governor of Brighton College – were soon to move to Cuckfield, Sussex, and were living temporarily in Brunswick Square.

Unlike two of his brothers, Bevan did not go into banking. Instead, he studied art in London and Paris where he was influenced by the Post-Impressionists. He was friendly with Renoir and Gauguin. He became a founder-member of the Camden Town Group of artists. His works now hang in Tate Britain, the National Portrait Gallery, Brighton Museum and Art Gallery, the Ashmolean, and other public collections in the UK and abroad.

Alma Lillian Birk, later Baroness Birk (1917–1996)

POLITICIAN AND JOURNALIST
10 Belgrave Place

Alma Wilson was born at this address on 22 September 1917, the daughter of Barnett Wilson (formerly Woolfson) of Stamford Hill, London, and his wife, Alice. Her father ran a successful greeting card company, and hers was a comfortable upbringing, attending South Hampstead High School, London and the London School of Economics.

A woman of great energy and matching ambition, she and her husband, Ellis Birk, were committed to the Labour Party and, as well as involvement through her life in various charities, she unsuccessfully stood for Parliament three times.

She was also a journalist working for, among other publications, the *Daily Herald*, and associate editor of *Nova*, which heralded a new kind of women's journalism.

Created a life peer in 1967, in 1974 Birk was made a government whip, and later that year Parliamentary Under-Secretary of State at the Department of the Environment. Shortly before the general election of 1979 she became Minister of State in the Privy Council office. During the years of Labour's opposition she held various shadow posts.

Hector Bolitho (1897–1974)

WRITER
1 St Nicholas Road

Bolitho, the author of more than 50 works, from biographies to novels and travel books to radio plays and short stories, some published to international acclaim, concealed his homosexuality in his homophobic native New Zealand. He finally left for Australia shaken by a sex scandal, and arrived in England in 1923, a practised journalist and published author. After a short stay working in South Africa, he returned to England in 1925.

In 1949, the year that saw the last of his four lecture tours of the USA, he met Derek Peel, a former army officer, with whom he collaborated in writing *Without the City Wall* (1952). They moved in together and came to the address above in 1956.

While living here Bolitho continued to write – eight books, including an autobiography, a revised edition of his much-praised *Albert, Prince Consort*, along with an edited volume, appeared in these years.

Aged 65, he became chairman of a panel of teenagers in a television series, *The Young Elizabethans*, but television was not his medium. He also raised large sums for polio research as chairman of the Committee for Writing and Reading Aids for the Paralysed. When in the privacy of his home he liked nothing better than to play 'Home Sweet Home' on the piano with his nose.

He suffered the first of several strokes in 1965 and his last book, *The Drummonds of Charing Cross* (1967), was completed in collaboration with Peel. The onset of arteriosclerosis caused Bolitho's health to decline rapidly, so that Peel wrote all the articles and book reviews that appeared under Bolitho's name.

Bolitho died at **Lee House Nursing Home**, 61 Dyke Road on 12 September 1974, and was cremated at Downs Crematorium, at a private service with only Peel and their housekeeper in attendance. After his partner's death, Peel became an alcoholic and was found dead on 28 April 1979.

Margaret Bondfield (1873–1953)

FIRST WOMAN CABINET MINISTER
14 Church Road, Hove

Born in Chard, Somerset, Bondfield first came to Brighton when she was eight to stay with her widowed sister. When she was 14 she was visiting relatives in Brighton and was offered a job in Mrs White's ladies' outfitters, then at this address. Here she was befriended by one of the customers, **Louisa Martindale** (*qv*), who took her under her wing, helped to educate her and lent her books, and generally contributed much to her young friend's political development.

When Bondfield left Mrs White's she became an improver – doing window dressing and stock taking – for W Hetherington's in Western Road for two and a half years. There she would 'live in', which meant ill-ventilated, sparsely furnished accommodation in a dormitory (possessions were kept in boxes under residents' beds) that had communal washing facilities and was cold in winter.

While in the town she was a member of the Clifton Road Congregational Church, where she sang in the choir.

In 1894, having saved £5, Bondfield moved to London where she became involved in trades unionism. In 1923 she became chairman of the Trades Union Congress (she had been the first woman elected to its executive). That same year, at the third attempt, she was elected MP for Northampton, one of the first three women Labour MPs to be elected. The next year she both became the first woman minister (Parliamentary Secretary to the Ministry of Labour) and lost her seat. She returned to the Commons at a by-election for Wallsend in 1926. In 1929 she was made Minister of Labour in the second Labour government, the first woman to achieve Cabinet rank. However, her political reputation collapsed with her support for a cut in benefit rates and for Ramsay MacDonald's formation and leadership of the National Government, but which she did not join. Defeated in 1931, she never again sat in the Commons.

Sara Forbes Bonetta (c 1843–1880)

WEST AFRICAN PRINCESS
17 Clifton Hill

Orphaned in an inter-tribal war in West Africa, Sara was rescued by Captain Frederick E Forbes from being made a human sacrifice. He gave her a Western name and convinced King Ghezo of Dahomey to make a present of her to **Queen Victoria** (*qv*). Impressed by her exceptional intelligence, the queen took her under her wing and gave her an allowance, and she studied literature, art and music, and spent time at Windsor Castle.

At the age of eight she was sent to school in Sierra Leone and returned to England at the age of 20 and married Captain James Pinson Labulo Davies, a Yoruban businessman. She prepared for the event by being sent to live with a Mr and Mrs Welsh in Clifton Hill. But she was unhappy there: she knew no one, and she referred to the house as 'a desolate little pig sty'. However, the wedding, at St Nicholas' Church, Church Street, in August 1862, befitted the status of the bride and groom: the wedding party arrived in ten carriages drawn by pairs of greys, accompanied by bridesmaids. The breakfast was held at **West Hill Lodge**, Montpelier Road, before the couple left for London en route for Sierra Leone. Their daughter was christened Victoria and the queen took an interest in her welfare.

The family moved to Nigeria, where Sara was baptised and had two more children in Lagos. She was 37 when she died of tuberculosis.

When Sara died, the queen wrote in her diary: 'Saw poor Victoria Davies, my black godchild, who learnt this morning of the death of her dear mother'.

Dion Boucicault (1820–1890)

DRAMATIST AND ACTOR-MANAGER
6 Cavendish Place Ⓟ

Before he was 20, the Irish-born Boucicault, hiding his acting career from his family by adopting the pseudonym Lee Moreton, cajoled provincial managers in Brighton, Bristol, and Hull into staging his early work, which led to his first major triumph, *The London Assurance*. In 1862 he came to live at Cavendish Place until, in 1867, he was forced to sell his London mansion and offer manuscripts of his most successful plays to his creditors, after being declared bankrupt. A wheeler-dealer who never took things lying down, within six weeks he had successfully applied for his bankruptcy to be discharged. Within a year he was again London's most well paid and successful playwright, buying a house in the capital's Regent Street.

Slight and bald, with a domed forehead, he seems to have been irresistible to women. (He was 65 when he married Louise Thorndyke, his 21-year-old third wife in 1885, whom he had first married bigamously, a charge he countered by denying the legality of his second marriage.)

In 1867 he appears to have purchased another house in Brighton and it may be that much of the time his second wife Agnes, an actor, and their six children lived here while he pursued a London life that comprised prolific writing, touring, litigation, money making schemes (he was so down on his luck at the end of his life that he advertised cigars) and adultery.

Constant work produced a nervous breakdown during the time he was in Brighton. He gave up the house in Brighton and in September 1873 he and Agnes left for America (the children remained at school), became US citizens and divorced there. He continued to write and toured from coast to coast.

Mary Elizabeth Braddon 1835–1915

AUTHOR AND ACTOR
26 and 34 New Road (26 is now Mrs Fitzherbert's pub)

Toward the end of 1859, a year before Braddon left these lodgings, where she had lived since 1857 when acting (often at the Theatre Royal), she began working on short stories and a collection of poems, *Garibaldi and other Poems*. These were published in 1861 and the following year she wrote her most famous novel *Lady Audley's Secret*, which helped to create the genre of the 'sensation' novel. She was helped in this by an admirer, John Gilby, who gave her enough money to take a six month break from acting, which she had pursued from an early age to lift her mother and brothers from the genteel poverty into which they had plunged after the breakup of the parents' marriage. (Her older brother Edward left for India when she was ten and eventually became Premier of Tasmania.)

Braddon met John Maxwell on the seafront at Brighton in 1860 and that year he began publishing her 'penny dreadful' short stories in his periodicals. That year, too, her first novel, *Three Times Dead*, appeared. She and Maxwell began living together the next year (and took her mother with her) and by 1864 they had two children. However, Maxwell was married with five children, with a wife in an asylum in Ireland. When she died, the couple married in 1874 and had six more children, including the novelist William Babington Maxwell. Braddon returned occasionally to Brighton: for example, she spent a week there in November 1880, going to the theatres and seeing old friends.

After the success of *Lady Audley's Secret*, which has been in print ever since and has been filmed and dramatised, and which made her name and fortune, Braddon went on to write more than 80 novels.

Edward Bransfield (c. 1785–1852)

ANTARCTIC EXPLORER
11 Clifton Street
61 London Road (now The World's End pub)

The man who may have been the first person to sight Antarctica and was certainly the first to partially chart it, spent the last decade of his life in Brighton.

Edward Bransfield was born in Ireland, and after being press-ganged into the Navy at 18 he rose through the ranks from ordinary seaman. When in Valparaiso, Chile, he was commanded to take charge of a hired, two-mast brig, the *Williams*, to chart the recently discovered South Shetland Islands, near the North Antarctic Peninsula, where he arrived in January 1820. He landed on the previously unknown King George Island, of which he took possession for the Crown. His journey then took him past Deception Island, and he discovered and charted Tower Island and Ohlin Island. Crossing what is now Bransfield Strait, on 30 January 1820 Bransfield sighted and charted Trinity Peninsula, the northernmost point of the Antarctic mainland, noting 'high mountains, covered with snow' (later Mounts Bransfield and Jacquinot). It is claimed that Fabian von Bellingshausen, a German-Russian explorer, had sighted Antarctica three days previously. However, it may be that Bellingshausen did not realise what he was looking at as he records only icebergs and not a land mass.

On his return, Bransfield spent several years as master on merchant ships and by 1841 he and his wife, Anne, were living in Bognor. They later moved to the Clifton Street address and by 1851 had moved to London Road. He died on 31 October 1852 and his wife survived him by a decade. They are buried in the same grave in the **Extra-Mural Cemetery**.

Frederick Hervey, 1st Marquess of Bristol and 5th Earl of Bristol (1768–1859)

POLITICIAN, LANDOWNER AND PHILANTHROPIST

19–20 Sussex Square

From 1801 to 1804 the then Lord Hervey, later Earl of Bristol, served as Under-Secretary for Foreign Affairs in the government of Lord Addington. Created the first marquess in 1826, he lived here, at Sussex Square, between 1831 and 1859.

A local landowner, he was generous in his benefactions. In 1836 he gave nine acres for the opening of St Mary's Hall School, Eastern Road, as a boarding school for 100 daughters of clergymen. He also gave other land and buildings, part of which went for the infants' school. At the time of its creation in 1838, the marquess had thought that St Mark's Church, Church Place, Kemp Town, which he also paid for, could serve as a chapel to St Mary's Hall School. The argument about this delayed its consecration until 1849, when it became Kemp Town's parish church. (It was later to serve as the school's chapel after being declared redundant in 1986.)

In 1856 Bristol donated 20 acres to create the Lewes Road Parochial Cemetery. Now the **Woodvale Cemetery**, it is where he is buried. In1859, he gave eight acres of land, known as the Bristol Ground, to augment the **Extra-Mural Cemetery**, which had been opened in 1851 and was becoming crowded. He also paid for the chapel of the Royal Sussex Hospital.

Clive Brook (1887–1974)

ACTOR

Garden House, 13 Clifton Place (gone)

Brook was the last owner of this house, which was demolished in 1964. It was formerly the old rectory of the Church of St Nicholas of Myra and later called Saxon Lodge. He was a major Hollywood star and among other roles he played opposite Marlene Dietrich in *Shanghai Express* and also played Sherlock Holmes three times. One of his films was *The Brighton Strangler*.

Sir Samuel Brown (1776–1852)

CIVIL ENGINEER, NAVAL OFFICER AND BUILDER OF THE BRIGHTON CHAIN PIER

48 Marine Parade 🅟

Usually known as Captain Brown, he saw action in the Napoleonic wars but his naval career ran parallel with his civil engineering interests. Before constructing the Royal Suspension Chain Pier (commonly called the Chain Pier) he had produced a prototype suspension bridge which Thomas Telford adapted for the Menai Bridge, and which was also used for the Union Bridge across the Tweed.

The Chain Pier was opened in 1823 in the conventional catenary (hanging chain) style. Its purpose was to allow easier embarkation and disembarkation for cross-channel traffic, and for a while Brighton became the busiest port to serve the Channel. However, a storm on 5 December 1896 destroyed the pier, although it had been closed on safety grounds two months before.

Hablot Browne (1815–1882)

ILLUSTRATOR

8 Clarendon Villas, Hove 🅟

In 1848, Browne, better known as 'Phiz', **Charles Dickens'** (*qv*) illustrator, came down to see Dickens who, that year, had finished writing *Dombey and Son* in the town. He brought with him the frontispiece for the novel for the author's approval.

In 1864, it was a far less happy occasion that brought Browne to Brighton. It would seem that Browne's wife, Susannah, had brought their son, two-year-old Arthur John, to the town to improve his health. The youngest of their 12 children, he died here and was buried in the **Extra-Mural Cemetery**.

It was in 1880 that, enriched by a pension from the Royal Academy, which also gave him public recognition, Browne decided to seek a healthier climate away from London. He moved to this address, a modest house, 32 years after his first visit to Brighton, with his wife and four daughters and two maidservants. Soon they were joined by two of his grandchildren. This prompted his daughters to open a nursery school, which was attended by **Eric Gill** (*qv*).

Browne was happy here, surrounded by his family and under no pressure to work, which allowed him to paint and benefit from sea breezes. Before he came here his work had deserted him, he had four dependent children and he was in poor health. But in Hove, wrote a friend, 'he seems to have recovered much of his gaiety and strength'. Yet his happy state was not to last. He died on 8 July 1882 and is buried in the **Extra-Mural Cemetery**.

Dora Bryan (1923–2014)

ACTOR AND COMEDIENNE

108 Crescent Place
Clarges Hotel, 115–119 Marine Parade
(now apartments)
Springfields Nursing Home,
11 Langdale Road, Hove

Dora Bryan, born in Southport, had a career on stage, screen and television that lasted into her 80s. She was directed by Alfred Hitchcock, appeared on stage in Ibsen and Pinter and *A Taste of Honey* and *Hello, Dolly!*, and on television in *Absolutely Fabulous* and *The Last of the Summer Wine*.

She lived in Brighton for many years with her husband, the Lancashire and England cricketer, **William 'Bill' Lawton** to whom she was married for 54 years. Latterly, they lived at **Springfields Nursing Home, 11 Langdale Road, Hove** (he died in 2008).

At one time Bryan and Lawton owned the Clarges Hotel, to which they moved from Crescent Place. Here exterior shots were used in *Carry on Girls* and *Carry on at Your Convenience* (though Bryan did play in *Carry On* films, she did not appear in either of these). However, bankruptcy forced the couple to sell most of the building. They retained a flat with a sea view on the first floor.

Jack Buchanan (1891–1957)

ACTOR AND THEATRE MANAGER

19 Lewes Crescent **P**

Scottish-born Buchanan was the epitome of sophistication. Internationally renowned as an entertainer, he popularised the American-style double-breasted dinner jacket and was the urbane man-about-town – effortless insouciance incarnate. He was always dressed immaculately, was tall and slim, with good looks, grace and charm. His form was romantic comedy, often musical, and he also appeared in films, including two Hollywood productions.

Buchanan was also a businessman, which included building and owning the Imperial Theatre, North Street, Brighton (later the Essoldo Cinema). This opened in 1940 with his own show, *Top Hat and Tails*.

In 1949 he married his second wife (his first marriage had been dissolved), an American, Susan Bassett, who was 25 years his junior. They lived with Theo, her daughter from a previous marriage. They moved to Brighton in 1955 when Buchanan was terminally ill with cancer, something he kept a secret. He travelled to Glasgow for the opening of Scottish ITV at the Theatre Royal in August 1957 but died in a London hospital in October.

Edward Bulwer-Lytton, later Ist Baron Knebworth (1803–1873)

WRITER AND POLITICIAN
The Vicarage (later The Grange, now The Grange Museum and Art Gallery), The Green, Rottingdean

Bulwer (he adopted his mother's maiden name to create the double-barrelled name in 1844) had lost his father, the drunken General William Bulwer, when he was four. Aged eight or nine, he is reported to have asked 'Pray, Mamma, are you not sometimes overcome by the sense of your own identity?' It was time, she decided, that he was sent to school.

He was intellectually precocious – he could read at four and wrote verse at seven – and had inherited a love of reading from his mother. However, in the first three schools he attended in two years he learned little and made no friends. In 1814 his mother moved him to the school run by **Dr Thomas Hooker** (*qv*) in Rottingdean, where boys were prepared for Eton and Harrow.

At The Grange, Bulwer came under the influence of inspiring teachers and found friendship with other boys. He discovered Scott and Byron. As he said, he 'made a leap': he flourished physically – he took to boxing, at which he excelled – and wrote poetry for the school magazine.

His entry in the *Oxford Dictionary of National Biography* says of him at this time: 'Tall and athletically proportioned, already sporting whiskers and a moustache, at fifteen Bulwer carried himself with a self-assurance verging on arrogance. The outward air of confidence, however, masked a nature which at heart was acutely self-conscious and deeply insecure. It was a contradiction that increased with the passage of time.'

At that time, too, Hooker said that Bulwer had 'a mind of very extraordinary compass . . . an emulation rarely found, and an anxiety and attention, and care about his business, very uncommon'. But he said he could do no more for the boy and urged that he be sent to Eton. The 15-year-old Bulwer persuaded his mother otherwise and he went to a private tutor, a clergyman in Ealing, and then to Cambridge.

He served as an MP and Secretary of State for the Colonies for just over a year from 1858. His more lasting fame, however, comes from his literary work, especially his novels.

Anthony Burgess (1917–1993)

NOVELIST, CRITIC AND COMPOSER
78 Tisbury Road, Hove

The man then still known as John Burgess Wilson rented the two-room, ground floor flat of this undistinguished-looking house for a few months between 1959 and 1960. He and his wife Lynne had determined upon Hove by sticking a pin in a map of southern England. He wrote of the town: 'I did not care for it much. It was full of ancient people who had come here to die.'

They stocked the furnished flat with gin and cheap white wine and he bought a typewriter. And it was here that he drew on Hove to write his quartet of Enderby novels. The town's pubs, the 'gull-clawed air, New Year blue, the tide crawling creamily in' were his inspiration. The interior of Francis Xavier Enderby's flat, in the fictional 81 Fitzherbert Avenue, was modelled on Burgess's own furnished lodgings. Though the first of the comic Enderby novels, *Inside Mr Enderby*, did not come out until 1963, half of it was written in Hove.

While living here Burgess was diagnosed with an inoperable brain tumour, and told that he had a year to live. He did not quite believe the diagnosis but could not afford to ignore it. Thus, it became the impetus for a furious commitment to writing – initially to write enough books in what time was thought to be left of his life to support his wife after his death – that remained with him always. He wrote five and a half novels in that year.

Sir Edward Burne-Jones (1833–1898)

PAINTER
North End House (now Aubrey House), The Green, Rottingdean

According to the novelist **Edith Bagnold** (*qv*), who later lived in what became known as North End House, Sir Edward was walking over the South Downs as a young man and came upon a cottage which was the south end of Prospect Cottage House, and bought it. When older and wealthier, he bought the cottage next door and created the L-shaped house. This is a nice story but it can't be true as he bought the cottage in 1880, when he was 47 and well established as a Pre-Raphaelite painter and craftsman. At the time, too, he also purchased the adjoining Aubrey House.

His granddaughter **Angela Thirkell** (*qv*) said that he had bought the place for its beauty with almost his last £8, which, for the same reasons, seems unlikely.

It was originally a three-storey cottage, one room deep, and Burne-Jones eventually united it with the house at right angles to it. He called it North End House partly after North End Road, where he and his wife, Georgiana, had their London home, but also because it was within measurable distance of the north end of the village street which ran from the beach and past The Green. (The house has now been subdivided again into three properties.)

Burne-Jones made a painting in the corner of a bedroom to amuse the children made to stand there.

During his years in Rottingdean, Burne-Jones continued to paint and exhibit to much acclaim. St Margaret's Church, across The Green, where the Burne-Joneses' ashes are interred opposite the grave of their granddaughter, has seven of his stained-glass windows, on which he had worked with William Morris.

Frequently finding it hard to complete works, during his last decade he continued on projects begun, in some cases, many years earlier.

He became a baronet in 1894, something that would never have impressed his wife. Two years later the Burne-Joneses were deeply affected by the death of their great friend Morris. The *Oxford Dictionary of National Biography* writes that he 'remained at heart disaffected and unimpressed by society or the artistic establishment. All his life he indulged a fiendish sense of humour, which was utterly self-mocking, as well as undermining of the pretensions of others.'

The same writer says that Burne-Jones seems to have grown old before his time, with an overbearing sense of work not done and life's short span. By the late 1890s he was distinctly frail and he died of angina at his London home in 1898.

Peter Burton (1945–2011)

JOURNALIST, PUBLISHER, EDITOR AND AUTHOR
5 Arundel Terrace
33 Bristol Gardens

Burton, a pioneer of gay journalism, was a literary institution in Brighton. Yet he left school without qualifications to work as an office junior for the publishing firm of Hamish Hamilton. Among other diversions, he worked in a bookshop and managed a gay night club in London. His break into his future career came when he was asked to write for *The Stage*, but his true course was set when he began to write in the late 1960s for *Spartacus* which was run at that time from a guesthouse in Brighton, a lonely example of gay journalism. Burton later edited *Jeremy* and, in 1973, he began writing for *Gay News*, as literary editor, under its founding editor Denis Lemon. When this folded in 1983, he came to be literary and features editor of *Gay Times*, a job he held until 2003.

Burton was also the last publisher of the merged Millivres Books/Gay Men's Press imprint. He wrote or contributed to 30 books, including six anthologies, three of which were nominated for Lambda literary awards. He wrote two volumes of memoirs, *Parallel Lives* and *Amongst the Aliens: Some Aspects of a Gay Life*. He worked for a time for Rod Stewart's manager, Billy Gaff, handling the American press, and his authorised biography, *Rod Stewart: A Life on the Town* (1977), allowed him to buy a flat in Brighton.

In 1968 Burton got to know the novelist **Robin Maugham** (*qv*), and, acting as his amanuensis, helped him to complete his final books. At least one, *Conversations with Willie*, about Maugham's uncle Somerset Maugham, it has been claimed, was entirely Burton's work.

Burton reviewed for the *Daily Express* and wrote obituaries for *The Independent*. He organised the literary programme for the local Clifton Montpelier Powis Festival for the five years leading to his death.

His work output was the more remarkable for his using a manual typewriter, the ribbons of which he could not change. He revered friendship and was a famed cook, who loved nothing better than to entertain his friends with food, wine, whisky, music, gossip, ideas and advice at his book-filled home.

CA Busby (1786–1834)

ARCHITECT
11 Waterloo Place
1 Stanhope Place (2 Lansdowne Place, Hove) **P**

With his one-time business partner, **Amon Henry Wilds** (*qv*), Charles Busby has left a grand and indelible stamp on his adopted city, making Brighton the great Regency creation that it remains today. By the age of 22 he had published two volumes of architectural designs, which brought him several commissions. He had worked in various places, including the United States, exhibited and won a gold medal at the Royal Academy, and patented a water-saving hydraulic system, before he came to Brighton at the invitation of **Thomas Read Kemp** (*qv*), MP and wealthy property developer. It was he who brought Busby into partnership with Wilds, a local architect, who had a successful partnership with his father, **Amon Wilds**, a builder and carpenter.

In 1823 Kemp commissioned the younger Wilds and Busby to create Kemp Town. We do not know exactly which work belongs to which of them as they signed their plans with both names and there is insufficient surviving documentary evidence to tell one's creation from the other. But Busby was responsible for the chapels of St Margaret in 1924 (demolished in 1959) and St George (1824–5), and Portland Place (1824–8). Their partnership was dissolved after only 25 months and Busby claimed that many of the buildings were his.

Kemp Town has been compared to Nash's Regent's Park, and the span of Lewes Crescent is 200 feet wider than Bath's Royal Crescent, but the development was neither architecturally nor financially successful. Busby and Kemp were allowed no part in the building, and there were lengthy delays which caused their design to be compromised. Compared to this, in Brunswick Town when Busby was architect, builder, and manager, the development sped on. He also patented a steam-driven central heating system to provide his houses with hot and cold water.

In January 1830 Busby moved, with his wife and two children, from Waterloo Place to 1 Stanhope Place (now 2 Lansdowne Place, pictured). At the back, what is now **Brunswick Cottage, Brunswick Street West**, was his drawing office, reached by a passage.

A radical Whig, who assisted with Hove's agitation in favour of the Reform Bill, Busby served on the Hove vestry and was one of the first Brunswick commissioners created under the Brunswick Square Act 1830. He was the estate's surveyor at £40 a year until his death. In 1831 he became high commissioner of Hove.

A keen astronomer, Busby also designed and built a small paddle-steamer, which he sailed off the shore locally. However, he was arrested for debt in 1829, sued in 1832 and the following year was declared bankrupt, owing £12,644. His friends ensured that his debts were paid but he was now a broken man and died at Stanhope Place on 18 September 1834. He was buried in the churchyard of **St Andrew's Church**, Church Road, Hove.

RA ('Rab') Butler, later Baron Butler (1902–1982)

POLITICIAN

The Wick, The Wick School, Furze Hill (now the site of Furze Croft apartments, St Ann's Well Gardens), Hove

The man, who was to become Conservative President of the Board of Education (Education Secretary), Chancellor of the Exchequer, Home Secretary, Foreign Secretary and deputy prime minister, spent five years at this school. The future writer and critic **Lord David Cecil** was a contemporary and his younger brother John was to follow a decade later.

Butler was born in Attock, India (now Punjab, Pakistan), into a family of Cambridge dons and Indian governors. Like other children of his class and generation born in the Empire, he was sent home to attend prep school at the age of eight. This one was run by a brother and sister, Laurence and Mary Thring, who were related to Edward Thring, the famous headmaster of Uppingham School.

Education here was far more formal than the boy had hitherto known, and to help his adjustment, his mother, Ann, took a house in Hove. She became friendly with the Thrings and would often play the piano at the school or help out with theatricals and concerts. Laurence Thring, Butler wrote, was 'remarkable', but he remembered less of him than Mary, who was very stern with the children. 'The Captain Scott tragedy happened during my early time there', he wrote, 'and if we were ever careless with our food, Mary Thring would say: "Captain Scott would have given his eyes for that egg." We became less and less appreciative of the great explorer.'

Dame Clara Butt (1872–1936)

SINGER

27 Adur Terrace, Southwick
4 St Aubyns Mansions, Kings Esplanade, Hove 🅿 *

Dame Clara was born in Adur Terrace but by the time she came to St Aubyns Mansions in 1903, she was renowned world-wide as a recitalist and concert singer. She lived here with her husband, the baritone **Robert Kennerley Rumford**, whom she had married three years previously. They would give many successful and lucrative concerts together.

Butt was famous for her deep and agile singing (and particularly her association with Edward Elgar) and her imposing height of 6 feet 2 inches.

When they moved in the mansion block on the seafront was comparatively new. It was constructed in 1899 as part of an ambitious scheme that was never completed. It consists of four principal floors, each with two flats. Her grand piano was kept in the large hallway.

Butt and Kennerley Rumford lived in St Aubyns Mansions (pictured) for only three years, and as their main residence remained in London this was not their primary home.

They had a daughter and two sons. Two years her senior, Kennerley Rumford outlived Butt, remarrying in 1941 and dying in 1957.

* *When a plaque was placed here in 2012, her birth date was given as 1848. The residents' association, who paid for the commemoration, made a mistake in their submission to Brighton Council, who erected it. It has been corrected.*

Douglas Byng (1893 –1987)

COMIC SINGER AND SONGWRITER
Flat 2, 6 Arundel Terrace

Byng was a familiar, dapper figure in Kemp Town, to which he moved in 1964, when he was already a star. At 70 years, his was one of the longest careers in show business. He had first known Brighton, a town to which he confessed himself 'devoted', in his early teens when he would stay there with a distant relative. He took delight in the fact that his great-grandfather, Mr Shelley, had been the Beadle and was buried in St Nicholas' Church. Other relatives, in past generations, had lived in the town, and his grandfather Byng had played at the Theatre Royal, where he himself was to appear 112 years later. Before moving to Brighton, Byng would stay with friends, delighting in the *Brighton Belle*. With his later affluence he would take a large suite in the **Norfolk Hotel** (now the Mercure Brighton Seafront Hotel), Kings Road.

He was friendly with Brighton actors including **Lord Olivier** (*qv*), **Dame Flora Robson** (*qv*) and **Dora Bryan** (*qv*).

Byng appeared in cabaret in London, Monte Carlo and New York (one act was described by Noel Coward as 'the most refined vulgarity in London'). He was the lead in comedies and musicals, made films and wrote and recorded songs. Cole Porter wrote 'Miss Otis Regrets' for Byng, who was the first to perform it, dressed as a butler. At the end of a performance, he would say: 'It's the best I could do for the money'.

He was also renowned not only as a pantomime dame but as a female impersonator in other kinds of performance, thus paving the way for stars like Danny La Rue. His camp performance and risqué humour can also be seen in the later careers of Kenneth Williams, Frankie Howerd, Paul O'Grady, Graham Norton and Julian Clary.

As a gay man living at a time when homosexual acts were illegal, Byng was very discreet about his sexuality. Claims have been made that he had affairs with both Coward and Porter, and he himself claimed a dalliance with the bisexual Prince George of Kent, brother of George VI. With the change in the law in the 1960s, Byng said: 'I don't know what all the fuss is about; I just got on with it'.

In his autobiography, he wrote: 'Actually I don't feel I have ever really worked, as everything I have done so far has also been my hobby'.

Shortly before his death he played a one-man show at the National Theatre in London before a sell-out audience. His ashes were scattered in the garden of his home.

George Canning (1770–1827)

PRIME MINISTER
Marine Parade (now Royal Crescent Mansions*)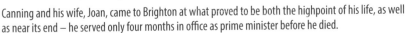

Canning and his wife, Joan, came to Brighton at what proved to be both the highpoint of his life, as well as near its end – he served only four months in office as prime minister before he died.

He was highly intelligent, cultured, a gifted orator and of outstanding personality and abilities – apart from politics his parodies had been performed on the London stage.

In January 1827, Canning, when Leader of the Commons and Foreign Secretary, had caught a severe cold while waiting for two hours for the arrival of the coffin of the Duke of York, brother of **George IV** (*qv*), at the funeral at St George's Chapel, Windsor. He then travelled to Bath to see the prime minister, Lord Liverpool (himself recuperating from illness), but by the time Canning reached Brighton he was seriously ill, the worst symptoms being agonising rheumatic pains in the head, upon which vapour baths and quinine had no effect. By February he was writing to a colleague that 'H.My' (George IV) was laid up with gout in the Royal Pavilion 'and I at the eastern extremity of the cliff'. They exchanged gifts – the king sent Canning whey and fruit and he sent the other an 'unexpected quadruped' (wild pig).

However, news came that Liverpool had been paralysed with a stroke and Sir Robert Peel, then Home Secretary, travelled to advise the king. Canning visited the Pavilion four days later. Although Canning was sufficiently recovered to speak in the Commons on 1 March, his illness never went away.

Liverpool eventually resigned. After long delays, much uncertainty as to who was to enter Downing Street, and resignations by those who would not serve under him, Canning became prime minister in April 1827. In July he caught another chill, which led to inflammation of his liver and lungs, and he died in August at Chiswick House in London.

* *In 1848 three storeys were added to the house.*

Sir Herbert Carden (1867–1941)

LOCAL POLITICIAN AND MAYOR OF BRIGHTON
19 West Hill Road
103 Marine Parade Ⓟ

Carden was a visionary local politician, who, in his way, put as much of a lasting mark on Brighton as did the architects **Amon Henry Wilds** (*qv*) and **Charles Busby** (*qv*), the builders **Thomas Cubitt** (*qv*) and **Amon Wilds**, or the developer **Thomas Kemp** (*qv*) in earlier times.

Born in West Hill Road, Carden was a solicitor, and was elected to the council as a socialist in 1895, becoming an alderman eight years later. In 1916 he was elected mayor for three years and also served on Hove Council from 1902 to 1905.

Carden was largely responsible for Brighton Council developing the electricity, telephone and tramway systems, and building council homes, as well as protecting the downlands and buying land for what is now Dyke Road Park. He personally bought Devil's Dyke and Ditchling Beacon from their private owners and then re-sold to the council for the same amount to defeat a hike in prices.

Fortunately, however, he did not succeed in his plans to rebuild the sea front from Kemp Town to Hove in the art deco style, to redevelop the area of the Lanes, and to replace the Royal Pavilion with a conference and entertainment centre.

Earl of Cardigan (1797–1868)

SOLDIER AND COMMANDER OF THE LIGHT BRIGADE
45 Brunswick Square, Hove

Lord Cardigan's stay in Brighton in 1840 was not a long one and, while he and his wife lived in some splendour and freely entertained, one event proved unwelcome.

His regiment, the 11th Hussars, was billeted in the local barracks at Preston, and Lord and Lady Cardigan took up residence in Brunswick Square, having moved from the **Royal York Hotel** (now the Youth Hostel), Old Steine. They were seen on the seafront, in 'an elegantly styled chariot', accompanied, at the rear, by footmen in full livery. The Cardigans gave dinners both at the hotel and the house and, on one occasion, he took a party by private train to Shoreham, where they danced and had a lavish dinner. On another day the regiment engaged in 34 horse races with £13,000 stake money.

But on 12 September 1840, Cardigan fought a duel with a former officer, Harvey Tuckett, on Wimbledon Common. This was occasioned when, at a ball at Brunswick Square, Cardigan was asked by a female guest why Captains JW and RA Reynolds were not present. Cardigan disliked the two so much that he said that as long as he lived neither would enter his house. The conversation was reported to RA Reynolds, who asked Cardigan to deny it, and when he refused Reynolds challenged the earl to a duel. To accept would be against the rules of the army; to refuse would imply cowardice. This was stated in a letter to *The Morning Post* by Harvey Tuckett, a former officer, which caused Cardigan to challenge *him* to a duel, during which Tuckett was wounded. Both men were arrested and Cardigan was tried in April 1841 before the House of Lords. He was found not guilty on a legal technicality, but Cardigan, a notoriously vain man, was booed and derided in public.

Thirteen years later, though, Cardigan was engaged in an action that brought him public acclaim and honours. After some misunderstanding among commanders, he led the Light Brigade 'into the Valley of Death'. One hundred and thirteen of the 673 men, who were to be immortalised by Tennyson's poem, fell to the Russian guns and 247 were injured.

Edward Carpenter (1844–1929)

CAMPAIGNER FOR GAY EQUALITY
AND SOCIALIST WRITER
45 Brunswick Square, Hove Ⓟ

Carpenter was born in this house in Brunswick Square, the seventh of the ten children of prosperous, middle class parents, and his unconventional, rebellious nature was very much shaped by his upbringing. His father was a magistrate and chairman of the Hove commissioners. The family had moved there the year before Carpenter's birth when, as he was to write, the town was 'just growing into importance, and yet retained some of its old-world character'. Fields separated Hove from Brighton.

The house had enough space for a veritable menagerie — pigeons, seagulls with clipped wings, rabbits, tortoises, guinea-pigs and an aquarium. The square's large garden was 'overrun, despite the efforts of the gardener and other authorities, by all the children of the surrounding houses'. The **Rev Frederick W Robertson** (*qv*) and **Henry Fawcett**, the local MP, were frequent visitors.

Carpenter was educated at Brighton College from 1854 to 1863 but came to regard life in Brighton as 'fatuous', 'idiotic', and 'artificial'. There, and later in Cambridge and London, he ' had had my fill of balls and dinner-parties and the usual entertainments'. It was 'a would-be fashionable world which I hated'.

While the town's social life was 'chilly in the extreme', and its scenery and surroundings 'bare and chilly enough', Carpenter gained great consolation from the sea and the South Downs. Three or four miles away it was 'a world remote from man'.

He left in 1863, but when his father died in 1882 (his parents were buried together in Hove cemetery), he spent several months back in the family home, to which he had returned periodically, sorting out the estate. His unmarried sisters remained in Brighton for a few more years and then moved to London, and in 1886 the house and furniture were sold.

Lewis Carroll (1832–1898)

WRITER, MATHEMATICIAN AND PHOTOGRAPHER

11 Sussex Square Ⓟ
4 Park Crescent

On 2 January 1885 Carroll (Charles Lutwidge Dodgson) recorded in his diary that his sister 'Henrietta left for Brighton, in pursuance of her new plan of living by herself'. Carroll knew the town well because he had stayed many times in Sussex Square, at the home of his old Christ Church, Oxford, friend, the Rev Henry Barclay. Henrietta, one of Carroll's six unmarried sisters (he was the eldest son among 11 children), sought new independence and the peace and solitude she seemed to enjoy, by moving from the crowded family household in Guildford to Park Crescent, Brighton. She was to die here in April 1922. Eleven years younger than her brother, who supported her financially in her new but simple life, she lived with an elderly maidservant and several cats, and made new friends. A young resident of Park Crescent described her as 'a rather starchy person who did not like to see us play too close to the house' and claims that 'she had an uncanny knack of enticing the cats to her'.

Carroll would often stay with Henrietta and visit with young friends. On one occasion, he and 25-year-old May Miller (somewhat more mature than some of Carroll's female friends) took the steamer from Eastbourne to Brighton with the intention of visiting Henrietta. They enjoyed standing on deck as the waves came over the side. They were soaked, turned straight back and skipped the visit.

THE REV. CHARLES LUTWIDGE DODGSON (LEWIS CARROLL) STAYED HERE FREQUENTLY BETWEEN 1874 AND 1887.
Erected by the Regency Society

In 1887 Carroll and Henrietta, who tended to disapprove of the theatre, went to see a theatrical production of *Alice in Wonderland* at the Theatre Royal. (He is said to have got inspiration for the rabbit hole in the novel from the small underground tunnel in Sussex Square running down to the sea.) He also went to see Louey Webb's aquatic entertainment on the pier – she did sewing, writing and other activities while submerged in a water tank – with which he was so taken that he went back to see it again.

Shortly after his death an inaccurate anecdote about Carroll appeared in the *Sussex Daily News*, which prompted a swift, corrective response by Henrietta, who signed herself 'one of his mourning relatives'. When another erroneous story appeared she did the same again.

Sir Edward Carson (1854–1935)

IRISH UNIONIST POLITICIAN AND LAWYER

Northgate House, Bazehill Road, Rottingdean (now the site of Northgate Close)

Immensely wealthy from his practice as a QC – he earned £20,000 in fees in 1900 – Carson had this house as a weekend country retreat. His neighbour **Philip Burne-Jones** painted his portrait and Burne-Jones' cousin, **Rudyard Kipling** (*qv*), another neighbour, was, like Carson, opposed to Home Rule for Ireland. The children of another Kipling cousin, **Stanley Baldwin**, called Carson the 'Black Man', possibly because of his saturnine looks. Carson provided a loan for the purchase of the village's reading room in 1909.

Carson embarked on a national tour to promote the Unionist 'solemn league and covenant', which gained half a million signatures, and to advocate civil disobedience against Home Rule. (When the Home Rule Bill was before Parliament, Carson raised the Ulster Volunteers, the first Loyalist paramilitary group, which became the Ulster Volunteer Force in 1913.)

On the night of 4 October 1912 Rottingdean villagers assembled, with torch lights, to welcome Carson home. The local Conservative and Unionist Association presented him with an illuminated address and, in his speech of thanks, he said: 'As you know, I came to Rottingdean not for politics. I came to it as a place I have learned to love and where I might rest.' Six months later Annette, his first wife and mother of four of his five children, died and her funeral took place in the village. The next year Carson gave up the house. It was later used by the St Dunstan's charity and also as a school before demolition in the 1970s.

Deryk Carver (c. 1505–1555)

PROTESTANT MARTYR

Black Lion Pub, 14 Black Lion Street

A popular pub by this name has stood on this site since the 16th century and it is to its very earliest times that it owes its greatest claim to fame. For in the 1540s Deryk Carver, a Flemish Protestant, who had fled religious persecution in his home country to settle in the village of Brighthelmstone, which was to become Brighton, purchased the Black Lion brewery. (The name refers to the black lion of Flanders.)

Carver, who was about 40, became a wealthy member of the community and may have grown hops on the Hempshares, the areas of open land where hemp was also grown for rope making.

However, Catholicism was restored with the accession to the throne of Mary Tudor in July 1553. Fifteen months later, Carver was arrested at his home, where he spoke as a lay preacher, while praying with 11 others, three of whom were also arrested and eventually executed. He was tried in London in 1555. At his trial he refused to recant his Protestantism and then attacked the Catholic faith as 'poison and sorcery . . . Your ceremonies in the Church be beggary and poison.'

He was found guilty and burnt at the stake in Lewes on 22 July 1555. His profession was mocked by his being placed in a barrel before he was executed, becoming one the nearly 300 Protestants put to death during the reign of Queen Mary Tudor.

The Black Lion Brewery, one of the oldest buildings in Brighton, ceased brewing in 1901, was demolished in about 1970 and rebuilt in 1974 as a replica of the original building. In the 1970s the pub bore Carver's name.

Thomas Hayter Chase (1814–1874)

CHIEF OFFICER OF POLICE
37 Duke Street

In 1844 Chase was appointed as successor to the murdered **Henry Solomon** (*qv*) and held the post for nearly ten years.

The Brighton commissioners were afraid that, if they appointed a local man as successor to Solomon, they might find their police force compulsorily amalgamated into the East Sussex Constabulary. They advertised for a single man, but Chase kept the fact that he was married quiet until he got the job. He was 30 years of age and came to Brighton from the Isle of Wight, where he was chief superintendent of the Isle of Wight Division of the Hampshire Constabulary. Before that he was a member of the Metropolitan Police. Chase was one of the most colourful inhabitants of the office: before joining the police he had served as an artillery officer in the Spanish Carlist Wars and, at the end of his time in Brighton, was declared bankrupt.

He was adept at taking advantage of the divisions within the governance of local Brighton policing at that time. In 1847 the Brighton commissioners dissolved their own police committee, replacing it with a larger body in the misplaced hope of quelling dissent. Chase had soon realised that the committee supported (as he did) an increase in police numbers, whereas the full body of commissioners did not. Making an unfavourable comparison with the size of the local force and that of another fashionable watering hole, Bath, the commissioners agreed to an increase that they had formerly opposed. A year later, Chase compared Brighton police pay rates with those in London and secured an increase, much to the annoyance of his opponents.

Chase's power to make decisions independently lasted only so long as the commissioners and the committee were at loggerheads. But Chase's frequent high-handedness got him in trouble not only with the commissioners but also the press.

Eventually, in 1851 he was censured over various complaints, the police committee resigned, was reformed and his decision-making, hitherto rubber-stamped, came under scrutiny. There was evidence enough to sack him – he was reluctant to dismiss constables found drunk on duty and there were criticisms of poor policing during the 1852 borough elections – but he stayed in office.

However, while he was a man with powerful enemies he also had powerful friends. In his relationship with a woman imprisoned for fraud and then debt, he became accessory to further fraud because when she was in Lewes debtors' prison he acted as a referee and offered an accommodation address for her.

Threats of civil proceedings against him were halted on his plea of making innocent mistakes and because the Brighton commissioners wanted to avoid a local scandal that would inevitably focus on their lack of supervision of their chief of police. But further investigation then revealed that he had been pocketing money made from sales of old uniforms rather than paying it into the superannuation fund. This time the commissioners didn't believe it was just another honest mistake. They dismissed him, and in doing so distanced themselves from any further allegations of fraud.

Chase then became station master at Burgess Hill, emerging, curiously, as chief constable of Portsmouth six years later, although he was only in post there for a year. During the American Civil War he ran a large spy network in England, passing the US Government details of firms that were covertly supplying goods and ships to the Confederate States.

Sir Winston Churchill (1874–1965)

PRIME MINISTER, WRITER, NOBEL LAUREATE
Lansworth House, 29–30 Brunswick Road, Hove 🅿
(🅿 also in Lansdowne Road)*

'I am well and happy', the ten-year-old Churchill wrote to his father, Lord Randolph from his school in Hove. A month before, his mother, Lady Randolph (Jennie), had written to her husband, with perhaps some relief, to say that 'he is working so much harder this term'. These are unremarkable statements only if one ignores how unhappy were Churchill's schooldays.

Between the ages of two and six he had lived in Dublin, where his grandfather was the viceroy, and he had been well tutored by a governess. But upon return to England he went to school in Ascot, where birching was a common punishment. In 1883 (according to his *My Early Life*) or 1884 (according to his son Randolph's biography) he was moved to Brunswick Road, where the sisters Kate and Charlotte Thomson ran a kindlier regime for 22 pupils. It had been chosen by the Churchills partly because the family doctor, Robson Roose, had his main practice in the area and he believed that 'fresh sea air' would benefit young Winston, whom his parents regarded as frail. (This proved to be a fateful choice: soon after he came to the school Churchill caught pneumonia, which was to prove a recurrent ailment throughout his life, and though close to death for several days, he survived thanks to Roose.)

In the 1880s there was open land to the north of Brunswick Road, and what is now St Ann's Wells Gardens was then a wooded area, with a spring, known as The Wick or Chalybeate. The school, Churchill was to write, was 'cheaper and less pretentious'. It had a matron, a cook, four servants and a small back garden.

The school's dancing teacher was Miss Eva Moore, born in Brighton and later a noted actor and active suffragist who was to become the mother of Jill Esmond, actor and first wife of **Laurence Olivier** (*qv*). The boy enjoyed her lessons but Miss Moore found him naughty and there was criticism of his behaviour when the school attended services at the Chapel Royal, North Street.

Churchill left in 1888 for Harrow. His experiences there suggest that Hove was a rare respite. 'I was allowed to learn things which interested me: French, History, and lots of Poetry by heart, and above all Riding and Swimming,' he remembered. He played cricket and rode three times a week and remembered 70 years later the pleasures of collecting butterflies while there.

---

* *Both plaques were erected by the former Hove Council and adopt Churchill's date of starting at the school rather than that of his son and biographer, Randolph. Both, too, misspell the name of the Misses Thomson by the insertion of a 'p' and the apostrophe in the name is misplaced*

Sir John Clements (1910–1988)

ACTOR AND THEATRE MANAGER

Kay Hammond (1909 –1980)

ACTOR
7 Royal Crescent

The marriage of Clements and Hammond in 1946 was the second for each of them and united in matrimony one of the great couples of the English theatre. In 1944 they had appeared in a West End revival of Noel Coward's *Private Lives*. They appeared together in Clements' own play (appropriately titled) *The Happy Marriage* in 1952.

Clements was also a successful radio broadcaster, and Hammond joined him in the weekly discussion programme *We Beg to Differ* that gave vent to their comic rivalry.

Hammond was paralysed with a stroke in 1960 and spent the rest of her life in a wheelchair. The following year Clements joined the Old Vic Company, where his first appearance was as Macbeth in New York in 1962. Four years later he succeeded **Sir Laurence Olivier** (*qv*) as director of the Chichester Festival Theatre, where he also acted.

Clements and Hammond were a devoted couple and he left Chichester in 1973 to spend more time with her.

In Brighton they were part of a theatrical community, which included their immediate neighbours Olivier and his wife, **Joan Plowright**, as well as **Terence Rattigan** (*qv*) and **Dame Flora Robson** (*qv*).

Hammond died in 1980 in Brighton, and Clements died in 1988 in a nursing home near Midhurst, Sussex, where he had spent the last two years of his life.

Sir Charles (CB) Cochran (1872–1951)

THEATRICAL IMPRESARIO
15 Prestonville Road

When he was seven years old, Charlie Cochran went to see *Sinbad the Sailor*, the Christmas pantomime at the Brighton Theatre Royal and Opera House (as it was then known). He was enraptured, and his passion for the stage was to develop into a career that combined collaborations with Noel Coward, popular musicals and international seasons featuring Diaghilev's Ballets Russes, Sarah Bernhardt, and Anna Pavlova.

Cochran was born in this house on 25 September 1872, into a fairly prosperous family (his father, James, owned a tea and cigar importing business at **49 North Street**), the fourth of nine children. He attended kindergarten in Lewes and on his first day at Brighton Grammar School became friends with **Aubrey Beardsley** (*qv*), who, he was later to say, had a great influence on his life. 'Neither of us did a great deal of work' at the school, he later wrote, but he and Beardsley masterminded school theatrical productions at, among other places, the Dome and the Royal Pavilion.

When his father's business was sold to meet debts, Cochran was taken away from school for the boredom of an office boy's job in an estate agents. He took to performing smoking concerts in Brighton and elsewhere, and then, 'borrowing' money from his office, he and another old grammar school pupil, **GF Scotson Clark** (who became a well-known artist), took off for France and then for America.

Sir Edward Codrington (1770–1851)

NAVAL OFFICER, COMMANDER OF COMBINED FLEETS AT THE BATTLE OF NAVARINO AND MP

Hampton Lodge, 140 Western Road, Hove 🅿

Codrington lived here for only four years (1828–32) of a distinguished life. He purchased Hampton Lodge after its compulsory vacation by the banker and forger, **Henry Fauntleroy** (*qv*). Hampton Lodge adjoined what was Codrington Place (and was partly on land now the corner of Western Road and Hampton Place). He also developed Codrington House (now gone) and Sutton Lodge (corner of Hampton Place and Western Road). He developed, too, nine houses in Codrington Place, and owned 1 and 2 Western Cottages, which later became 1 and 2 Sillwood Road (now site of the old bank building on the corner of Sillwood Road and Western Road).

Codrington is commemorated in Greece by a large obelisk because of his role in the Battle of Navarino in 1827 when the combined British, French and Russian fleet, of which he was Commander, destroyed the Turkish and Egyptian fleet during the Greek War of Independence. (The Greek ambassador unveiled the Brighton plaque.) He was also involved in the blockade of Cadiz and the Battle of Trafalgar.

At one time an MP, in 1839 he was made commander-in-chief at Portsmouth and his active career ended with the termination of that command on 31 December 1842. He died at his London home on 28 April 1851.

Levy (or Levi) Emanuel Cohen (1796–1860)

NEWSPAPER EDITOR AND OWNER AND SOCIAL REFORMER

2 Clarence Square
34 North Street (gone)

Clarence Square was Cohen's childhood home where he lived as the eldest son of German-born **Emanuel Hyam Cohen**. Born in Munich, Cohen *père* was one of the founding members of Brighton's Jewish community. He ran a boarding school for Jewish boys in Artillery Place until 1816.

When his father died in 1823, Cohen became head of the family. He was a theatre critic for the *Brighton Herald* and then, in 1827, started the *Brighton Guardian*, with the help of his sisters, Zippora and Rossetta, with offices in North Street. This was a radical paper that campaigned for the repeal of the Corn Laws (one of the great reformist causes of the time), supported universal suffrage and argued that poverty was the cause of crime. Circulation at one time reached 60,000. Cohen attacked magistrates, describing them as 'crabbed nervous, passionate, fiery mouthed, vain and bombastic justices – the bare sight of them turns one's feelings bitter'. He refused to be sworn in as a special constable by one magistrate, claiming to be a minister of religion (he was active in the local Jewish community).

In 1833 Cohen was prosecuted at Lewes Assizes for criminal libel after publishing a story about 'incendiary fires in the area of Arundel & Horsham'. He received a fine of £50 with six months in prison, but from his cell he still wrote the paper's leading articles.

He was twice president of the Newspaper Society (the newspaper owners' association) from 1841 to 1843. In 1845 he attended a conference to choose the Chief Rabbi, in his capacity as vice-president of the Brighton congregation.

He was the brother-in-law of **Henry Solomon** (*qv*), while his brother, **Hyman Lewis Cohen**, as a town commissioner, is thought to be one of the first Jews to serve in local government.

When he died, the newspaper was run by his brother Nathan and closed in 1901. He is buried in the **Florence Place Jewish Cemetery**, Florence Place, Ditchling Road.

Lewis Cohen, later Baron Cohen (1897–1966)

LOCAL POLITICIAN, PHILANTHROPIST AND BUSINESSMAN
55 Dyke Road Avenue

As a young man Lewis Cohen became a socialist after being shocked by the poverty and poor housing he saw in Brighton when working as a rent collector.

A collateral descendant of **Levi Emanuel Cohen** (*qv*), Cohen was educated in Hastings and at Brighton Grammar School. Today he is remembered for two things. First, he was founder and chairman and managing director of the Alliance Building Society, which he created from a local society (the Brighton and Sussex Building Society), and aided by mergers and acquisitions, he turned it into a financial institution of national importance. (It later became the Alliance and Leicester, converted to a bank in 1997, and was later swallowed up by Santander Bank.) He is also remembered for proposing a marina in 1963, with the Black Rock site chosen the next year. The harbour opened in 1978 but commercial and residential development didn't start until 1983. The development changed forever the cliff views beyond Kemp Town.

Cohen also saved the Theatre Royal, obtained the land for the University of Sussex, and was a driving force in the creation of the Brighton Festival, which started a year after his death.

However, other ambitious ideas were (fortunately) not realised. He wanted the Clock Tower demolished and also a music and entertainments pavilion built on the front, which would include a dance hall, conference centre, restaurant and ballroom. Another proposal was for a chain of gardens from Preston Park to the sea, which would have entailed the loss of many buildings.

He stood unsuccessfully for Parliament six times, five of them for Brighton seats (Brighton and Hove in 1931 and 1935 and Brighton Kemptown in 1951, 1955 and 1959).

Cohen was also a property developer who built extensively in the suburbs, while offering affordable housing and mortgages.

Dame Ivy Compton-Burnett (1884–1969)

NOVELIST
20 The Drive, Hove 🅿

In December 1891* Dr James Compton-Burnett, his second wife, Katherine, and their nine children moved to The Drive. Some of the children were susceptible to pneumonia and one son, Guy, was to die of pneumonia in 1905, while Ivy nearly succumbed to it. Their father, a homeopath, believed sea air to be the remedy. Indeed, the *Homeopathic Dictionary* actually pointed out: 'From August to the end of December the climate of Brighton is probably the best in England, but the spring is boisterous, windy and often very cold.' Dr Compton-Burnett had had his own ranking of coastal resorts advisable for delicate children – a year in Brighton ranked second after one in Worthing, followed by 'a year or two' in Eastbourne or Folkestone.

A directory of the time says that one 'cannot but help be struck with the air of wealth and refinement' of the area. The house, which had 13 bedrooms, was of red brick with white facings. The children called it 'the hideous house'. While the first motor car had been seen in The Drive in 1895, carriages stood two or three deep outside each house every afternoon as calls were made. The Compton-Burnetts had no carriage but had about nine servants.

The young Compton-Burnett will have passed the mother of **Margaret Powell** (*qv*) in the street, as the latter worked in The Drive as a kitchen maid and later cook at this time, but, as a child, Compton-Burnett never went below stairs in her own home. The general who lived opposite objected to having a homeopath as a neighbour. A homeopath for a father meant compulsory porridge each day, fruit and vegetables and a mostly vegetarian diet. There were family prayers, with the servants included, hymns and Bible readings.

Hove at that time was a fast-growing place, helped by the fact that Dr Compton-Burnett's own speculative building was developing in several places. It was, by the time of the Compton-Burnetts' arrival, 'a wilderness of raw, red brick', according to the biographer Hilary Spurling, with a population of 26,077. It had five churches, newly built or being constructed. The town hall had been open only nine years and the public library opened the year of the family's arrival.

After private tutoring, at 14 Compton-Burnett went to a newly built Addiscombe College at 39 and 41 Tisbury Road, Hove. It was run by four women, three of whom were sisters, Catherine, Laura and Frances Cadwallader, one of whom also later educated **Patrick Hamilton** (*qv*).

In the quarter of a century that the family spent here, speculative building grew apace. Yet the children walked in meadows, picked flowers and fed the donkey in the field next to the town hall. Compton-Burnett was once taken to see the Prince of Wales, the future **Edward VII** (*qv*), pass by.

When Dr Compton-Burnett died in 1901 he left a not inconsiderable empire of 100 properties, most of which were shops and terraced houses on the outskirts of the town. His wife died in 1911and in 1915 Compton-Burnett moved to London. She was left with a deep dislike of Hove, so much so that she refused ever to visit friends in Brighton. 'It's a horrid, horrid place', she said just before she died. She came to see the Hove years as ones of wasted youth, though, in fact, she had spent some time away at boarding school and at Royal Holloway College, and her first novel, *Dolores*, had been published in 1911 when she was in Hove.

* *The plaque wrongly gives the date as 1897*

John Constable (1776–1837)

PAINTER
11 Sillwood Road P

Constable was already spending a few months a year in Hampstead away from his central London home for the sake of the health of his wife, Maria, when he was advised to 'try the sea' in Brighton. He came in 1824. This was the first of several extended stays, though he would often leave his wife and the children and travel down from London

on his own. Maria's health was always delicate and proved a constant anxiety to her husband. Brighton's air, it was believed, would counter her tuberculosis, but she died in 1828, leaving him with seven children under the age of 11.

This address was then known as 9 Mrs Sober's Gardens, after Ann Sober, sister of **Thomas Kemp** (*qv*). In 1817 she built a house called Western Lodge on the site of what is now Sillwood Terrace. Constable wrote that where he lived was 'so called from Mrs Sober, the Lady of the Manor – & rich in estates here – which are more so now by their new buildings'.

As Hampstead and his native Suffolk had attracted his professional attention, so did Brighton. He wrote to a friend: 'I am looking for a month's quiet here and I have brought with me several works to complete. What a blessing it is thus to be able to carry one's profession with me.'

He had not enjoyed the coast for such long periods since honeymooning in Dorset in 1816 and was taken with the magnificence of the sea. However, he did not take to Brighton entirely. It was, he told a friend, 'the receptacle of the fashion and the off-scouring of London' where the 'everlasting voice' of the sea was often drowned by noise from the beach which was like 'Piccadilly or worse by the sea-side'. Maria, however, called the town 'Hampstead by the sea'.

Constable sketched and painted – he had a studio in his house – and 200 works are attributed to his stays in the town. The images of some small scale works of people and boats were used to create, among several others, *The Chain Pier*, displayed in the Royal Academy Exhibition of 1827. He also painted *Brighton Beach, Beaching a Boat, Brighton**, and *The Gleaners, Brighton*. In 1826 he stayed for two weeks and produced *The Sea near Brighton*.

* *In 2014 the Tate Gallery in London announced an intention to return Constable's Beaching a Boat, Brighton (1824) to the descendants of its owner after it was discovered that the painting had been stolen by the Nazis in Hungary during the Second World War.*

Alfred Edgar (AE) Coppard (1878–1957)

SHORT-STORY WRITER AND POET
25 Gladstone Place

Coppard was born into poverty in Folkestone, one of the four children of a journeyman tailor and a former housemaid. The family's lot improved when Coppard was five after they moved to Brighton, where lived several relatives on both sides. It was in Melbourne Street, their second home, that for the first time they were able to live as sole tenants of a house. Coppard attended the board school in Fairlight Place, at a cost of a penny a week, but ill health is said to have forced him to leave when he was nine and work as an assistant to a street vendor of paraffin and firewood. When his father died, the family's poverty worsened and his mother's job as an auxiliary kitchen maid at the Lion Mansion Hotel (now part of the Royal Albion Hotel) allowed her to bring home unwanted food scraps to feed the children, a subsistence eked out with parish relief. The family were later forced to move to two rooms in Hollingdean Road and then to Newmarket Road, and finally to Gladstone Place.

Despite the obvious hardship Coppard's posthumously published autobiography recalls boyhood freedom and pleasures. He educated himself by reading voraciously at the town's public library, where 'so much of the English imagination had, like a kindly stranger, taken me by the hand'. At ten, he went to live with an uncle in London and started work as an errand boy. At 13 he came back to Brighton. He worked as a bookkeeper in the engineering works near the barracks, and, by the age of 20, he had also worked for an auctioneer, a cheesemonger, a soap agent, and a carrier.

Although disparaging of the town – oddly, he said, it had 'no fine architecture, no fine history, no cultural context' – he also called it 'that paradise of brightness'.

In 1905 Coppard was married in the town to Lily Richardson, daughter of a local plumber, and in 1907 they moved to Oxford, where he became a confidential clerk in an ironworks. In 1919 Coppard became a full-time professional writer.

Bob Copper (1915–2004)

TRADITIONAL FOLK SINGER, COLLECTOR OF FOLK SONGS AND WRITER
1 Challoner's Cottages, Falmer Road, Rottingdean **P**

Copper was the most famous in a family, now based in Peacehaven, renowned for its singing and passing down of Sussex folk tunes. They lived in this cottage from 1898 to 1969, although their origins in Rottingdean can be dated to the 16th century. A local man called Copper is mentioned briefly by **Rudyard Kipling** (*qv*) in *Rewards and Fairies*.

Copper's grandfather James 'Brasser' Copper (1845–1927), a farm bailiff, and his brother Thomas, a pub landlord, had sung at the home of **Sir Edward Carson** (*qv*) and were honorary members of the English Dance and Folk Song Society.

Kate Lee, secretary of the newly formed Folk Song Society, collected songs from James and Thomas Copper in 1898 when staying with Carson. Lee's publication of the songs and her account of the experience might have been the last records of the Coppers. It would seem that no other folk song collectors visited the Coppers after her.

In his youth Copper did light manual farm work, became a barber's lather boy and, as a teenager, a supplier of seafood to the local hotel. At the age of 18 he joined the Life Guards. His parents bought him out so he could join the West Sussex Constabulary. In 1941 he married Joan Deal, whose parents ran the Central Club in Peacehaven and in due course they took over this members-only drinking club, which later hosted folk nights. However, even as a boy Copper was aware of the passing nature of the culture into which he was born. He wrote: 'I became aware at an early age that I was witnessing the very last chapter of a long story and that what I was seeing and hearing would be quickly finished and gone forever. This made me doubly anxious to absorb everything I could while there was still time...'

Copper collected songs and sang with his friend and cousin, Ron Copper, learning the old ways of singing from their fathers, although in the inter-war years some of that kind of music was unfashionable and thought by some to be out-moded and dreary. They made a handful of recordings, including *Traditional Songs from Rottingdean*.

There was a revival of interest in folk singing in the 1950s, which brought the family fame. In 1950 family members were recorded by the BBC (Copper was last recorded by the BBC in 2002 in conversation with Pete Seeger in New York), and the family has also performed at the Royal Albert Hall. Other members of the family, by blood or by marriage, have been drawn into the performances.

Copper wrote several books about the family and its songs, as well as *Across Sussex with Belloc*, about the travels of the novelist. Copper's obituary in *The Independent* referred to him as 'England's most important traditional folk singer'.

Copper's six grandchildren Mark, Andy and Sean Barratt and Ben, Lucy and Tom Copper now also appear independently as The Young Coppers, singing the same family repertoire.

Thomas Cubitt (1788–1855)

BUILDER
13 Lewes Crescent Ⓟ

Cubitt was often called an architect, but preferred the title builder. By the time that **Thomas Kemp** (*qv*), assisted by the architects **Charles Busby** (*qv*) and **Amon Henry Wilds** (*qv*), commissioned Cubitt to build his visionary Kemp Town development in 1823, Cubitt had a well-established reputation. Among many major projects, he had worked on speculative building in Belgravia and Bloomsbury, London, for aristocratic property owners.

Instead of negotiating with other master craftsmen, Cubitt had developed a system whereby he directly employed workmen of all the building trades, among them brickmakers, masons, plasterers and painters. This was innovative for speculative residential building and it helped make his name in the building industry.

But in Kemp Town, sales did not take off as planned and Kemp conveyed large sections of land to Cubitt to pay his debts. When Kemp went abroad to flee his creditors, Cubitt continued the work in partnership with his near neighbour **Frederick Hervey, Earl of Bristol** (*qv*). Cubitt lived in this house, which he built himself, from 1846 to 1855.

Marcus Cunliffe (1922–1990)

ACADEMIC
8 Lewes Crescent

Cunliffe lived here, with his wife, the sculptor **Mitzi Solomon**, in the 1960s until 1973, although they were divorced two years earlier.

After his appointment to the first lectureship in American studies at Manchester University in 1949, he became professor of American studies at the University of Sussex in 1965, where he was one of those who helped develop the discipline into what it is today.

However, he left after becoming entangled in the 'Huntington affair'. In the name of free speech he had opposed the opposition provoked by an invitation to Samuel P Huntington to lecture at Sussex.

Huntington was a distinguished political scientist, who had been an adviser to the Johnson administration during the Vietnam War.

Cunliffe left Sussex in 1980 and spent the rest of his life as a distinguished teacher and writer in the USA, where he died. The university's Marcus Cunliffe Centre for the Study of the American South is named in his honour.

Antony Dale (1912–1993)

HISTORIAN AND CONSERVATIONIST
46 Sussex Square

Dale is one of a small group of people whose influence in helping to maintain Brighton's architectural glory can be seen at every street corner. He founded the Regency Society in 1945 and was its secretary for 40 years, which would be achievement enough. But he also fought to save Brunswick Square and Adelaide Crescent from demolition, whilst stopping an over-ground car park being placed in Regency Square.

Educated at Brighton College and Oxford University, his conservation interests spread far wider than Brighton. From 1962 to 1976 he was chief listing investigator for the Ministry of Town and Country Planning. This led to ministers listing buildings of special architectural and historic interest.

His books include *Fashionable Brighton, The History and Architecture of Brighton, About Brighton, Brighton Town and Brighton People*, and *Brighton Cemeteries*.

Gerald de Gaury MC (1897–1984)

DIPLOMAT, EXPLORER, WRITER, SOLDIER AND ARABIST
Flat 3, 18 Sussex Square

De Gaury, who lived at this house for the last 20 years of his life and died here at the age of 86, was a diplomat who assisted the creation of the Arab states that came into being between the two World Wars.

Wounded once at Gallipoli and three times in France during the First World War, he was awarded the Military Cross for action at the Battle of Arras. He was an enthusiastic and skilled photographer, an accomplished watercolourist and sketch artist, and was also the author of many books on the Middle East, including his autobiography *Traces of Travel*.

De Gaury also served in various diplomatic posts in the Middle East and rejoined the Army to raise and command the Druze Cavalry.

William George Spencer Cavendish, 6th Duke of Devonshire (1790–1858)

WHIG GRANDEE AND CONNOISSEUR OF THE ARTS
1 Lewes Crescent (now Fife House)

Born in Paris, baptised in London, and educated at Harrow and Cambridge, the duke paid £1,800 for this house in 1829 and kept it until his death. **Prince Metternich** (*qv*), **William IV** (*qv*) (whose Lord Chamberlain he was from 1830 to 1834), **Lord Palmerston** and **Sir Edwin Landseer** (*qv*) were

numbered among his guests. He must also have stayed here with Eliza Warwick, of whom we know little, during their ten-year liaison, which began in November 1827 and remained a well-kept secret. He never married.

The Duke's prolific spending included £26,000 of his own money on his entourage as official representative at the coronation of Tsar Nicholas I in St Petersburg in 1826; a loss of £40,000 on the sale of a collection of coins and medals; vast redevelopments at the family home of Chatsworth; and the acquisition of several libraries. Such expenditure caused the sale of many of his estates, but not Lewes Crescent. However, he may not have come here after 1854, when he suffered a paralytic seizure from which he never recovered.

Kay Dick (1915–2001)

WRITER AND EDITOR
Flat 5, 9 Arundel Terrace

Dick began life as unconventionally as she was to live it. She was 'baptised' in the Cafe Royal by bohemian friends of her mother, Kate Coleman, a part-Irish actor, who had taken her there after leaving Queen Charlotte's Hospital, London, with 2s 6d in her purse, no husband and no home.

Educated at boarding schools in Geneva and South Kensington, at 26 Dick became the first woman director in English publishing at PS King & Son. She later switched to journalism (at the *New Statesman*) and also became prominent as an editor, encouraging young and unknown writers. She also wrote seven autobiographical novels, as well as non-fiction, but she suffered from bouts of writer's block. She campaigned tirelessly for the introduction of the Public Lending Right (PLR), which pays royalties to authors when their books are borrowed from public libraries.

Dick was an arresting presence: good-looking, with a great crest of hair, an eye-glass, a cigarette always to hand, and clothed in shirts from Jermyn Street. In later life she would be seen out walking with her dogs in Arundel Terrace (to which she moved in July 1968).

The independent income of her long-time partner, writer **Kathleen Farrell**, enabled Dick to concentrate on writing, and when their relationship came to an end Farrell remained in Brighton.

Her closest friends included the writers **Neville** and **June Braybrooke**, and the novelists **Brigid Brophy** (a fellow PLR campaigner), **Pamela Hansford Johnson**, **Francis King** (*qv*), **Gillian Freeman** and **Shena Mackay**. They and others were entertained at Arundel Terrace, where cigarettes, cream teas and martinis were supplied in quantities that belied her financial situation. Her basement flat was lined with floor-to-ceiling bookshelves crammed with editions of most of the 20th century's notable writers, many of which were inscribed by authors grateful for her editorial help, including George Orwell (in her copy of *Animal Farm*, he wrote: 'Kay – To make it and me acceptable'), while LP Hartley inscribed 'with gratitude and admiration'.

The journalist and newspaper editor, Roy Greenslade, a Brighton neighbour for 30 years, wrote that he found Dick 'both exasperating and exhilarating', but her 'vendettas were outweighed by her acts of kindness and generosity towards her friends, especially young people'.

She died from lung cancer at the **Dane House Nursing Home, Dyke Road Avenue**.

Charles Dickens (1812–1870)

NOVELIST
Bedford Hotel (now site of Holiday Inn), Kings Road 🅿 *
16 Lansdowne Place, Hove 🅿
148 Kings Road
Old Ship Hotel, Kings Road

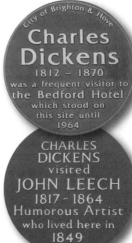

In 1848, while staying in Brighton, Dickens wrote to his friend, the painter Frank Stone: 'I don't in the abstract approve of Brighton – I couldn't pass an Autumn here – but it's a gay place for a week or so and when one laughs, and cries, and suffers the agitation that some men experience over their books, it's a bright change to look out of the window and see the gilt little toys on horseback going up and down before the mighty sea and thinking nothing of it.'

He wrote parts of some of his novels in the town, while a local ale – the Brighton Tipper – is referenced in *Martin Chuzzlewit*. Brighton is also mentioned in *Sketches by Boz, Bleak House* and *Nicholas Nickleby*. Some of *Dombey and Son* is set in the town. Like the author, the elder Dombey stays at the Bedford, while Chichester House, 1 Chichester Terrace, is said to be 'Dr Blimber's Academy for Young Gentlemen', which Paul Dombey, *fils*, attends.

Dickens' first visit appears to have been in October 1837, when he came to Brighton with his wife Catherine, who was pregnant with their second child, Mamie, to have a week's break at the Old Ship Hotel. He was 25 and already the brilliant reporter and sketch writer for *The Morning Chronicle*. The well-received *Sketches by Boz, Oliver Twist* (appearing in instalments) and the contemporaneous run of *The Pickwick Papers*, had made him the greatest literary sensation since Lord Byron. He wrote to his friend and future biographer, John Forster, that 'unless I am joined by some male companions' he was 'unlikely to see anything but the Pavilion, the Chain Pier and the sea'.

In May 1847, when Dickens was not well after an accident and Catherine was recovering from the birth of their seventh child, Sidney, they stayed for ten days at 148 Kings Road, the lodgings owned by a William Bennett or Dennett. Dickens worked on *Dombey and Son* from the 17–23 May and corresponded with **Hablot Browne** (*qv*) ('Phiz') about his sketches for the book. He also took in a large order for alcohol: 'half a dozen bottle of dry sherry, half a dozen of dry old port and two or three bottle of Chichester Punch if the latter were available', as he said. The health of husband and wife and Catherine's lack of evening dress caused Dickens to decline a dinner invitation from the **Rev Henry Wagner** (*qv*).

In March 1848 he was back again for at least two weeks with Catherine to concentrate on writing the final double number of *Dombey and Son*, 'that immortal story', he joked in a letter, while staying at **5 Junction House**, **Marine Parade** (gone), 'where we are comfortably (not to say gorgeously) accommodated', having moved from the Bedford. (The addresses suggest a room had been taken at what may have been the Junction House Hotel (gone), where the historian Clifford Musgrave says Dickens stayed, and was likely to have been in what is now Grand Junction Road.)

Dickens returned on 22 November 1848 to finish writing the short Christmas book, *The Haunted Man*. He stayed at the Bedford Hotel, where fellow guests included Queen Victoria's uncle, the Duke of Cambridge, who, with his wife, was celebrating his daughter's birthday. Dickens complained to his friend **Frank Stone** that they were 'driving me mad by having Life Guards under the windows…!'

No doubt Mark Lemon, writer, actor and founding editor of *Punch*, coming to visit to discuss his dramatisation of the book, made matters more bearable. Dickens went to the Theatre Royal for some light entertainment that included the fifth act of *Richard III* played as burlesque.

From 14–21 February 1849 Dickens and Catherine were in Brighton again, when he was turning over in his mind problems he had with David Copperfield, staying with his illustrator **John Leech** (*qv*), and his wife at Junction House. But a few days later, they all had to decamp to the Bedford Hotel when the landlord's daughter, already mentally ill, became 'much more mad' and the father, too, 'horribly mad', as he wrote to **Ada Lovelace** (the Countess of Lovelace), the computer pioneer and mathematician. That same year Dickens visited Leech and his family at Lansdowne Place (pictured).

Dickens wrote to John Forster: 'If you could have heard the cursing and crying of the two; could have seen the physician and nurse quoited [*sic*] out into the passage by the madman at the hazard of their lives; could have seen Leech and me flying to the doctor's rescue; could have seen our wives pulling us back, etc'.

In March 1850 Dickens retreated again to Brighton for two weeks, some of the time with Catherine, at the lodgings at Kings Road 'to pursue Copperfield in peace', as he wrote to Angela Burdett-Coutts **Harriot Mellon** (*qv*). To another friend, he wrote: 'Such weather here! So bright and beautiful! And here I sit, glowering over Copperfield all day.'

In February 1852 he and Leech came overnight to the Bedford for a walk on the Downs and 'a nice little dinner … in some snug corner'. They seem to have made a habit of this because in November Dickens wrote to Leech to ask him if he was disposed for a 'Hout' – a day in Brighton, a good walk, fresh air – and a week later they were there and had dinner at the Bedford.

When in Brighton Dickens would sometimes attend Trinity Chapel and hear the **Rev Frederick Robertson** (*qv*) preach.

In February 1852 he was working on *Bleak House* and *A Child's History of England* and editing his magazine *Household Words*, had invitations to 'feasts and festivals', and was engaged with Angela Burdett-Coutts on the charitable venture, Urania House in London. Not surprisingly, he told John Forster that 'my head would split if I remained here [in London]' and so he was off to Brighton for two weeks and he stayed at 1 Junction Road (again, despite the different but similar address as previously, this, too, may well have been the Junction House Hotel), with Catherine and her sister, Georgina Hogarth. He wrote that the weather was made for walking and not for writing and that he had not even made a start. A year later he complained to Mrs Lavinia Watson, a friend, that 'I was brayed and brassily blasted into imbecility of mind by German bands'.

In March 1857 Dickens had a three-day break with his friend, the writer **Wilkie Collins**. This is curious in that Collins disliked the town, which brought him out in 'cold perspiration', and where he found it difficult to eat and sleep.

Dickens also visited Brighton to give some of his famous public readings. On 11, 12 and 13 November 1858 he gave readings at Brighton Town Hall, returning for three days in November 1861, with two readings at the town hall (7th and 8th) and one at the Royal Pavilion (9th). On19 October and 2 November 1868, he gave readings at the Grand Concert Hall (gone), West Street (on the site of where **Dr Johnson** (*qv*) once stayed with **Hester Thrale** (*qv*) and her husband, **Henry Thrale**). After one of these readings the *Brighton Gazette* reported that 'the dialogue throughout was delivered by [Dickens] in his liveliest and most felicitous manner'. These latter readings were part of what was planned to be a farewell tour of 100 performances due to end the next year, although, in fact, he was still reading in London shortly before his death.

Poignantly, given Dickens' happy, past visits to the town with Catherine, Frederic Ouvry, his lawyer, pursued Dickens' wife here, where she and her mother were staying for two weeks so that she could find some respite from the distress of their domestic situation, to sign the deed of separation on 4 June 1858 which would end their marriage.

* *When the Bedford burned down in 1964, a cache of Dickens' letters, written to the manager, Mr Ellis, which were in a display cabinet on the ground floor, was saved. At that time, though, the first Dickens plaque on the hotel, erected in 1925, was lost.*

Clarissa Dickson Wright (1946–2014)

BROADCASTER, COOK, BARRISTER, WRITER AND BOOKSHOP OWNER
Convent of the Sacred Heart School, The Upper Drive, Hove (now site of Cardinal Newman School)

Baptised Clarissa Theresa Philomena Aileen Mary Josephine Agnes Elsie Trilby Louise Esmerelda, Dickson Wright became one half (with Jennifer Patterson) of the *Two Fat Ladies* TV cookery team.

Aged 11, she was sent to board at the Convent of the Sacred Heart School after years of physical abuse by her father, the distinguished surgeon and alcoholic, Sir Arthur Dickson Wright (he also physically assaulted her mother). She wrote of the school: 'I suddenly realised I was in a safe place. From that moment on I loved boarding school if for no better reason that I was safe'. Her lasting memories were how beautiful everything smelled: 'beeswax polish, flowers and incense'. She savoured this, she wrote, in beautiful surroundings and was inspired by the grace, dignity and authority of the nuns.

The school, which closed in 1966, was not only suffused with an emphasis on spiritual wisdom but also offered practical advice – 'don't carry scissors in your pocket' – and, unusually for the day, a variety of academic subjects for women.

Dickson Wright left the school, where, according to the present day Cardinal Newman School, she is 'fondly remembered as a spirited and intelligent young woman', in 1964 when 18. At the age of 21, she was the youngest woman at the time to be called to the Bar.

Jane Elizabeth Digby, Lady Ellenborough (1807–1881)

ARISTOCRAT AND ADVENTURESS

Norfolk Arms (site now the Mercure Brighton Seafront Hotel), 149 Kings Road

Jane Digby and her first husband, **Edward Law, later 1st Earl of Ellenborough** (1790–1871), made the inn, built around 1824, famous by their patronage between 1828 and 1830. He was Lord Privy Seal in the government of the Duke of Wellington and would later be appointed governor-general of India.

(The inn was completely rebuilt in 1866 in the French Renaissance Revival style, then called the Norfolk Hotel. That year, according to one guidebook, it became 'more beautiful than any other building in Brighton'.)

However, in 1830, by which time Ellenborough was president of the Board of Trade, the couple's divorce by Act of Parliament caused great scandal. Digby, who had numerous lovers and was to marry four times, was regarded as promiscuous for the age in which she lived. On this occasion, her affair was with Prince Felix of Schwarzenberg (1800–52), the Austrian statesman, who at the time was his country's London attaché. (He was a protégé of **Prince Klemens von Metternich** (*qv*) and was later Austrian Minister-President.)

The inn was obviously a venue for their trysts as its fame changed to notoriety and in 'Brighton!! A Comic Sketch', a poem published in 1830, the building became the subject of satire: 'But ladies, use, when you next come/The Schwarzenberg Hotel'.

It is claimed that Ellenborough fought a duel with Schwarzenberg and received £25,000 from him (a cuckolded husband could then sue his wife's lover).

In 1829 Digby left for Basel to await Schwarzenberg and the birth of their child, a daughter, Mathilde Selden, born in late November 1829, who was later to he brought up by her father's family.

Digby and the prince lived together in Paris in 1830, where some would still admit her to society. The couple had a son, Felix, later that year who lived only a few weeks. Schwarzenberg, conscious of career and his Roman Catholic family, deserted Digby in 1831. This earned him the title of 'Prince of Cadland' in London society.

However, the inn had regained its reputation by 1841 when a guidebook could describe it as 'a capital family hotel, which has long enjoyed the patronage of many persons of rank and distinction'.

Lord Alfred Douglas (1870–1945)

POET AND LOVER OF OSCAR WILDE
**28 Brunswick Square, Hove
35 Fourth Avenue, Hove
Flat 1, St Anne's Court, Nizells Avenue,
Hove** Ⓟ

Douglas looked back fondly in old age to the time when, as a child, he had stayed in lodgings in Oriental Place, with his sister, Edith, and their overbearing and degenerate father, the 9th Marquess of Queensberry. And it was the marquess who was to prove, much later in life, to be the nemesis of Douglas's lover Oscar Wilde.

In the summer of 1894 Wilde was staying with his family at a house in Worthing, where he worked on *The Importance of Being Earnest*. Douglas visited the house, disliked it and got Wilde to take him to the Grand Hotel, Kings Road, in October, where Wilde developed influenza. Wilde was later to claim that when Douglas was ill he hardly left him, but when the roles were reversed, Douglas was never in the room.

In 1902, two years after Wilde's death, Douglas (nicknamed 'Bosie') married Olive Custance, a bisexual poet. The marriage produced one son, Raymond, who was to spend much of his life in mental hospitals. When Douglas became a Catholic in 1911, the marriage became stormy, and while Olive later converted, her lapse from the faith caused her to leave the marriage. She lived (and was to die) in Viceroy Lodge, now replaced by flats of the same name at **143 Kingsway, Hove**. The couple never divorced but remained on friendly terms and met most days.

Douglas's first Brighton home was a flat in 28 Brunswick Square. In 1927, he and his mother, Sybil, moved to 35 Fourth Avenue, or what one biographer calls 'a small, dingy house in Hove' (dingy it may have been but it is not small). However, in 1935, when his mother died, Douglas's nephew, by now the 11th Marquess of Queensberry, rented the distinctly non-*fin de siècle* flat in St Anne's Court (pictured) for Douglas, and in this small apartment Douglas lived out the sad coda of his life.

Douglas was penniless, reliant on the help of friends and the Civil List pension granted to him after friends had petitioned on his behalf. During the Second World War, he described watching from the windows of his flat as German bombers came over Hove and, in fact, two houses were destroyed in Nizells Avenue and four of his neighbours were killed.

Even with his penurious existence, on his deathbed Douglas managed to place two bets (he lost both). He could be charming but he was also self-centred and vindictive. He made enemies easily and quarrelled incessantly and was litigious and fiercely anti-semitic, characteristics that waned only slightly with age. He died in Lancing Hospital and is buried, with his mother, in the small cemetery of the Franciscan Friary, Crawley, West Sussex.

Christiana Edmunds (1828–1907)

MURDERER

16 Gloucester Place (gone)

Edmunds, the infamous 'Chocolate Cream Poisoner', was born in Margate, the daughter of an architect. She was living with her widowed mother at this address when she began an affair or a flirtation – the details are uncertain – with a married man, an eminent local doctor, Charles Beard, who lived at **64 Grand Parade** (site of University of Brighton), almost opposite where she lived.

In the summer of 1870, he broke off the relationship and Edmunds purchased strychnine from Isaac Garret, a chemist at **10 Queens Road**, saying that she needed to get rid of stray cats. She then bought a box of chocolates from JG Maynard's at **39–41 West Street**, and injected them with the poison before taking them to Beard's wife. The next day Mrs Beard became violently ill but recovered. Beard later claimed he suspected his former lover of attempted poisoning but said nothing for fear of the relationship becoming public.

Edmunds returned the chocolates to the confectioner, who exchanged them for ones she said she preferred, and he then unwittingly sold the returned chocolates to other people who fell ill. To allay suspicion, Edmunds then used intermediaries to buy more chocolates and poison.

But in June 1871, four-year-old Sidney Albert Barker, on a day trip to the town with his family, died after eating chocolates purchased in Maynard's. An inquest found the death to be accidental but David Black (see **Constance Garnett** (*qv*), the Brighton coroner, later said that only poisoning could account for the death.

Undeterred, Edmunds started to send parcels of poisoned fruits and chocolates to prominent local people. As the police had connected the large numbers of ill people with the chocolates, Edmunds also sent them to herself, saying that they had come from Maynard's, to pretend that she, too, was a victim of the poisoner.

When Dr Beard finally told the police of his suspicions, Edmunds was arrested and charged with the murder of Sidney Barker and the attempted murder of Mrs Beard. She was to appear at the Lewes Winter Assizes but it was ruled that a fair trial was impossible locally due to sensational local press coverage of the case (one of the magistrates had also been a recipient of a parcel). Thus, she was sent for trial at the Old Bailey in January 1872, charged with the boy's murder.

Edmunds was found guilty and sentenced to death. At first she claimed to be pregnant, as expectant women could not be executed, but that claim was found to be false. However, mental illness having been established at the trial she was committed to Broadmoor Criminal Lunatic Asylum and died there in 1907.

Edward VII (1841–1910)

MONARCH

8 Kings Gardens, Hove 🅿

Fife House, 1 Lewes Crescent 🅿
**(plaque, now obliterated, to Duke of Fife
and Duke of Devonshire)**

As monarch, Edward would sometimes stay with his
eldest daughter, **Princess Louise** (who lived here until
1924) and her husband, the **Duke of Fife**, at Fife House,
when the gardens would be set aside exclusively for his
use. However, he also stayed several times with his friend,
the banker **Arthur Sassoon**, of the wealthy Anglo-
Jewish merchant family, at his home at Kings Gardens, Hove (pictured). Sassoon, whose half- brothers,
Nathan and Reuben, had equally sumptuous houses nearby, lived in great splendour with 40 servants.

In 1898, when he was Prince of Wales, Edward rode twice on the Volk's railway along the seashore. The
first time he went on his own to Rottingdean and back but returned later when **Magnus Volk** (*qv*), the
railway proprietor, disappointed to have missed the king, sent him a personal invitation.

Edward liked the air in Brighton. He loved to be driven fast and was proud to have exceeded 60mph on
the Brighton Road in 1906. He came to stay with Sassoon for a few days in December, January and
February in the last three years of his life. The last stay was occasioned by his health. In late 1909 those
who saw him in Brighton were shocked at how old, tired and ill he looked. At dinner, he sat silent and
morose. On a trip to Worthing he fell asleep in his car and crowds gathered to stare silently through the
windows. He was depressed about the prospect of a Liberal re-election at the forthcoming general
election because of the attacks on the House of Lords and his fear that the monarchy would be dragged
into a party political dispute. These were issues he may have mulled over, on 14 January 1910, when his
diary records: 'In the morning, walk on the beach at Shoreham – in the afternoon, motor to Worthing
and walk on promenade.' On 10 February he was visited at Kings Gardens by Herbert Asquith, the Liberal
Prime Minister, to discuss the situation of the Irish nationalists siding with the Tories over the Finance Bill.

Sir Elwyn Jones, later Baron Elwyn-Jones (1909–1989)

POLITICIAN AND LAWYER
17 Lewes Crescent 🅿

When Labour were elected in 1964, Jones became Attorney General and two years later, the Welsh-born
lawyer and his wife, the writer and artist **Pearl 'Polly' Binder**, moved to this to house. They had married
in 1937.

The son of a tin-plate rollerman and educated at Cambridge, Jones was a member of the prosecution
team at the Nuremberg Trials and had first been elected to Parliament in 1945. As Attorney General he
established the Law Commission, was counsel for the tribunal for the Aberfan inquiry, and prosecuted
the Moors Murderers. When Labour returned to power in 1974, he became Lord Chancellor with the title
of Lord Elwyn-Jones.

He died of cancer of the prostate at Lewes Crescent, on 4 December 1989. His wife died seven weeks later.

Rev Richard Enraght (1837–1898)

CLERGYMAN AND CONTROVERSIALIST

36 Russell Square
5 Station Road (formerly 5 Courtney Terrace), Portslade

Enraght was born in Ireland and was ordained an Anglican priest in Corsham, Wiltshire, where he served as a curate (in those days essentially the priest). He then served as a curate to **Arthur Wagner** (*qv*) at St Paul's, Brighton, living in Russell Square between 1867 and 1871. He moved to become curate-in-charge of St Andrew's with St Helen's, Hangleton. Here one of his six children was born (three others had been born in Brighton).

He shared Wagner's Anglo-Catholicism and was active, through letters to the local newspaper and a book and a pamphlet, in promoting that cause and its rituals, as well as campaigning for the abolition of rented pews. However, there was much antipathy in Brighton to High Churchmen (although their influence was strong in the town) and the *Brighton Gazette* was vitriolic toward clergy who introduced English Catholic rituals.

When he moved in 1874 to become a vicar in Birmingham, the Church Association, a radical Protestant group, prosecuted Enraght under the Public Worship Regulation Act 1874. He served 49 days in Warwick Prison in 1880–81, before being released on a technicality. But while the sentence cost him his post, it also gained him international attention. He then moved to become priest to Bromley-by-Bow, London, and South Bromley, Kent, and spent the final period of his life in a quiet rural living in Norfolk.

Henry Fauntleroy (1784–1824)

BANKER AND FORGER

Hampton Lodge, Western Road, Hove (gone but part was on land now at the corner of Hampton Place and Western Road; the porch is at Hampton Lodge, 140 Western Road)

Fauntleroy was the last person in the UK to be hanged for forgery. He gained this unenviable distinction on 30 November 1824 when he was put to death by a near neighbour, **James 'Jemmy' Botting**, the public hangman, who was born in Brighton off West Street and was to die in Hove.

Fauntleroy had risen from clerk to partner at the bank, which his father had founded. Fauntleroy was arrested on a charge of forgery. He was known in the town for his extravagant living, with his finely furnished houses, handsome carriages and beautiful and expensive mistresses.

Fauntleroy had charge of the day-to-day business, but the bank suspended payment in 1824, and he was charged with forging the trustees' signatures.

An Old Bailey trial heard him plead guilty but claim that he was using the money – said to amount to £250,000 – to pay off the firm's debts. Despite his plea and 17 business people attesting to his integrity, he was sentenced to death, but only after the case was twice argued before judges on points of law. Although there was an offer by an Italian to take his place on the scaffold, Fauntleroy met his death before an estimated crowd of 100,000 outside Newgate Prison, London.

Ken Fines (1923–2008)

PLANNING OFFICER
74 Northease Drive, Hove
23 North Road P

Appropriately the plaque that commemorates Hove-born Ken Fines is situated on a building near the North Laine area, which he not only successfully preserved in 1976, but which he also gave its name.

The son of a stage electrician on the Palace Pier, he became the council's planning officer in 1974 at a time when demolition was in the air. He urged the cause of preserving working class streets and villas.

He thought up the name North Laine from the old open field system, which had surrounded the town of Brighthelmstone. North Laine, he believed, was 'full of charm and character'.

He fought opposition in the council and the business community which favoured what is now North Laine being replaced by high-rise blocks and offices, and the construction of an elevated road from Preston Circus to a huge car park off North Street, which would have gone through North Laine.

He retired in 1983 and a tree was planted in Sydney Street in Fines' honour. He continued to play a role in local conservation and also wrote *A History of Brighton and Hove*.

The plaque bears the phrase 'Our Hero', a name given to him by the North Laine Association.

Maria Fitzherbert (1756–1837)

MORGANATIC WIFE OF GEORGE IV
55 Old Steine (now Youth Hostel) P

Church of St John the Baptist, Bristol Road P

This twice-widowed Catholic was unusual for a woman associated with the Prince Regent – she appears, despite claims, to have refused to become his mistress and accepted only marriage. The marriage, which took place in 1785 in the drawing room of her house in Mayfair, was secret because illegal – it breached the Act of Settlement 1701 which disbars Catholics, and those in the line of succession to the throne being married to Catholics. This would have ruled out 'Prinnie' (as the prince was known) from following his father George III as king. Yet the marriage was declared valid by Pope Pius VII, after Cardinal Thomas Weld, nephew of Mrs Fitzherbert's first husband, Edward, petitioned him.

In 1795 the prince married his cousin Caroline of Brunswick but never divorced Mrs Fitzherbert. George also wrote a will, bequeathing 'worldly property . . . to my Maria Fitzherbert, my wife, the wife of my heart and soul'. Although he later turned against her and claimed the marriage false, when he was dying he asked that her eye miniature, which he wore, be buried with him.

Mrs Fitzherbert lived in the listed house in Old Steine from 1804 and died there. It is still a handsome place, despite unfortunate alterations, and sits, appropriately enough facing the prince's **Royal Pavilion**, Old Steine. She and the prince would sit on the balcony, acknowledging the crowds.

The relationship between Mrs Fitzherbert and George underwent several vicissitudes. In the autumn of 1806 the Prince embarked on an affair with Lord Hertford's wife, Isabella, during which time he treated Mrs Fitzherbert contemptuously. However, at other times he declared his love for her. But in December 1809, she had grown so tired of his repeated declarations that she turned down his invitation that she stay with him at the Marine Pavilion (as the Royal Pavilion then was), citing the 'very great incivilities' she had received there. The final break came 18 months later in 1811.

Mrs Fitzherbert had helped to endow the Church of St John the Baptist in Bristol Road and it was opened two years before she died. It was only the fourth new Catholic Church in the country to be consecrated since the Reformation. (In 1791 the Catholic Relief Act had permitted the building of Catholic churches.) Before then she had had a priest say mass in her home and would invite local Catholics.

She rests in a vault, marked by a simple plaque, in the central aisle. Her adopted daughter, Mary Seymour (sometimes rumoured to be the child of Mrs Fitzherbert and her royal husband), had a marble memorial placed in the church and her mother's kneeling effigy has three rings on her finger, one for each of her marriages. The inscription reads: 'One to whom she was more than a parent has raised this monument to her revered and beloved memory'. Engraved on a book which the effigy faces are the words: 'It is a more blessed thing to give than to receive', a reminder of her generosity.

Robert Flemyng (1912–1995)

ACTOR
Flat 4, 6 Arundel Terrace

Flemyng lived between his small house in Clapham, London, furnished with what one obituarist called 'the no-nonsense austerity of an urban rectory where equally no-nonsense fare was offered such as grilled chops and red wine', and this apartment. This was said, by that same writer, to be 'luminously awash with marine light but again a refuge of simplicity and tranquillity which reflected the taste of his beautiful Peruvian wife, Carmen'.

Flemyng's acting abilities, combined with good looks and a commanding voice, earned him a solid 60-year career on stage, television and in film. Never a star, he was, though, popular and instantly recognisable. His stage appearances included Terence Rattigan's *French without Tears*, T.S. Eliot's *The Cocktail Party*, and Somerset Maugham's *The Constant Wife*. His films included *The Blue Lamp*, *Funny Face*, *The Man Who Never Was*, *Young Winston* and *Shadowlands*. On television he was in two long-running series in the 1960s, *Compact* and *Family Solicitor*.

William Henry Fox Talbot (1800–1877)

PIONEER OF PHOTOGRAPHY
The Vicarage (later The Grange, now The Grange Museum and Art Gallery), The Green, Rottingdean

Born in Melbury, Dorset, Fox Talbot was five months old when his army officer father died, leaving £30,000 worth of debt which forced the boy and his aristocratic mother, Elizabeth, into various (albeit desirable) homes. In 1804, she married Captain (later Rear-Admiral) Charles Feilding (1780–1837), who effectively became the child's father.

Fox Talbot, a brilliant student and eager to learn, but painfully shy and reclusive by nature, was initially educated at home by his mother and tutors. As a boy he had shown great curiosity about the world and remarkably wide interests, particularly in mathematics, languages, politics, botany, optics and astronomy. He had enjoyed chemistry and got himself into trouble over causing explosions while experimenting with chemicals. In 1808, when he was eight, he met the astronomer William Herschel. That year, too, he entered the small Rottingdean boarding school, run by **Rev Thomas Redman Hooker** (*qv*).

To lessen the wrench of boarding for both mother and son young William was allowed to return home in the evening for several weeks, as his mother was living temporarily in Brighton. That first year, Hooker could write to Lady Elizabeth: 'He seems to be of a very sweet & amiable disposition and . . . I have not a moment's hesitation in pronouncing him to be of a very superior capacity', but he added: '. . . everything should be done to induce him to play more and think less'.

The boy and his mother exchanged a lively correspondence on many subjects, including politics (as he did with others), during which he said how happy he was at the school. By his last year they could write to one another fluently in French, interspersed with Latin and Greek.

In 1811 William was accepted at Harrow School, after which he entered Trinity College, Cambridge.

He invented the calotype process, the precursor of photographic processes of the 19th and 20th centuries. He was also a notable photographer who contributed to the development of photography as an artistic medium.

William Friese-Greene (1855–1921)

DEVELOPER OF THE CINEMATOGRAPH
20 Middle Street Ⓟ

9 Worcester Villas, Portslade Ⓟ

The modest terraced, bow-fronted building in Middle Street, which has been a private home, offices and a youth hostel, may be one of the most culturally influential places in the world. 'May' because while the commemorative tablet states that it was here that Friese-Greene, the inventor of cinematography, 'carried out his original experiments which led to a world-wide industry', the evidence for this being the spot – or even Brighton being the town where this was done – is not cast-iron. Street directories and electoral registers do not place Friese-Greene at the address. In *Pike's Directories* for 1904 and 1905 a Captain W Lascelles Davidson and Dr Benjamin Jumeaux had a 'laboratory for natural colour photography' here. However, although Ray Alister, Friese-Greene's biographer, confirms this, he also states that Harvey Harrison, his subject's brother-in-law, 'had come to help at **[203a] Western Road** and the new, elaborate laboratory at Middle Street, where there were also other assistants.' Another source suggests that Friese-Greene may have been employed by Davidson and Jumeaux.

There is also dispute about the application of Friese-Green's 'chronophotographic camera', which allowed the creation of moving picture images, for which he gained a patent in 1899. Or rather, his was not the method which came to be adopted internationally. Business problems forced him to sell his method, he went bankrupt in 1891 and the patent lapsed.

It was from the late 1890s that Friese-Greene started to focus on creating moving pictures in colour. By 1905 he had developed a working system in which successive images were taken through alternating filters (for example, red and blue-green), with the printed frames then being dyed these colours. If projected at sufficient speed, they created an impression of colour. By this time he and his family were living in Brighton. (They also lived in Arundel Street.)

The young Friese-Greenes thought Middle Street the best playroom in the world. Not that their father allowed them to play there, but he sometimes let them come and watch him. In the centre room an airship about six feet long was suspended above a complicated system of railway lines. The boys might stand in the outer room and look through a glass panel.

As Alister also describes, 'Friese-Greene, from a third room, would move model trains about the railway lines, directing them by some black magic of his own. They were being directed by a wireless beam . . .'

Constance Garnett (1861–1946)

TRANSLATOR
58 Ship Street (now a restaurant)
40 Buckingham Place

Garnett was born in Ship Street (pictured) and was christened in the Chapel Royal in North Street. The house had been numbered 45 in 1845 when her parents, David and Clara Maria Black, had come to live there and where her father also had his solicitor's firm's office.

David Black had first lived and worked at number 56 after he returned from time in Canada before his marriage, although before that he had lived in the town with his brother Peter and completed his schooling there in 1832. He then took articles at the solicitors Freeman and Cornford, at 58 Ship Street, who 16 years later offered him a partnership. He later became town clerk (in 1863) and coroner of Brighton. Clara, who had literary interests, heard **Charles Dickens** (*qv*) give one of his readings in Brighton.

Garnett was the sixth of eight children. Her eldest sister, also born in Ship Street, was **Clementina Black**, the writer, suffragist and political activist. The family would holiday for a month each year in Uckfield, Sussex, or nearby Sharpsbridge.

For two years from the age of four until she was nearly six, Constance was confined to an invalid carriage with tuberculosis of the hip joint. She was taught at first by governesses and was then an unhappy boarder in a school in Sussex Square. It was when she was at the school, too, that the family moved to Buckingham Place, which was smaller and less expensive than the house in Ship Street. In 1876 she transferred to the Brighton High School for Girls (now Brighton and Hove High School) at Milton Hall, 75 Montpelier Street, which had opened that year.

Garnett went up to Newnham College, Cambridge in 1879 and found liberation. She had not been happy in Brighton, what with her mother's death in 1875 and her father's gloomy temperament, and Buckingham Place, with its cramped quarters, as well as her unhappy time at the Sussex Square school.

In 1899, Constance married Edward Garnett, editor and book reviewer, at Brighton Register Office and two years later the couple moved to a rented cottage at Henhurst Cross in Surrey. A year later, their only child, **David Garnett**, who would become a novelist and a member of the Bloomsbury Group, was born in Buckingham Place, to which Constance had returned because she trusted to the ministrations of the family doctor in Brighton, Dr Humphrey. Afterwards, she could not wait to get home: 'Brighton is a hateful place', she wrote. A year later, it proved to be literally so for, in 1893, her unsuccessful, lonely and isolated brother Arthur shot dead his mentally ill wife, Jessie, and one of their children, Leslie, before killing himself with chloroform at their home, **27 Goldstone Villas**, Hove.

George IV (1762–1830)

MONARCH
Royal Pavilion, Old Steine
Marlborough House, Old Steine

George first came to the village of Brighthelmstone when he was 21 and Prince of Wales. Its vivid life of balls, promenading and assemblies attracted him. Here was wit, beauty, and style far removed from the dull court of his father, George III, in London.

Having married **Mrs Maria Fitzherbert** (*qv*) in 1785, he leased a 'superior farmhouse' from Thomas Kemp, MP, wool merchant and local landowner, and father of **Thomas Kemp** (*qv*) in what was becoming an increasingly fashionable village. The water cures of **Dr Richard Russell** (*qv*), which had done so much to popularise the place, were recommended to the prince by his doctors.

At that time there was hardly a house on The Steine and George's house had a full view of the sea. George had the architect **Henry Holland** enlarge the building into the Marine Pavilion, a modest building in Graeco-Roman style in 1787, after Parliament gave him £161,000 to pay his debts and increased his income from the Civil List by £10,000 a year.

The prince had contracted his disastrous marriage in 1787 to Princess Caroline and they stayed for two months at Marlborough House, Old Steine, while Marine Pavilion was being redecorated. (He was also to stay there again soon after his succession to the throne in 1820.) In 1808, the grand stables (now **The Dome**) were completed. After later enlargement, in 1815–23 George commissioned the architect John Nash to transform the Marine Pavilion, whereby he placed a cast-iron frame over the building to support the towers, minarets, pinnacles and onion domes in an extravagant 'mixture of Moorish, Tartar, Gothic and Chinese, and all in stone and iron', as Dorothea Lieven, the wife of the Russian ambassador, sought to describe it. (The writer William Hazlitt was to call it 'a collection of stone pumpkins and pepperpots'.)

George's garden has now been restored as it was in his day to make it probably the only complete Regency garden in the UK. The gorse, heather and other native plants evoke, horticulturally, the love of nature found in contemporary Romantic art and poetry, as do the winding paths and the views through the trees, but there are also Indian and Chinese varieties brought back at the time.

All of this created work for an army of workmen, tradesmen, labourers and craftsmen, and the prince's patronage helped increased the population of Brighton from 3,620 in 1786 to 40,634 in 1831, the year after he died.

When in the town 'Prinny', as his friends called him, would send to the hotels every morning for a list of their guests, so that he could invite whomever he knew. 'Come directly, do not bother about clothes. The Queen does nothing but embroider flowers after dinner', he would urge his old friends.

After staying at the palace, Lady Warncliffe wrote: 'The King was in very good spirits but one was afraid of *encouraging* him, as he was rather inclined to be *improper* in his jokes.' His sister-in-law (later Queen) **Adelaide** forbade women to dress *décolleté* to her parties, whereas George liked 'ample expansions'.

For George, the theatricality of the meal was as important as the food. He employed table deckers, artists of the table, whose job was far more than to lay cutlery correctly. Often dozens of courses were served. After eating, guests would then go off to dance or play cards before a cold supper.

George's weight problems – at one time he weighed 20 stone – made him fear ridicule in public and so in 1822 he had a 65-yard tunnel constructed to run from the palace to the stables that he might go from one to the other unseen. It cost him £1,783. The cylindrical, arched ceiling lowers slightly from one end to the other. (At one time open for special visits, the tunnel is now closed to the public but its route can be traced above ground in the Pavilion gardens by the tarmac that covers most of the apertures that used to let in daylight.)

The interior of the Pavilion was not finished until 1823 and, in ill health, grossly overweight and prematurely aged, his once good looks ravished, George became increasingly unable to make the journey to Brighton. He visited only twice after the work was over, the last time in 1827.

Eric Gill (1882–1940)

SCULPTOR, TYPOGRAPHER AND WOOD ENGRAVER
32 Hamilton Road **P** *
2 Prestonville Road
17 Clifton Road
Preston View, Highcroft Villas

Gill, who was born in Hamilton Road, looked back on Brighton in later life as 'a shapeless mess' and 'not a place at all; an urban sprawl'. Yet his childhood was an unusually happy one; 'moralistic, strict, emotional, cosy and contained', says his biographer Fiona McCarthy. For Gill, the adult pacifist, it was also imperialistic and patriotic.

He was the second child of a family of seven boys and six girls (two of whom died during Gill's childhood) of the Rev Arthur Tidman Gill and his wife Rose, both of whom rest in Brighton's Extra-Mural Cemetery. It was a plain living and high thinking home, with a family income of £150 a year. He himself had the household job of cleaning the knives and laying the table. The family entertained themselves with puns and word games and the children produced a homemade journal, *The Monthly Magazine of Fun and Frolic*. Gill long remembered the fireworks for the jubilee of **Queen Victoria** (*qv*) set off on the West Pier. Mr Gill pinned up a large card in the breakfast room, illustrated with a great eye: 'Thou God seest me'.

The Hamilton Road house is a small Victorian one with a semi-basement but its modern additions have destroyed the original character of what McCarthy calls 'amiable primness'.

McCarthy sees that Gill's later seeking-out of mountain dwellings – Capel, north Wales, Piggotts Hill, Buckinghamshire and the Pyrenees – dates from the vistas of Brighton that Hamilton Road afforded the young Gill.

When Gill was two, the family moved to Prestonville Road, and then Clifton Road and finally to Highcroft Villas or 'a succession of small, tightly packed houses near the railway line in Brighton', as McCarthy puts it in her entry on Gill in the *Oxford Dictionary of National Biography*.

These homes were not far from the North Street chapel, where the senior Gill, first ordained as a Congregationalist minister, was assistant minister for the Countess of Huntingdon's Connexion, a sect of Calvinistic Methodists, founded by the **Countess of Huntingdon** (*qv*) in Brighton in 1760. (The chapel was in what had been her house.)

Having been educated in the nursery at home, when he was six Gill was sent to a kindergarten run by the Misses Browne, daughters of 'Phiz', **Hablot Browne** (*qv*), illustrator of **Charles Dickens** (*qv*). He was a slow learner and, ironically, given his later career as a typographer, at eight could only read three-letter words. He then went to the Arnold House School, Montpelier Terrace (gone), a boys' day school, where his father had taught on arrival in Brighton (it was then called Western College). Gill was a 'fairly happy' but indifferent scholar, apart from arithmetic, unexceptional for one who was so rebellious as an adult. He was also keen on cricket. 'It's a pity he's so easily led', wrote one teacher.

Gill inherited his mother's musical ability and had a gift for performance. He and his father loved mechanical contraptions like microscopes and telescopes. With his brothers and sisters he visited the Booth Museum, in Dyke Road, near their home, and very likely the chalk fossil collection in Brighton Museum. He would visit Brighton Station to watch and sketch the trains.

When Eric was 14 his father joined the Church of England, as a result of which the family moved to Chichester in 1897. The spiritual fluidity of his father may perhaps explain how Gill attached himself to Anglicanism and agnosticism before being received, with his wife Ethel (Ettie), into the Catholic Church in 1913. For this he came to Brighton weekly to receive formal instruction from Canon Connelly prior to his reception into the Church at Sacred Heart Church, Norton Road, Hove. (Ettie took her instruction at a Brighton convent.)

Toward the end of his school days, Gill discovered his penis: 'What a marvellous thing was this that suddenly transformed a mere water tap into a pillar of fire – and water into an elixir of life'. As one who was, in later life, to go through all kinds of sexual turmoil, and commit adultery and incest with his daughters, but came to be regarded publicly as a sexual prophet, he spent much of the next 45 years acting upon that discovery.

* *Gill's most public work in Brighton today is the several commemorative plaques on buildings (the first in the city), commissioned by the council.*

William Ewart Gladstone (1809–1898)

PRIME MINISTER

20 Brunswick Square, Hove
Lion Mansion Hotel (now west wing of
the Royal Albion Hotel), Kings Road **ⓟ**

Gladstone's first visit to Brighton may have been when he was
the 32-year-old vice-president of the Board of Trade, when he
stayed at 20 Brunswick Square from March to April 1842; and he may have stayed at number 27 in
February of the following year. In June 1844 he stayed a few days at 5 Sussex Square, which his brother,
John Neilson Gladstone MP, had taken for nine months. His final visits were respite from onerous
parliamentary sessions as prime minister, in the final year of the fourth of his four governments, such as
his visit in 1893, when he managed five days away. Even then he returned for a sitting that encompassed
his 84th birthday on 29 December that year. The following January he managed only a weekend, and his
last visit was just after retirement that year.

There were several other visits in the intervening years. In April 1850 his fourth child and second
daughter, five-year-old Catherine Jessy, died of cerebral meningitis and Catherine, his wife, was prostrate
with grief in Brighton. It was to there that Gladstone reported to her the funeral in London, which he, but
not she, attended. He then went to Brighton to spend time with Catherine and the younger children.
Gladstone holidayed in the town during the parliamentary Easter Recess of 1866.

In 1891 he came to visit his friend and private secretary, Sir Edward Walter ('Eddie') Hamilton, who was
recuperating from a serious illness. This may well have been at the Lion Mansion Hotel, with its porticoed
entrance in Kings Road, where Gladstone often stayed. Hamilton noted in his diary: 'They [presumably
Mrs Gladstone had come with him] were delighted with the hotel (especially as they did not have to pay
the Bill, which Armistead settles); and they enjoy themselves here.' (George Armistead was the former
MP for Dundee, one of Gladstone's wealthy benefactors.)

In the Easter Recess of 1893 he returned for a month to the Lion Mansion Hotel, again courtesy of
Armistead, during which he went back occasionally to London, and also visited Lord Rosebery, the
Foreign Secretary, who was to succeed him as prime minister, at his home, The Durdans in Epsom, Surrey.
Gladstone noted that he found 'Pier and salt air perfection' in Brighton. Toward the end of his stay he was
interviewed by the police about an 'intruder' named MacCurran.

A few weeks later he returned again to refresh himself after the difficulties at Westminster. The year
ended with a Christmas break in Brighton, where, he recorded, 'Backgammon with Mr A Wood. Worked a
little on the Odes'. (He was translating the *Odes* of Horace.)

It was Armistead's generosity which again allowed Gladstone his final stay in March 1894, less than two
weeks after he had retired. That September, he pronounced himself 'thoroughly content with retirement'.

Graham Greene (1904–1991)

NOVELIST

Hotel Metropole, Kings Road
Royal Albion Hotel, 35 Old Steine

Graham Greene first came to Brighton when he was six to convalesce after illness, which he believed to have been jaundice. He was taken to the town, at his mother's request, by his Aunt Maud, a neighbour in Berkhamsted, Hertfordshire.

Greene must have known the town very well by the time he came to write *Brighton Rock* in 1937 because in *Ways of Escape*, reflecting on the criticism which the Brighton local authorities had made of the novel when it first appeared, he wrote that 'for me to describe Brighton was really a labour of love, not hate'. He went on: 'No city before the war, not London, not Paris or Oxford, had such a hold on my affections ... It was there I saw my first film, a silent one, of course, that captured me forever: *Sophie of Kravonia*'.

In *Brighton Rock* he immortalised Sherry's Dance Hall (gone), West Street, referred to as 'one of the town's most famous temples of pleasure' by the historian Clifford Musgrave.

The town was somewhere where Greene could 'watch others without being watched', according to biographer Michael Shelden, but fame spoiled that: 'I am too well known in Brighton nowadays', said Greene in the 1960s.

In October and November 1958 he stayed at the Hotel Metropole, with the film director Carol Reed, while working on the screenplay of *Our Man in Havana*. They shared a suite, with two bedrooms. Greene would rise early, write, hand the pages to the secretary (who had a room in the suite) to type and then they would be handed to Reed in bed. The two men would meet at lunchtime to discuss progress and the routine would continue in the afternoon. 'In the evenings we amused ourselves', said Greene. While there he sent a telegram to his former lover Catherine Walston (the relationship had ended the previous year) and muse of *The End of the Affair*: 'FAIR WINDS AND HAPPY WINDFALL LOVE GRAHAM'.

It appears that Greene would often go to Brighton to work (the Royal Albion [pictured] offered him 'tranquillity' said his daughter). In 1960 he sought peace to finish *A Burnt-Out Case* 'but my dream of getting down to Brighton is shattered', he wrote to Walston.

In 1969 Greene published *Travels with My Aunt*, in which Henry Pullinger, a retired bank manager goes with his eccentric Aunt Augusta, first, to Brighton, which 'proved to be a bizarre taste of what was to come'. Here he meets one of his aunt's old acquaintances, and gains an insight into one of her many past lives. A psychic, too, predicts many travels in the near future. However, before they set off for new places and adventures, among other things, Henry and Augusta stay at the Royal Albion, where, otherwise comfortable, the lights of the Palace Pier do not allow Henry to sleep; they have a drink in the old Star and Garter, 16 Kings Road (now Dr Brighton's); and they dine at the Cricketers pub*, 15 Black Lion Street. They leave on the *Brighton Belle* to Victoria Station in London.

In November 1981 Greene was in Brighton to finish *Monsignor Quixote*, and, according to his friend and travelling companion, Fr Leopold Duran, 'to stay at the same hotel in which he wrote part of *Brighton Rock*'. This may well have been the Metropole.

* *The Cricketers pub has a Greene room devoted to the novelist (and Jack the Ripper!), displaying memorabilia.*

Martha Gunn (1726–1815)

'QUEEN OF THE DIPPERS'

36 East Street P (now a restaurant)

Gunn excelled so much as the operator ('dipper') of a bathing machine used by women that she was described by the local *Morning Herald* as 'The Venerable Priestess of the Bath'. She was also called 'the Queen of the dippers'. The dipper pushed the machine and helped the bather in and out of the water. This required great physical strength.

Her fame spread nationally and she featured in popular engravings and cartoons. She was said to be a favourite of the Prince of Wales, with free access to the royal kitchens in the Royal Pavilion. She did not retire until her 80s and is buried in **St Nicholas' churchyard**, Church Street.

James Orchard Halliwell-Phillipps (1820–1889)

ANTIQUARY AND LITERARY SCHOLAR

Hollingbury Copse (the street of the same name stands on the site)

In 1878–9, seeking sea air for his health, Halliwell-Phillipps moved to Brighton under doctor's orders. He was suffering from depression and migraines, was drinking heavily and dependent on opiate draughts to sleep. His work, professional squabbles and his own quarrelsomeness had exhausted him. Henrietta, his wife, disabled for many years, was terminally ill and died soon after the move.

Amid dense woodland, Halliwell-Phillipps built what he called a 'bungalow' or a 'rustic wigwam', which contained his very extensive library or 'workshop'. In effect, it comprised a vast spread of single storey buildings, rooms and outhouses, connected by wooden corridors, and all clad in wood with an outer casing of what was said to be fireproof, vulcanised sheet iron. The property was surrounded by gardens and groves that he himself planted, and had splendid views across the fields and downs to the distant sea. A year or two after moving here, he married Mary Rice, his second wife. The marriage and the surroundings revived him and he returned to work. As a vice president of the British Archaeological Society he would invite members to 'entertainments' at his home.

Halliwell-Phillipps had been born in London. He was educated privately, at one point at William Henry Butler's school in Brighton, before entering Cambridge. It was at the Brighton school that he first began to collect manuscripts and books, especially on the history of science and mathematics. He was only 19 when elected a fellow of the Royal Society.

In 1842 he eloped with Henrietta, the daughter of the noted bibliophile Sir Thomas Phillipps, having been unable to provide a dowry and having exchanged acrimonious correspondence with his future wife's implacable father. (He took his second surname after his father-in-law's death.) In 1845 he was accused of stealing codices from Trinity College, Cambridge (he had left without a degree and in considerable debt), for which he was never prosecuted. However, he is said to have destroyed more than 800 17th century books by cutting them up to paste 3,600 cuttings in scrapbooks.

He was also a prodigious collector, author, editor (his *Nursery Rhymes of England* (1842) contains the first printed version of the story of the three little pigs), curator and cataloguer. An astute seller of literary works when hard up, he donated works to places as varied as the Smithsonian Institution in Washington DC and the local authority in Plymouth. Halliwell-Phillipps gave 500 volumes to the Shakespeare Birthday Trust Library, which he had been instrumental in setting up, as he was in saving Shakespeare's birthplace in Stratford-upon-Avon.

On his death, Mary, his widow, moved to Dorset and 'the wigwam' was up for sale for what prospectuses called the 'upset price of 6,000 guineas'. There were no takers and within a decade the wrecker's ball had done its work.

Under Halliwell-Phillipps' will 300 volumes of literary correspondence and other papers were left to Edinburgh University. His main Shakespearean collections are now in the Folger Shakespeare Library, Washington DC, while he gave about 1,000 in 1876 to Brighton Library, where they are kept in a special collection. Halliwell-Phillipps is buried in the churchyard of **All Saints, Church Hill, Patcham**.

Patrick Hamilton (1904–1962)

NOVELIST AND PLAYWRIGHT

12 First Avenue Ⓟ

The Childhood Home of PATRICK HAMILTON 1904 – 1962 Playwright and Author

Hamilton was born in Hassocks, Sussex, the youngest of three children in an affluent upper middle class family – his parents were minor novelists, his father was also a non-practising barrister – who moved to Hove in 1908, first to a series of flats, and then settling in a rented house in Palmeira Avenue that December. The following January they bought this four-storey house and remained here, with three or four servants, until soon after the outbreak of the First World War, when they moved to Chiswick. Hamilton attended the school run by a Miss Cadwallader, one of the three sisters who had run the school a decade or so before, when **Ivy Compton-Burnett** (*qv*) had been a pupil.

Toward the end of his life Hamilton wrote of 'the grey, drab, tall, treeless houses leading down to Kings Gardens and the sea' and the petty, complacent snobbery of the neighbours. He said his childhood was happy and he was well cared for. However, he suffered childhood anxieties and neuroses at the hands of a succession of nurses, to which he attributed the alcoholism which was to kill him.

As she walked Hamilton and his brother along the seafront, Nellie Gates, a beautiful nurse, for whom both boys experienced a sexual awakening, treated them to tales of her love life. Her sexual conquests (she said) included local stars like **C Aubrey Smith** (*qv*), county cricketer-cum-Hollywood star, and Ernest Longstaff, the Brighton and Hove Albion outside right.

He later attended Holland House, a prep school in Cromwell Road, Hove, where he was happy and led a gang. While he attended the plush Queen's Picture House, Nellie banned other cinemas as 'common', but the children did go to the Brighton Hippodrome.

Hamilton spent much of his life in small boarding houses, rented rooms and private hotels in London, Hove and Brighton, and there encountered those who would populate his novels, like *The Gorse Trilogy*, *Hangover Square* and *Slaves of Solitude*.

In 1921 he came to Brighton as a member of a repertory company at the Grand Theatre. He stayed at lodgings in Over Street, then a slum area near the station. Two of his characters lived here – Esther Downes in *The West Pier* and Jackie Mortimer in *Twopence Coloured*.

What may have been Hamilton's last visit to Brighton was a sad one. In 1952 his life was in a mess – he owed the tax man; he was divorcing, as was his lover, the novelist (as Laura Talbot), Lady Ursula Stewart or La (they had lived for a while in Hove the previous year and later married, in 1954); and he was drinking heavily. His ever-faithful brother Bruce, home from abroad for a while and wanting to stoke some happy memories for his return, suggested a holiday in Brighton. They stayed at the Queen's Hotel, Kings Road, but staff in bars and the hotel looked at the frequently inebriated, shambling Hamilton with contempt.

Gilbert Harding (1907–1960)

TELEVISION PERSONALITY
20 Montpelier Villas

The man who was born in the Hereford Workhouse, where his mother and father were master and matron, became, comparatively late in life, 'the most famous man in Britain', one of the first television personalities, known particularly for his on-screen rudeness and irritability.

It was his success on *What's My Line?* that enabled Harding to buy this delightful house in April 1956, while keeping his six-room London flat near the BBC. It cost £4,000 and he spent as much again on improvements. Also living in the house were his secretary, Roger Storey, his chauffeur, David Watkins, and Joan Smith, his companion, whom he would take for 'treats' to the Theatre Royal, although Harding had a tendency to sleep during plays. However, once, when in that theatre, he heard the line 'I've been offered a part in Manchester Rep' spoken by a particularly inept actor Harding bellowed from the stalls: 'Take it!'.

Harding's public reputation belied his private self: a deeply unhappy and lonely man, he could, though, be kindly, generous, warm-hearted, witty and amusing. He was learned, cultured and well read (he had been a professor of English in Canada and a school master) and also loved pubs – he frequently drank too much – and restaurants, but also enjoyed cooking.

Alan Melville (*qv*), his friend and neighbour, told how Harding was dogged with a sense of non-achievement: he had never created anything, he would say. He despised what he called his 'tele-notoriety'. Harding, at a loose end between programmes and personal appearances, would often pop round to Melville for 'liquid elevenses', which caused Melville 'dread' as he, as a writer, had deadlines to meet, but Harding came to see that he should call when he knew Melville to be free.

Among other Brighton residents, he also shared convivial lunches and dinners with **Robin Maugham** (*qv*) and **Hector Bolitho** (*qv*).

Harding was a Catholic convert at the age of 22 (this had ended his training for the Anglican priesthood), and it was when he came to Brighton that he became aware of the annual practice of burning an effigy of the Pope in nearby Lewes. In a letter to the Brighton *Evening Argus*, he branded this 'a gross insult to the Pope' and 'disgraceful', and started a highly unsuccessful campaign to have the practice stopped. The following year effigies of the Pope *and* Harding were burned.

He died on the front steps of 1 Portland Place, London, opposite Broadcasting House, where he had just recorded *Round Britain Quiz*, the programme which had brought him to public attention just over ten years previously.

Sir Hamilton Harty (1870–1941)

COMPOSER, SONG WRITER AND ARRANGER
33 Brunswick Square, Hove Ⓟ

Harty had suffered from a brain tumour since 1936, which had necessitated surgery and also the removal of his right eye. He continued to transcribe, write, conduct and travel. But in 1940 the war had put paid to much concert-giving, and Harty's St John's Wood house in London suffered massive bomb damage. He had to leave London and after a month of searching and staying in an hotel, he moved to this house, where search lights and the sound of distant guns were the accompaniment of the night. He gained some consolation by taking short walks to the shore. The nearest place with equipment for his continuing treatment was London, 60 miles away. He conducted the BBC Symphony Orchestra for the last time at Tunbridge Wells on 1 December 1940. Two months later a chill, from which he ought to have recovered, put him to bed and he died of septic pneumonia at his Hove home.

Sir Hamilton Harty
Composer and Conductor
died in this house
on 19th February 1941

ERECTED BY THE REGENCY SOCIETY

Sir Rowland Hill (1795–1879)

INVENTOR OF THE PENNY POST AND REFORMER OF THE LONDON–BRIGHTON RAILWAY
11 Hanover Crescent Ⓟ

In 1840 Hill made what was to be an indelible mark on our daily lives when he inaugurated the penny post, but in 1842 he was dismissed from his Treasury post. However, he applied the reforming zeal and administrative abilities that he had brought to Post Office reform throughout the three and a half years he subsequently spent as a director, and then, from February, 1845, chairman of the board, of the London and Brighton Railway Company. He took on the job in 1843, buying this house, where he lived until 1848. The last of the three stages of opening the line had occurred in 1841 and his appointment came in the wake of inexperience, inefficiency, breakdowns, accidents and delays which ignited criticism and hostility among shareholders and public alike.

Hill's investigations revealed damaging incompetence – a dividend was paid when there was no profit. Sure of his own abilities, he invested substantially in the company and persuaded family and friends to do likewise. He cut extravagance and waste and developed the neglected third class market. He cut fares and revised the timetable. He introduced a proper excursion programme, and the Easter Monday excursion to Brighton in 1844 had 45 carriages and four engines from London Bridge, with six carriages and an engine added at New Cross and six more with a sixth engine at Croydon for a four and a half hour journey. **Queen Victoria** (*qv*) felt the elegant watering place being cheapened by such innovations and even fellow directors feared that an influx of working class Londoners would damage Brighton as a 'superior' resort. Cheap fares, season tickets, faster (regular) services were a major step in commuting. Five months after Hill took over, shares, which had fallen from £50 to £35, rose to £75.

In his time, the Shoreham to Chichester line was built and he promoted amalgamations and co-ordination, including with cross-Channel steam packet companies.

As he left the railways job, he was presented with a publicly raised testimonial of £13,000 for his initiation of the penny post.

Hill was sufficiently taken with Brighton to continue to live there two years after he left the company, during which time he was again working, as secretary to the Postmaster-General, on further postal reforms.

Sir John Hindmarsh (1785–1860)

ADMIRAL AND FOUNDING GOVERNOR, STATE OF SOUTH AUSTRALIA
30 Albany Villas, Hove Ⓟ

Hindmarsh joined the Navy as a volunteer at the age of nine (his father was a gunner) and by 13 had experienced conflict, including at the Battle of the Nile. At 20 he served as lieutenant at Trafalgar. By the time that he and his wife, Susannah, came to live in this house in 1857, he had just retired from a distinguished career as a naval officer and a more questionable one as a colonial administrator.

His request for the post and influence secured Hindmarsh the first governorship of South Australia in February 1836. The settlement grew and he made a large profit from land speculation. However, his gift for money-making was not matched by administrative talents nor an understanding of his role. He was accused of being dictatorial and interfering, and of undermining the settlers' confidence by trying to make the new colony his own creation, rather than that of those who were promoting it. There was much conflict. After a lot of private and public criticism, he was recalled in 1838. From September 1840 until 1856 Hindmarsh was Lieutenant-Governor of Heligoland.

He had been knighted in August 1851 and promoted to rear admiral on his retirement in January 1856. However, in April 1859 his wife died and Hindmarsh moved to London, where he died the following year, leaving £4,000, his library, oil paintings, engravings and china to his four children.

Sir John Berry ('Jack') Hobbs (1882–1963)

SURREY AND ENGLAND CRICKETER

13 Palmeira Avenue, Hove Ⓟ
32 Furze Croft, St Ann's Well Gardens, Hove

Hobbs, one of the greatest batsmen, with the highest number of runs scored and centuries made in first class cricket, moved to Palmeira Avenue, from which he could see the Hove cricket ground at the back, soon after the end of the Second World War. In the early 1960s he moved to the more utilitarian Furze Croft, where he was to die.

Cricket had generously rewarded him financially, but he remained a humble and unassuming man. He would go to the Hove ground to watch a game, sitting unrecognised near the end gate. Until a few weeks before his death he would also go to his sports shop in Fleet Street, London, three days a week, keeping the books, settling accounts and meeting callers.

From 1953, the year in which Hobbs was knighted, on 'The Master's Birthday' (16 December) he met with friends and admirers, including the cricketers Alf Gover, Doug Insole, Colin Cowdrey, and Eric and Alec Bedser; Sir Alexander Durie, later president of Surrey CCC; and the journalists Morley Richards and John Arlott, for a celebratory lunch at various Brighton venues and, later, in London.

Hobbs' wife Ada had been increasingly frail and ill for many years, and the burden of care fell primarily upon him. He refused to employ a nurse, which he believed would interfere with the intimacy of their relationship. She died in 1963. Suffering from cancer, he died in his sleep at home, a few months later.

William Holford, later Baron Holford (1907–1975)

ARCHITECT AND TOWN PLANNER

133 Marine Parade

Born in South Africa, Holford studied in Italy before coming to England in 1933. He lectured in Liverpool and worked as an adviser on post-war reconstruction.

He was a planning consultant to the City of London and Liverpool and Exeter Universities, and architect of Corby New Town. His plans for St Paul's Cathedral's precincts and Piccadilly Circus received prolonged criticism. He also had commissions in Australia and Brazil.

He later held academic posts and public offices. Knighted in 1953, he was the first architect and town planner to be made a life peer, taking his title as Lord Holford of Kemp Town in 1965.

He was a man of his time whose faith in large-scale redevelopment accorded with the spirit of reconstruction and modernising zeal in city centre replanning in the 1950s and 1960s. However, nowhere have his ideals fallen to the cause of conservation more than in his adopted town of Brighton.

George Jacob Holyoake (1817–1906)

SECULARIST, JOURNALIST, TRADE UNIONIST AND CO-OPERATIVE PIONEER
36 Camelford Street 🅟 *

Eleanor, Holyoake's first wife, who retained her religious beliefs and took no part in his public life, died in 1884. In 1886 he married his second wife, 40 year-old widow Mary Jane Pearson, and that same year they moved to this tall, narrow house. They lived here with her nine year-old daughter, his 17 year-old niece and a servant. He might have moved to Brighton in 1877 had a Mr Mayall managed to purchase a newspaper in the town for which he had proposed to make Holyoake the chief writer. However, Holyoake had been active in Brighton, anyway, before making it his home. For example, in 1879, he wrote a petition to persuade a Quaker, who had given £500 to open a library in the town, to ensure that it was open on Sundays.

The author of more than 20 books, an editor and journalist, Holyoake was the last person in Britain to be jailed for blasphemy. This happened in Cheltenham in 1842 after he suggested, at the end of a lecture on socialism, that religion was a luxury the poor could not afford. He was also the last person to be charged with publishing an unstamped newspaper, but the prosecution was dropped when the tax was repealed. He was the founder of secularism and also served as president of the Co-operative Congress, a movement he supported in England and in Italy and France. He was an active supporter of the Italian liberator Giuseppe Garibaldi, and at home he was a member of virtually every reform group. He stood three times for Parliament in the Liberal interest, each time withdrawing before the poll.

Holyoake continued his writing, including his autobiography, *Sixty Years of An Agitator's Life*. He travelled to speaking engagements and played a part in local civic life. (He had only been in Brighton two years when he had to be informed that he could not be made an alderman, implying he had sought the office.)

The year after his arrival in Brighton he travelled to the USA, where a journalist who interviewed him noted 'a pleasant, elderly gentleman of unassuming manners, a concise use of English language, great clearness of thought and precision of statement'.

Despite some journalism, Holyoake seems to have been hard up and friends subscribed £700, half invested to produce an annual £40 pension, the rest given to him.

At the end of his life, Holyoake's bed was placed in his library, as he was determined to die among his books. From his death bed he dictated an appeal to working people to vote for the Liberals at the coming election (as they were to do to usher in the reforming Liberal government of Henry Campbell-Bannerman), and he died on 22 January. His wife died the same year.

* *Holyoake moved to Castleford Road in 1886 and not 1881 as stated on the plaque.*

Rev Thomas Redman Hooker (1762–1838)

CLERGYMAN AND HEADMASTER

The Vicarage (later The Grange, now The Grange Museum and Art Gallery), The Green, Rottingdean

Hooker's career prospects were cut short when his father lost his fortune. He became private secretary to the Duke of Dorset, learned French, took holy orders and, through the Duke's influence, established the school in the village in 1800, where he was also a popular vicar from 1792 until his death. The house was a vicarage when he acquired it and he extended it to make it suitable to serve also as a school.

His pupils included **William Henry Fox Talbot** (*qv*) and **Edward Bulwer-Lytton** (*qv*).

A skilled horseman, Hooker also had a sideline as a lookout for local smugglers. It is is said that an underground tunnel ran from the house to the beach for this purpose.

There is a fine and prominent bust of him in St Margaret's Church, Rottingdean.

Sir Michael Hordern (1911–1995)

ACTOR

Brighton College, Eastern Road

Today a room at his old school, with a bronze portrait bust, is named in his honour, but Hordern, who was to become an acclaimed stage actor – from Shakespeare to Pinter, Chekhov to Stoppard – as well as a screen and television actor, was a decidedly undistinguished pupil.

He went to Brighton College when he was 14 to join his brother, Peter Hordern. While himself no good at sport, for a time he basked in the glory of his brother (later an Oxford Blue and England rugby international). He excelled at nothing other than singing, although he could not read music.

It was a shooting school and Hordern took to the sport, and while he was not much good, it did allow him to avoid cricket and also to smoke. Hordern also joined the Officer Training Corps and wrote in his autobiography: 'It was a great school for getting up in khaki, shouldering a rife and drilling. We were all little soldiers every Friday.'

However, as an intimation of what was to come later in his life, each year the school staged a Savoy opera by Gilbert and Sullivan. His first part was that of the Duchess in *The Gondoliers*, and a friend and fellow pupil, Christopher Hassall, encouraged him in a theatrical career.

In those days, though, Hordern wrote, Brighton College was a poor school academically – cricket and rugby were more important than classics. It grew in numbers under Canon Dawson but the larger it became, the worse the education.

Selina, Countess of Huntingdon (1707–1791)

RELIGIOUS REFORMER

North Street (now the site of Huntingdon House, 20 North Street)

Apart from St Nicholas' Church, Church Street, the oldest place of worship in Brighton at one time was the chapel built by the countess in the garden of her house in North Street in 1761.

A woman of great force of personality, she came to Brighton in 1755, hoping that the sea air would be beneficial for her ailing youngest son, but in 1757 both her sons died of smallpox.

The countess had been converted to Methodism largely under the influence of John and Charles Wesley, against much opposition from members of her family. She became known for her own powerful extempore addresses. She brought the famous preacher George Whitefield to speak in Brighton. He had brought her to an appreciation of what she saw as a truer form of faith and she had appointed him her chaplain. He addressed a large crowd in a field behind the White Lion Inn at the top of North Street, and soon after she opened her chapel as the first building of the evangelical Calvinist Methodist sect, which nevertheless followed the liturgy of the Church of England, and came to be known as the Countess of Huntingdon's Connexion.

But enthusiasm by local people was such that the building proved to be too small and by 1767 the chapel was enlarged (the first of four enlargements), funded by the selling of her jewellery for £698. In 1871 it was rebuilt in the Gothic style, in stone and flint with a spire, white marble pulpit, galleries and stained glass windows. It could accommodate 900 people. In 1972 the church was demolished, the proceeds going to the upkeep of other of the Connexion's places of worship.

Richard Jefferies (1848–1887)

WRITER, NOVELIST AND MYSTIC

3 and 8 (now 87) Lorna Road

Jefferies, who is noted for his depiction of English rural life in essays, natural history books, and novels, had only five years to live, when, in 1882, in desperate, chronic ill health, he moved to Brighton to convalesce, first, to one house in Lorna Road, and, then, from March and April 1883, to Savernake, Lorna Road. His wife Jessie and their two children accompanied him.

In December 1881 he had been ill with an anal fistula, and just before his move to Brighton he underwent four painful operations. Brighton and its hinterland proved an inspiration: the chalk grassland landscape and the presence of the sea, which had always meant much to him. This landscape, but also the shadow cast by his illness, drove him to write a spiritual autobiography, *The Story of my Heart*. It failed on publication in 1883, but is seen now as both central to his work and a mystical classic.

The family did not stay long in Brighton and afterwards lived in three places – Eltham, Kent; Rotherfield, Sussex; and Goring-by-Sea, Sussex. His plight, exacerbated by poverty, was made all the worse by the fact that, when living in Eltham, his 20-month-old son, Richard Oliver Launcelot, who had been born in Brighton, died suddenly of meningitis.

In April 1885 Jefferies' health gave way and a year later he vomited blood. In 1887 he had another haemorrhage. He was 38 when he died of a form of tuberculosis and was buried in Broadwater Cemetery, Worthing.

Sophia Jex-Blake (1840–1912)

DOCTOR AND CAMPAIGNER FOR WOMEN'S RIGHTS
13 Sussex Square

Jex-Blake was born in Hastings, the youngest of three surviving children of Thomas and Maria Jex-Blake. She was taught at home by her parents until she was eight and learned to read and write at an early age. She first attended boarding school in 1848.

In 1851 the family moved to this house and for two years she attended a local boarding school, but, as had happened before, her parents were asked to take her away. (In one eight year period she changed boarding schools six times.) On this occasion it may not have been entirely her fault as the teachers may have been more inflexible than before. However, even when teachers liked her they felt a 'need to rest from her vigorous presence', as her modern biographer writes. She displayed a 'native wildness'. A fellow pupil referred to 'a strong personality and [she] was so clever – in fact, far above our school mistress in natural intelligence'. Some of Jex-Blake's asides to her school teachers suggest not merely a maturity beyond her years, but impudence. However, another contemporary remembered that as a child, while she could be tactless and had a quick temper, she was also lovable: 'She came bounding into a room, bringing with her an atmosphere of gaiety and glee that is indescribable.'

In 1854 she was sent to board in Notting Hill, where she stayed for two years, and then came back to school in Brighton, where there was little attempt at serious teaching and she became bored. In 1857 she left boarding school for the last time with her sights set on being a teacher, and the following year was a student at Queen's College, London, to train in that profession.

Her true calling was medicine and it was a long and bitter battle for her to gain her qualifications to practice. Eventually, in Edinburgh, with four other women, she was permitted to take the matriculation examination and all passed. On 2 November 1869 they signed the matriculation roll, the first women medical students of a British university.

Jex-Blake founded the London School of Medicine for Women in 1874. In 1886 she began a similar school in Edinburgh and also started a hospital for women and children.

While she is noted on the family tomb in St Wulfran's Churchyard, Greenways, Ovingdean, she is buried in the churchyard at Rotherfield, Sussex, where she died.

Samuel Johnson (1709–1784)

WRITER AND LEXICOGRAPHER

Hester Thrale (1741–1821)

WRITER
77 West Street (gone) 🅟
St Nicholas' Church, Church Street 🅟

In 1769 Hester and Henry Thrale (1728–1821), politician and brewer, persuaded Dr Samuel Johnson to stay with them in Brighton. He was to pay many visits to the house, when he would worship at St Nicholas' Church, where the Thrales had a pew. At West Street, Johnson worked on his *Lives of the Poets*, the proofs of which Hester read.

In 1767 Thrale had purchased the property, a low, 'stone-coloured house' with bay windows, in fashionable West Street in Brighthelmston, where for many years they spent their autumns. (The house was demolished in 1866 and all that now remains is the garden post set in the pavement.)

In 1765, when the Thrales had been married for a year and had a small child (the first of their 12 children), Dr Johnson, the widowed and renowned creator of his *Dictionary*, came to dinner at their London home.

Henry was distant, unfaithful to his wife, severe and no great conversationalist, whereas Johnson was learned and a wit, and Hester was intelligent, well-read, multilingual, effervescent and talkative. Rumours would later suggest that Johnson and Hester enjoyed more than a close friendship. 'When I have no letter from Brighthelmston, think how I fret', he was later to write to Hester. He was so encouraged by her intelligence and her own early creative efforts that he would allow her to help him with his work.

However, Johnson never liked Brighton. 'The Journey to Brighthelmston makes no part of my felicity', he wrote to his host, adding that he visited because 'I love those with whom I go'. If one were minded to hang oneself there, 'no Tree could be found on which to tye the Rope'. 'The sea is so cold', he complained.

His beloved London was his social centre but Johnson found Brighton (like Bath) a 'blue stocking' place where women not only listened but argued. He would stay for weeks at a time – the diarist and novelist Fanny Burney and the painter Sir Joshua Reynolds were also occasional guests – but Hester came to see that Johnson was a demanding guest, who needed mothering and whose every demand had to be met. Burney wrote of Hester that she 'is extremely lively and chatty, and showed none of the supercilious or pedantic airs so frequently attributed by you envious lords of the creation to women of learning and celebrity; on the contrary, she is full of sport, remarkably gay and excessively agreeable'.

Burney's diary records visits to the New Assembly Rooms in the Castle Inn and the Assembly Rooms attached to the Old Ship in Ship Street. Thrale played cards and Fanny and Burney danced. They also went to Mr Thomas's Bookshop on The Steine.

In 1773 Henry became a town commissioner. Two years later, the Thrales' two-year-old son, Ralph, died of a brain condition in Brighton.

In 1782, Hester, by now a not very regretful widow of a year, 'picked up' (as she put it) Gabriel Piozzi, an Italian tenor, in Brighton. She engaged Piozzi as singing teacher to her eldest daughter, Hester, known as Queeney (later **Hester Keith, Viscountess Elphinstone**, literary correspondent and intellectual). Johnson was now ageing, past his creative best and not the person he was. Hester distanced herself from him – she had noticed, anyway, his eye for young women, including the teenage Queeney, whose patron he was. In 1784 Hester was to marry Piozzi, whom her three elder daughters would not accept as a stepfather, and Johnson was also violently opposed to the marriage. Thus, to avoid scandal she went to Bath and the daughters to Brighton.

Until 1856 Cecilia Margetta Mostyn, youngest daughter of the Thrales, lived with her husband, Bertie, at 9 Sillwood Place (gone).

Victoria Ka'iulani Kalaninuiahilapalapa Kawekiu i Lunalilo Cleghorn, Crown Princess Ka'iuni (1875–1899)

HEIR TO THE THRONE OF HAWAII

7 Cambridge Road, Hove

As second in line to the throne of Hawaii, after her elderly and childless aunt, it was decided that the princess, whose father was a Scottish financier, should have a British education. In 1889, aged 13, she was sent to a private school in Northamptonshire, where she excelled in Latin, literature, mathematics, and history and took classes in French, German, and sports, mostly tennis and cricket. Her aunt succeeded to the throne in 1891 in her absence, and in 1892 Ka'iulani moved to continue her education in Brighton at this address, home of Mrs Lena Rooke, a relative of Queen Emma of Hawaii. Here her curriculum included German, French and English and dancing, deportment and riding. The town delighted in the crown princess.

In 1893 her aunt was deposed and Ka'iulani sailed for the USA where, by meeting with President Grover Cleveland and by making speeches, she hoped to persuade that country to help restore the monarchy. But a republic was declared and within five years the USA had annexed the country. In 1899 she died, aged 23, in Hawaii, of inflammatory rheumatism.

Thomas Read Kemp (1782–1844)

PROPERTY SPECULATOR

The Temple (now Brighton and Hove High School), Montpelier Road Ⓟ
22 Sussex Square Ⓟ

Kemp's gift to Brighton is a vast and delightful impression on the eye known as Kemp Town. He did not, however, live to witness its completion.

The son of another Thomas, MP, landowner, and wool merchant, whose farmhouse in Brighton was rented by the Prince of Wales, the future **George IV** (*qv*), Kemp was born in Lewes, Sussex. He had been to Cambridge, practised law, was elected as MP for Lewes (he resigned the seat in 1816), and married to Frances Baring with whom he would eventually have ten children. The family moved to The Temple in 1819.

The house was at that time surrounded by fields, and its name is said to derive from the fact that Kemp designed it around descriptions on Solomon's Temple, as recorded in the Bible. As in Kemp's day, the tall flint stone boundary wall still surrounds it. Lions' heads are set on the pillars at the two entrances in Montpelier Road. Even after he moved in, Kemp had changes made – the place was much enlarged later in the century – and he built up the second floor and put in the four chimneys around the central dome, which has now gone and where the upper storey now stands. These mimicked the four minarets with which Nash surrounded some of the Pavilion domes.

Kemp and his wife's brother-in-law George Baring founded an evangelical sect and set up chapels in Lewes and Brighton, where Kemp preached. On return to the Church of England in 1823, he also returned to fashionable society, extravagant living, and politics (he was elected as MP for Arundel and in the general election of 1826 he regained a seat at Lewes, serving until 1837). His wife died in childbirth in 1825 (she is buried in St Nicholas' churchyard, Church Street) and in 1832 he married Frances Margaretta Harvey, a widow, with whom he had a son.

Kemp's wealth stemmed from the land inherited from his father, the most valuable part of which was the freehold of nearly half the parish of Brighton, outside the old town. Development had been taking place in a piecemeal way since before Kemp was born, and in 1823 he initiated the development of 40 acres of what is now Kemp Town or, rather Arundel Terrace, Chichester Terrace, Lewes Crescent, Sussex Square and associated service roads. There was money, he believed, in creating houses of the size and elegance of those being built around Regent's Park in London to suit the very wealthy.

CA Busby (*qv*) and **Amon Henry Wilds** (*qv*) drew up plans for the building of 106 houses. (Financial constraints cut the number from the planned 250.) In 1823, Kemp approached **Thomas Cubitt** (*qv*) to start building (he completed 37 houses).

The building boom collapsed in 1824–28 and tenants were slow in completing their houses. (There was an option to purchase at a fixed price and occupiers had to fit out the properties internally.) Income did not match the money required and it was only in the 1840s that profits started to come in, but it was too late for Kemp.

The houses were slow in selling and only 11 were occupied by 1828 and 36 by 1834. Ninety two houses, for which Kemp paid for the external building by the end of 1828, were let on 99-year leases.

He took his Sussex Square house in 1827, where he lived for ten years and entertained in a manner befitting his station, if not his financial situation. He donated a site for the Sussex County Hospital with £1,000 towards its cost.

A Whig, Kemp championed parliamentary reform and supported free trade. He was a Brighton town commissioner – he received **William IV** (*qv*) and **Queen Adelaide** on their first official visit as monarch and consort in 1830 – supported many charities, and rode with the Brighton Union Hunt. In William's reign he was a frequent dinner guest at the Royal Pavilion, sometimes with his eldest unmarried daughter and later with his second wife. This had not occurred under **George IV** (*qv*) because of Kemp's support of the Whigs.

Kemp's extravagant living and the slow growth of his enterprise did for him: his mortgages amounted to at least £84,000 and his creditors were in pursuit. In April 1837 Kemp resigned as an M.P., let his Kemp Town properties (Brighton land would be auctioned in 1842), and his London house, and went to live on the continent for the rest of his life. He came back once in 1840–41. It was only 11 years after his death that his plan, as envisaged, was completed.

After Kemp's death in Paris, his wife returned to live for most of the rest of her life in Kemp Town. She died in 1860 in Tunbridge Wells.

Edward Vaughan Kenealy (1818–1880)

BARRISTER
163 Wellington Road, Portslade (gone)

Born in Ireland, Kenealy lived here from the mid-1850s until 1874, with his wife and 11 children, commuting to Oxford and London.

A lover of the sea, he made Portslade his home because, as he wrote: 'Oh, how I am delighted with this sea-scenery and with my little marine hut! The musical waves, the ethereal atmosphere, all make me feel as in the olden golden days when I was a boy and dreamed of Heaven'.

He became nationally notorious for his unsuccessful representation of Arthur Orton, who claimed to be Sir Roger Tichborne, 'the Tichborne Claimant', in one of the great Victorian trials. During the trials Kenealy made groundless imputations against witnesses and various Roman Catholic institutions (he had abandoned the faith at university), was contemptuous of the judges, and prolonged matters to make this the longest trial on record.

The jury censured him but he started a newspaper, *The Englishman*, to support the claimant's cause and to attack the judges. His behaviour was so extreme that in 1874 he was barred from practising. He founded the Magna Carta Association to back the cause. In 1875 he was elected as 'the people's candidate', as MP for Stoke on Trent, lost his seat in March 1880 and died the next month. He is buried in the churchyard of **St Helen's Church, Hangleton Way**, Hove.

Francis King (1923–2011)

NOVELIST AND CRITIC
17 Montpelier Villas

King first lived in Montpelier Square ('tall, narrow and dark ... shoddily built') assisted by a large gift from his friend, the mystery novelist, **Clifford Kitchen** (1895–1967), who lived in two interconnecting houses in the square. King later bought 'one of the most beautiful houses in Brighton', 17 Montpelier Villas. He had to finance his Brighton life by becoming 'a Brighton landlady', renting rooms to students and other visitors.

However, while here King, author of 31 books, came to grief when he libelled a then friend and near neighbour, the vainglorious former Labour MP, **Thomas Skeffington-Lodge** (1905–94), who lived at **5 Powis Grove**. Skeffington-Lodge had served as MP for Bedford from 1945 to1950 and had unsuccessfully tried for re-election four times. His last parliamentary candidature was for Brighton Pavilion in 1969, when the Tory candidate Julian Amery, making a pun on his opponent's name and an important part of the town's economy, labelled him 'the bed and breakfast candidate'.

Skeffington-Lodge had seen a proof copy of King's gay novel *A Domestic Animal*, which belonged to the writer and novelist, **John Haylock** (1918–2006), his lodger at the time. He was not given to humour, and believed that King had featured him, in thin disguise, as a politician, Dame Winifred Harcourt.

However, King's real offence was to use words that Skeffington-Lodge had used about his prospects for a much-desired peerage. He had petitioned leading Labour figures to press his case. One of them, the former Labour leader Clement Attlee, had replied that he hoped Skeffington-Lodge would 'get what he deserved'. This caused the aspirant peer, who evidently also lacked a sense of irony, to announce at a dinner party, at which King was present, that the honour was 'in the bag'. King had Dame Winifred say this but thought that he had acted prudently in making the character a woman. King apologised but Skeffington-Lodge sought legal advice and a favourable opinion forced King to settle out of court in 1969. The book was withdrawn only days before its due publication date. The settlement and costs forced King to sell his Brighton house and move to London.

King substantially revised the book several times, at the legally bound requests of his adversary, and it sold so well as to be rarely out of print and was longlisted for the 'Lost Booker' prize. King used the experience in *The Action* (1978), which was about a neurotic woman who brings a lawsuit against a writer she is convinced has libelled her.

Dr William King (1786–1865)

SOCIAL REFORMER, CO-OPERATIVE PIONEER, PHYSICIAN AND MATHEMATICIAN
2 Regency Square P
23 Montpelier Road

Born in Ipswich, the son of a clergyman, it was originally intended that King should follow his father into the Church, but instead he studied medicine. After marrying Mary Hooker, daughter of **Rev Thomas Hooker** (*qv*), in January 1821 the couple moved to Brighton that following December. In 1825 he sponsored the founding of the town's Mechanics Institute, where he would often speak, and which fostered his interest in co-operation, as many of the workmen who were members were actively involved in the movement. In 1827 the Brighton Co-operative Benevolent Fund Association was founded to raise money to support the ideas of Robert Owen, the co-operative pioneer, which led to further fund raising through setting up a co-operative trading association. The couple lived in Regency Square from 1828 to 1830.

King founded the monthly *The Co-Operator* in May 1828, which, though it lasted only two years, was influential in advocating co-operative principles being applied to retailing, manufacture and self-employment, and eventually the full community.

The magazine's ideas were accepted by both the Rochdale Pioneers in 1844, recognised as being the founders of the modern co-operative movement, and the Christian socialists, who also set up co-ops.

But with King seeking support for co-operation through the patronage of the well-to-do, his doubts about Owenite radicalism and anti-clericalism caused other co-operative journals to attack him. Such radical ideas and his support for Catholic emancipation, he knew, were also damaging him professionally.

In 1842 he was elected physician to the Sussex County Hospital and held the same post with the Brighton Provident Dispensary from 1849. He was a town commissioner at the time when the commission acquired the Royal Pavilion in 1850.

He retired from his hospital post in 1861 and died in Montpelier Road (pictured) in October 1865. He was buried in the churchyard of **All Saint's Church, Church Road**, Hove.

Rudyard Kipling (1865–1936)

WRITER AND POET
The Elms, The Green, Rottingdean

Fourteen years before he came to settle in the village with his family, Kipling had stayed with his 'Auntie Georgie', Lady Burne-Jones, and her husband, the Pre-Raphaelite painter, **Sir Edward Burne-Jones** (*qv*), before he left for India to work as a journalist. His aunt and uncle had for some while taken a holiday home, North End House (now Aubrey House), The Green.

In 1897 Kipling returned to Rottingdean with his American wife, Caroline Balestier, and their American-born daughters, Josephine and Elsie, to live at The Elms. The following year their youngest child, John, who was later to die at the Battle of Loos, was born. The Kiplings were joining a ready-made family circle. For there were not only the Burne-Joneses but Kipling's cousin, the future Prime Minister Stanley Baldwin, had married Lucy ('Cissie') Risdale, whose family lived in **The Dene** (now sheltered housing), another large house on The Green.

And while the Kiplings spent several months each year abroad (in 1899 their eldest daughter Josephine died while they were in America), when home, the Kipling and Baldwin children had another playmate: Kipling's cousin, **Angela Thirkell** (*qv*) (then Mackail), later a novelist, who would stay, with her brother and sister, with their grandparents, the Burne-Joneses.

Their new home, wrote Kipling, rented at three guineas a week, 'stood in a sort of little island behind flint walls which we then thought high enough, and almost beneath some big ilex trees. It was small, none too well built, but cheap... there grew up great happiness between "The Dene", "North End House", and "The Elms". One could throw a cricket-ball from any one house to the other, but, beyond turning out at 2am to help a silly foxhound puppy who had stuck in a drain, I do not remember any violent alarms and excursions other than packing farm-carts filled with mixed babies – Stanley Baldwin's and ours – and despatching them into the safe clean heart of the motherly Downs for jam-smeared picnics.'

His house being 'none too well built' and needing more light in the attic, Kipling employed Ambrose Poynter, his cousin, an architect, to carry out improvements. In the Rottingdean years, Kipling published *Kim*, the *Just So Stories*, *Stalky & Co*, and the poem 'Recessional' in honour of Queen Victoria's Diamond Jubilee. He also wrote the poem, 'A Smuggler's Song', based on the tales of smuggling in the village.

Sir William Nicholson (*qv*), the artist, visited to make a woodcut portrait of the novelist. They became friends and collaborated on *An Almanac of Twelve Sports*. When **The Vicarage** came on the market, Nicolson bought it, renaming it The Grange, and had it enlarged by Edwin Lutyens.

Kipling loved rail travel and wrote *Railway Reform in Great Britain*, a humorous and fanciful story of the London, Brighton and South Coast Railway, where the towns have names reminiscent of those in *The Arabian Nights*.

The death of his uncle, Sir Edward Burne-Jones, preceded the outbreak of the Boer War by a year, a war which led to conflict between Georgiana and her nephew. He found himself at odds with his 'beloved aunt' over the role of Britain and he found some other 'Little Englanders' in the village, notably a local publican. When the news of the peace treaty arrived on 1 June 1902 Georgiana displayed a banner stating 'We have killed and taken possession', which angered lots of local people. Kipling was called and managed to calm matters.

Kipling remembered Rottingdean when there was one bus a day from Brighton, which took 40 minutes. But, now with a double-decker service run by the landlord of The White Horse, more people were arriving, often to stand around his house hoping to see the famous man, and he felt the need to seek a more isolated home. On 2 September 1902, the family left for Bateman's, near Burwash, in Sussex, where he was to live until his death.

Edward Knoblock (1874–1945)

PLAYWRIGHT AND NOVELIST
20 Clifton Terrace

Knoblock, born in New York but later a naturalised British subject, was the fourth of the 11 children of a businessman. He began piano lessons at the age of four. Today he is remembered chiefly as author of the one-act play, *Kismet*, which was to become, after its author's death, an award-winning stage and screen musical. He began life as a playwright living in London, his adoptive home, where he also acted a bit, produced plays and wrote novels.

In 1921 Knoblock adapted *The Three Musketeers* for the screen and *The Thief of Baghdad* and other films. He wrote more than 30 plays and four novels. He collaborated with **Arnold Bennett** (*qv*) and **Vita Sackville-West** (*qv*).

He lived in Clifton Terrace in the early 1920s, and his friend and fellow writer Somerset Maugham sometimes stayed with him. He also owned the Beach House, Worthing, where he entertained the writers **Arnold Bennett** (*qv*), Sir Compton Mackenzie, and JB Priestley.

Sir James Knowles (1831–1908)

ARCHITECT AND JOURNAL EDITOR
3 Percival Terrace **P**

Knowles served an apprenticeship in his father's London architectural practice and said that he worked on 'many hundreds of houses, besides several churches, hospitals, clubs, warehouses, stores, roads, and bridges' in his 30-year career. He also worked with his father on the latter's commission, the Grosvenor Hotel, London, and designed and laid out Leicester Square.

In Hove Knowles designed the Princes Hotel (now partly absorbed into the council offices and once the Brunswick Town Hall) in Grand Avenue, and the Stanford estate.

He was an associate and friend of some of the great intellectuals of his day, including **William Gladstone** (*qv*), Walter Bagehot, Alfred Tennyson, Cardinal Manning and TH Huxley. In 1883 Knowles gave up his architectural practice and devoted himself largely to intellectual interests. He was also a writer and edited *The Contemporary Review* from 1870 until 1877, when he founded *The Nineteenth Century*, which he edited (with a change of name to the *The Nineteenth Century and After*) until his death.

He lived in Brighton from 1903 until his death from a heart attack at his home on 13 February 1908. His funeral service took place at St Peter's, York Place, before his burial in the **Extra-Mural Cemetery**.

Peter Kropotkin (1842–1921)

ANARCHIST, SCIENTIST AND WRITER
9 Chesham Street

The years in Brighton, from 1909, when he moved here from London for his health, until he left in 1917 for a Russia wrought by revolution, were, in many ways, the most difficult and tragic of Kropotkin's life. When the First World War erupted in 1914, unlike many on the left, including anarchists most close to him, he had favoured the Allied cause as a way of curbing the power of Germany. He became isolated. The English and French authorities welcomed his support; the Bolshevik leaders, in his native Russia, attacked him. Few of his friends in England maintained contact and it tended to be the curious, not the comrades, who called. There were a few, though, who travelled to Brighton: the trades unionists Ben Tillett and Guy Bowman, and James Scott Keltie, the editor of *Nature*, for which Kropotkin wrote, and TJ Cobden-Sanderson, the artist and bookbinder, among them. A small group from the Brighton Trades and Labour Club came weekly to talk over their problems, and the neighbours were friendly.

In August 1914, Pryns Hopkins, the editor of the anarchist *Freedom* magazine, which Kropotkin had helped to found, visited him in Brighton. He later wrote: 'Mrs Kropotkin opened the door and if I recall rightly after so many years, she was small of figure but full of the warmth of welcome.' Kropotkin was seated in a big armchair because of his health. The writer went on: 'An enormous mass of whiskers bristled from his face in every direction. Within such a mane, one might have looked for a leonine type of countenance, but his was far too benevolent to be called that. He more truly radiated benevolence than anyone I had ever seen.'

Mrs Kropotkin offered cake and sweet Russian tea, and there was 'a long and most interesting discussion'. One matter on which they could not agree was Kropotkin's support for the war, which had broken out that month. However, lack of agreement – there were other points of divergence – 'in no way clouded the friendly intercourse of that delightful afternoon', wrote Hopkins. He added: 'As I was leaving, a few neighbours dropped in and I caught some hint of that veneration with which everyone regarded this mighty rebel, so warmly human.'

For much of 1915 and 1916 Kropotkin was prostrate with illness. He underwent two chest operations and was forbidden by doctors to travel to London.

In Brighton he started work on his *Ethics* and contributed to émigré and other publications. Here, too, on 12 July 1916, he marked an event of great significance in his life: it was 40 years since he had landed in Hull to begin his exile, which had seen him living in Switzerland, France (from which he had been expelled), Belgium, England, Canada and the United States.

Sir Edwin Landseer (1802–1873)

ANIMAL PAINTER AND SCULPTOR
65–66 Regency Square Ⓟ

Landseer's fame was at its height when he bought this imposing house in 1841. Yet the year before, he had had a nervous breakdown. This was beginning of his mental health problems, which manifested themselves as depression, melancholy, hypochondria and psychosomatic illnesses. They were to plague him ever afterward and ended with his family having him declared insane the year before he died.

The London-born son of an engraver and author, Landseer was a child prodigy, and in 1813 the Society of Arts awarded him a silver palette for his drawing of a spaniel. Two years later he was an honorary (on account of his age) exhibitor at the Royal Academy and elected an associate in 1826, when he was 24, then the youngest age for election. He became an academician in 1831.

His paintings of animals were, from a very early age, metaphors for human situations and emotions – so different from traditional British sporting art. In his early 20s he began painting his famous Scottish scenes.

The reasons for his initial illness are unclear. His mother had died a few months before; fatigue and anxiety have been suggested, as has the murder of a close friend, Lord William Russell. There is also the claim that the recently widowed Duchess of Bedford, reputedly his lover, had refused to marry him.

Landseer recuperated by touring Europe and returned to his house in London, which he never gave up (and, in fact, is where he died), even when he took his Brighton house. Sick and lonely, suffering from dementia, yet still inspiring public affection, he sought refuge in the stately homes of friends.

Despite the persistence and severity of his illness, exacerbated by heavy drinking and drug use, he continued to paint – *Monarch of the Glen* appeared in 1851 – and brought fame and wealth. While limited in his knowledge of sculpture, in a decade he created the four lions at the foot of Nelson's column, which were unveiled in 1867.

Penelope Lawrence (1856–1932)

Dorothy Lawrence (1860–1933)

Millicent Lawrence (1863–1925)

FOUNDERS OF ROEDEAN SCHOOL
25 Lewes Crescent Ⓟ
3 Arundel Terrace
37 Chesham Road
35–37 Sussex Square

ROEDEAN SCHOOL founded here as WIMBLEDON HOUSE SCHOOL in October 1885 with two teachers and ten pupils

Roedean, the most famous girls' school in the world, had its indirect origins in the foolhardy actions of its founders' father in 1869. Philip Henry Lawrence gave up his work as a solicitor to read for the Bar where he practised less than successfully. He also had a grandiose mansion built in Wimbledon. His financial plight (aggravated a few years later by a climbing accident that ended his legal career) became such that when the mortgage had to be paid, he could not afford to send Millicent (Milly), one of the 13 children with his second wife, to Newnham College, Cambridge. Thus, her Cambridge-educated half-sister Penelope (Nelly), the only child of her father's first marriage, paid from her salary for Milly to take a year's teacher training course as a demonstrator to women students in a physiological laboratory. (Their sister Dorothy had gone to Bedford College.)

Their mother, Charlotte, and Dorothy and Millicent started a school in their home to educate neighbours' children and take in boarders. When the sisters realised that they could not run a school in their invalid father's house – along with boisterous young brothers and sisters! – they wrote to Penelope to ask her to join them in setting up a new school. This was agreed and they settled on Brighton, renting Lewes Crescent (pictured). Ten pupils – 'six paying and four for show', as Penelope said – joined them for the opening in October 1885. (Two of those 'for show' were their sisters, Theresa and Christabel. In 1902 Theresa went to South Africa to found another Roedean near Johannesburg, while Christabel was to found the All-Women's Hockey Association.)

The first prospectus showed where the emphasis would be: 'Two or three hours daily will be allotted to out-door exercise and games'. In this, Penelope set an example. Learning to swim as a child in France, swimming became a life-long passion, and early Roedeanians were to watch her bulky form with awe as she swam between the two piers at Brighton.

So successful was the school that it soon expanded and took on Arundel Terrace in 1886, which housed 18 girls. The following year, they added 26 Lewes Crescent, and Chesham Road was used as a sanatorium for infectious illnesses. In 1890 they acquired 35, 36 and 37 Sussex Square (when the school became known as Wimbledon House School), previously occupied by a boys' school. 34 Sussex Square opened as a boarding house in 1892 and 29 Sussex Square was also used, officially opening the following year. All five of the other sisters helped with teaching, while Sussex Square also became home to Mr and Mrs Lawrence and the young brothers when the mansion was sold.

In 1895 it was decided to build new premises on the school's present site in Roedean Way on the cliffs above Rottingdean, and the school moved there in two stages in 1898 and 1899. A brother, Paul, later a judge and known as Uncle Paul by the school, donated the £50 he had made in his first year at the Bar.

Pupils adopted their own slang: 'aunt' for toilet; 'muck' or 'Thames mud' was chocolate blancmange; roly-poly pudding was 'boiled baby's arm'; and a 'Keenite' was a younger girl who had a crush on a senior one.

The three sisters governed the school together and were known by pupils as 'the Firm', although, in practice, Penelope, who had the dominant personality, took the lead and organised the academic side. Dorothy was regarded as the most accessible of the three but was dogged by ill-health and depression.

When they retired in 1924 all the founding sisters moved from Brighton.

Evelyn Laye (1900–1996)

ACTOR AND SINGER

20 Egremont Place*
York Place School (now Varndean School, Balfour Road)

Born in London, Laye attended York Place School from 1905. She made her first stage appearance at the Theatre Royal, Brighton, when she was 15. (Her father, Gilbert Lay — no 'e' — an actor, was briefly manager of the Pavilion Pier.)

One of the best known stars of her day, Laye appeared in some Hollywood musicals but was most noted for light and musical comedy.

* The school records give this as the Lay [sic] family's address but neither street directories nor electoral registers confirm this.

John Leech (1817–1864)

ILLUSTRATOR

16 Lansdowne Place, Hove 🅟
Bedford Hotel (now the site of the Holiday Inn), Kings Road

Leech and his family took this house in 1849 when **Charles Dickens** (*qv*), of whom Leech was both a friend and the illustrator of his Christmas books, visited them. Leech and Dickens would come to Brighton at other times to walk on the Downs and then have dinner at the Bedford Hotel.

Edward Fitzgerald, 7th Duke of Leinster (1892–1976)

GAMBLER AND BANKRUPT

6 Arundel Terrace

The seventh duke unexpectedly inherited the premier ducal title of Ireland from his eldest brother. He had been bankrupted once — in 1918 — before he inherited his title and then in 1922 (when he became duke), and again in 1936.

An addictive gambler, he sold his future £800,000 life interest in the family estate (which included the ancestral seat of Carton House and enormous associated estates), which he had never expected to inherit, for £67,000 and £1,000 a year for life, to a Tory MP and financier. He was married four times. Mary Etheridrge, his first wife, was, perhaps stereotypically, a chorus girl, while his fourth wife, Vivien Irene Felton Conner , whom he married in 1965, was a waitress and 28 years his junior. She died in Brighton in 1992. (His other two wives were an American socialite and an actor.)

He was known as 'the bedsit duke', long before he committed suicide by taking an overdose of pentobarbital in his flat in London.

Alan Lennox-Boyd, 1st Viscount Merton (1904–1983)

POLITICIAN
36 Brunswick Terrace, Hove

Lennox-Boyd left his post as a junior minister in the Ministry of Food to join the Royal Naval Volunteer Reserve and came to Hove to train in 1940. He lived in this house in 1954, the year he became Colonial Secretary under Sir Antony Eden and, later, Harold Macmillan.

Married into the Guinness family, he was on the right of the Tory Party (he had supported the Nationalist cause in Spain) and, with **Sir Winston Churchill** (*qv*), argued against the cause of Indian nationalism. Despite his almost mystical belief in Britain's 'imperial mission', he oversaw the cause of colonial liberation, if somewhat reluctantly at times. Among other places, Ghana and Malaysia gained independence in his time, which also took in the EOKA crisis in Cyprus and the Mau Mau emergency in Kenya.

Oscar Lewenstein (1917–1997)

THEATRE AND FILM PRODUCER
9 and 11 Hove Seaside Villas, Hove (now Western Esplanade)

Lewenstein was a central figure at London's Royal Court Theatre from the early 1950s until the mid-1970s, the time during which the theatre made an indelible mark on the English stage. He was a co-founder of the theatre's English Stage Company in 1956, the theatre's chairman from 1970 to 1972, and later its artistic director. He was also a film producer, whose films included *The Entertainer, Saturday Night and Sunday Morning, A Taste of Honey, The Knack*, and *Tom Jones.*

The son of Jewish immigrants, he was born in London but lived at number 9 as a child and died at number 11. He had returned to London when he was 14 when the family plywood and plastics business failed.

Victoria Lidiard (1889–1992)

SUFFRAGETTE
Flat 1, 14 Palmeira Avenue, Hove

Born in Clifton, Bristol, one of 12 children, Victoria Simmons was educated in a dame school, became a vegetarian at 10, left school at 14 and, with her mother and sisters, joined the Women's Social and Political Union in 1907, against her father's opposition. She said that her main reason for doing so was that 'the education of women – of girls rather – was considered of absolute unimportance and the boys – I had three brothers – the money was spent on them'. She chalked 'Votes for Women' on pavements and addressed meetings at the Bristol docks.

In March 1912, Lidiard took part in a window-smashing incident in London's West End and broke a window in the War Office. Arrested along with 200 other suffragettes, she served two months hard labour in Holloway Prison. She remembered one of her own sisters shouting encouraging messages from across the street, standing on a chair in her cell and singing out of the barred window, and the black beetle in her porridge. Under instructions from her mother, she did not go on hunger strike.

After school, Lidiard learned shorthand and bookkeeping at evening classes and worked in photographic studios. During the First World War she and a sister ran a guesthouse in Kensington, London, for professional women, and she worked at Battersea Power Station making anti-aircraft shells at weekends. She married Major Alexander Lidiard MC, a member of the Men's Political Union for Women's Enfranchisement, in 1918.

After the war, the Lidiards trained as opticians and later worked together as consultants at the London Refraction Hospital at Elephant and Castle where, in 1927, she became the first female refractionist. They later ran practices in Maidenhead and High Wycombe.

Lidiard was a member of the National Council of Women and in the last decade of her life worked for the ordination of women. She published a book, *Christianity, Faith, Love and Healing*, at the age of 99 and, at 100, *Animals and All Churches*. She canvassed MPs on conditions in the transport of live animals.

Lidiard died in Hove, at the age of 102, on 3 October 1992, the last surviving suffragette. The plaque on her home is, appropriately, in the movement's livery of purple, white and green.

Frederick Henry Horatio Akbar Mahomed (1849–1884)

DOCTOR
2 Black Lion Street (gone)
32 Grand Parade

Mahomed, who was to become a pioneering physician, was born in Black Lion Street, the son of Frederick Mahomed (1818–88), who taught dance, fencing, and gymnastics in Brighton, and grandson of **Sake Dean Mahomed** (*qv*). He was privately educated locally. At 18 he went to study medicine at the town's Royal Sussex County Hospital. When he was 20, he left for Guy's in London where he was universally praised for his work. In 1871 he won the Physical Society Prize for developing the sphygmograph (for measuring the pressure of the pulse) and had been runner up the previous year.

He qualified as a member of the Royal College of Surgeons in 1872 and soon after became resident medical officer at the London Fever Hospital. In 1874 he became a member of the Royal College of Physicians (and was elected a fellow in 1880), and was appointed student tutor and pathologist at St Mary's Hospital. He later returned to Guy's.

He gained academic distinction at Cambridge University and the University of Brussels. He wrote a series of papers on the results of the use of the sphygmograph, which he had modified, in the investigation of disease (his first paper was written when at Guy's). He also did pioneering work in understanding hypertension and the registration of diseases, and contributed to work on techniques such as blood transfusion and appendectomy for appendicitis.

Sake Dean Mahomed (1759–1851)

ENTREPRENEUR, TRAVELLER AND WRITER
2 Black Lion Street (gone)
32 Grand Parade

Mahomed's first business venture was unsuccessful but the results are seen everywhere today: in 1810 in London he opened the first Indian restaurant in England.

Early in life he had served in the Bengal Army and received a commission. His book, *The Travels of Dean Mahomet*, written in Ireland when he was 25, made him the first Indian to write a book in English.

In 1814, Mahomed, who was born in India, and his Irish wife, Jane Daly, moved to Brighton. He had done some shampooing work in London and when he first came to Brighton he worked in a bath house attached to the New Steyne Hotel, 11 Devonshire Place. He sold Indian cosmetics and medicines, like Indian tooth powder, hair dye, offered steam baths with Indian oils, and shampooing. In December 1815 he opened his own Battery House Baths, at the foot of the Steyne (as it was then spelt), but in 1820–21 he and a partner, Thomas Brown, built the magnificent Mahomed's Baths (on the site of which the Queen's Hotel, 1–3 Kings Road, now stands). While it was being built he briefly established a bath house on West Cliff. At the same time he published books on the medicinal benefits of shampooing.

He called his Brighton venture 'the Indian Medicated Vapour Bath (type of Turkish bath), a cure to many diseases and giving full relief when everything fails; particularly Rheumatic and paralytic, gout, stiff joints, old sprains, lame legs, aches and pains in the joints'. He was appointed by both **George IV** (*qv*) and **William IV** (*qv*) as their shampooing surgeon in Brighton, and he took to wearing ceremonial dress.

However, in 1841, Brown died and the baths went to public auction. Mahomed was unable to buy them but offered to work as manager. The baths were finally sold in 1843, but the new owner did not wish to employ him and so he moved to a rented house at 2 Black Lion Street, and attempted to work in competition with his old establishment.

Mahomed died at Grand Parade, his son Frederick's home, and, like Frederick, he is buried in **St Nicholas' Church, Church Street**. (There is some evidence to suggest that Jane Daly may have died earlier and that in 1807 he married another Jane. She may be the Jane who is buried with him.)

Gideon Mantell (1790–1852)

SURGEON AND GEOLOGIST
20 Old Steine **P**

Mantell was born in Lewes and, after apprenticeship and training, had his first medical practice there when he bought out his partner. He came to live here in 1833, assisted in his move by a £1,000 gift from the 3rd Earl of Egremont, for by this time he was already renowned. In 1822 he had published *The Fossils of the South Downs*, the first of his 12 books, with lithography by his wife, Ann. After exploring the rich vertebrate deposits of Tilgate Forest, near Cuckfield, East Sussex, he announced in February 1825 the discovery of Iguanodon, one of the various kinds of dinosaurs (a term not coined until 1842), for which he is best remembered. In 1827 he announced his discovery of a second kind of dinosaur, Hylaeosaurus. This creature was heavily armoured, thus confirming that dinosaurs were pedestrian and not amphibian, as had earlier been thought.

In Brighton Mantell was unsuccessful in establishing a medical practice but did found the Sussex Scientific Institution and Mantellian Museum, where he featured his collection in his own home, accompanying it with a library and reading room. In 1838, when he left the town for London, he sold his collection for £4,000 to the British Museum, the loss to the town of 'a most intellectual ornament', opined *The Times*.

Manuel II (1889–1932)

DEPOSED KING OF PORTUGAL
Eastern House, 9 Eastern Terrace

Manuel succeeded to the Portuguese throne on the assassination of his father, Carlos I and his elder brother, Luis Filipe, in 1908 (when Manuel was also wounded). However, he was ousted by the revolution of 1910. He lived in unremarkable exile in Britain, for some time at this house, until his death at his home at Fulwell Park, Twickenham.

Ebenezer John (EJ) Marshall (1832–1899)

HEADMASTER, BRIGHTON GRAMMAR SCHOOL (NOW BRIGHTON HOVE AND SUSSEX SIXTH FORM COLLEGE, 205 DYKE ROAD)
79 Buckingham Road 🅟 *

In May 1868 the boys were marched, in procession, to Buckingham Road, then the new home of the school, from its former site in Lancaster House, 47 Grand Parade, where it had been founded in 1859 as the Brighton Proprietary Grammar and Commercial School for the Sons of Tradesmen.

Marshall worked as headmaster from 1861 to1899 (the school became Brighton Grammar School in 1873). From their homes a few minutes away came **Aubrey Beardsley** (*qv*) together with his fellow pupils, **CB Cochran** (*qv*) and **Herbert Carden** (*qv*).

Marshall was well known for his skill in dealing with boys who were passed to his care because they could not fit in elsewhere. He would often stay friendly with them until he died. He was known for his irascibility and disputatiousness but also for dealing justly with his charges. He is buried in the **Woodvale Cemetery**, where his grave has been recently restored.

* *The tablet attached to this house stands adjacent to where the Brighton Grammar School (now Brighton Hove and Sussex Sixth Form College) once stood.*

Sir Edward Marshall Hall (1858–1927)

BARRISTER AND MP
30 Old Steine 🅟

Marshall Hall, one of the most renowned advocates of his day, was born here, the son of Alfred Hall, a well-known local doctor. His interest in law was quickened when he witnessed, as a 14-year-old, the opening stage of a local *cause célèbre*, the committal proceedings of **Christiana Edmunds** (*qv*), 'the

Brighton poisoner' before the Brighton magistrates. However, he started life as a clerk in a tea merchant's office, such was his housemaster's view of his abilities; but his father thought otherwise and he went to Cambridge.

In 1883 he married Ethel Moon, daughter of a local GP. But there was a terrible scandal when Ethel became pregnant during an extramarital affair in 1890, a year after her legal separation from Hall, and died as a result of a botched abortion. The lover, the abortionist and several other parties were charged with her murder. In 1896 Marshall Hall married a German woman, Henriette Kroeger, with whom he had a daughter, Elna, the following year.

At 39, Marshall Hall was a QC. A handsome man with a commanding presence and a reputation as a great orator, despite never regularly practising criminal law, the publicity of the cases he did take kept him in the public eye. Unsuccessful as defence counsel for George Joseph Smith, 'the brides in the bath' murderer, in the Camden Town murder he saved Robert Wood from the gallows, as he did with Robert Light in the 'green bicycle' murder case.

Louisa Martindale (1839–1914)

SUFFRAGIST AND FEMINIST
2 Lancaster Road

Born in Woodford Green, Essex, and privately educated, Louisa Spicer devoted herself to good works before marrying a 37-year-old widower, William Martindale, with four children, in 1871. He died in 1874, leaving her with two small daughters, the younger Louisa and Hilda. Having spent some time living in Europe, in 1885 they all eventually moved to this large house in Lancaster Road, so that both the children could attend Brighton High School for Girls (now Brighton and Hove High School).

Louisa held an 'open house' on alternate Saturdays for shop assistants and locally employed German governesses. One attendee was **Margaret Bondfield** (*qv*). While in Brighton Louisa senior helped found the Women's Co-operative Movement and the Brighton branch of the Women's Liberal Association (she was a speaker at public meetings, sometimes in support of her brother, the Liberal MP Sir Albert Spicer). She also founded the Lewes Road Dispensary for Women and Children, which was staffed by women. The dispensary moved to **101 Round Hill Crescent** and in 1910 to **8 Ditchling Road**, where it became the Lady Chichester Hospital, and which later opened as the New Sussex Hospital for Women and Children in **Windlesham House, Windlesham Road** in 1921. Her daughter **Louisa Martindale** (*qv*) was to become its senior surgeon.

Mary Agnes Hamilton, in her life of Margaret Bondfield, says of Louisa senior, that 'for many years [she was] a notable figure in Brighton, to whom women of two generations owe more than some of them know'. In 1903 she moved to Horsted Keynes, West Sussex.

Martindale's other daughter, **Hilda Martindale** (1875–1952), distinguished herself as a leading civil servant – one of the first women in that profession at a time when there were severe barriers to women's advancement – working in factory inspection, the Home Office and the Treasury.

GYNAECOLOGIST AND FEMINIST

2 Lancaster Road
11 Adelaide Crescent, Hove
Windlesham House (now site of York Mansions East), Windlesham Road, Hove

The younger Louisa (daughter of **Louisa Martindale** (*qv*)), and her sister Hilda attended Brighton High School for Girls (now Brighton and Hove High School) when the family settled in Brighton at Lancaster Road. They were not particularly happy at the school, to which they were accompanied each day by a governess. Louisa wrote that 'the teaching we received ... would nowadays be somewhat severely criticised'.

Martindale was to become senior surgeon in the New Sussex Hospital for Women and Children in Windlesham House, which had been founded by her mother as the Lewes Road Dispensary for Women and Children.

Earlier in her life, Martindale had travelled extensively abroad. After a period in Hull following qualification she returned to Brighton in 1906 to become one of the first three women doctors in the town.

In 1919 she opened her practice at her new home in Adelaide Crescent and in 1920 was listed at **10 Marlborough Place**. She became part-time medical officer in the school she had attended and at Roedean School, as well as working for the hospital. Martindale worked for women's interests and strived to open women's hospitals at home and abroad. She was a pioneer of radium treatment for uterine and ovarian cancer in the UK.

In the First World War, while living in London, she had spent her holidays working at the Scottish Women's Hospital in what had been Royaumont Abbey, France.

Martindale moved to London in 1923 but continued to work at the New Sussex, and also was appointed one of the first two JPs in Brighton in 1924. In 1939 she left the town for Forest Row, Sussex. Her life-long companion was Ismay Fitzgerald.

SOCIALIST REVOLUTIONARY

2 Manchester Street
6 Vernon Terrace Ⓟ

In March 1873 Eleanor Marx and her father Karl went to Brighton for what was to be a fortnight's holiday. He returned within a week, but she didn't. The day before his departure she had told him that she intended to stay in the town and earn her own living. Aged nearly 18, this was her bid for independence, her first example of being responsible for herself, a way of freeing herself from a 'very disagreeable' situation. This situation was due to the fact that she was in love with Hyppolite-Prosper-Olivier Lissagaray, an impecunious but colourful French journalist, insurrectionist in the 1848 Paris Commune, and a translator of her father's work. He was 17 years her senior and much disapproved of by Karl Marx. Eleanor claimed, too, that Lissagaray was treated badly by her sister, Laura, and her husband Paul Lafargue.

Marx signed up with an employment agency and asked some French friends living in Brighton to help her find private pupils (in April she was earning ten shillings [50p] a week through this work). In early May the agency found her a part-time teaching position in a girls' boarding school run by the Misses Hall in Sussex Square. She had rooms, first at Manchester Street and then at Vernon Terrace (pictured). She could have stayed with a friend, the Rev Pascal, a French socialist, through whom she hoped to get pupils, but she did not like his wife. Her father approved because 'if business questions take on a sociable form … independence and freedom are lost'. She also did extra-mural teaching because, she said, prices in the town were double those in London.

During this time her correspondence with Jenny, her mother, who visited her in Brighton, was at its most frequent and most loving, and kept her up with people and events. A friendly birthday letter to her father in May, asking him to send her history books and telling him of her two incomes reassured him that, after all, he had been a good father to her.

But while Jenny Marx empathised with her daughter's seeking independence, she also saw this period as a prolonged but misguided convalescence, and she doubted her daughter's decision to take up school teaching, fearing that the health of 'Tussychen' was not 'strong enough to recuperate on the treadmill of a boarding school with its strict routine and drudgery of business'. She also feared a stodgy and unappetising diet, offering to send whatever food Eleanor might want. She also urged Eleanor to seek medical advice after Eleanor herself admitted that she had been very ill when in the town and in one week fainted two or three times a day. Lissagaray visited her at weekends. They walked along the seafront to Hove, ate fish and chips, and clams and whelks on the pier, chain smoked, and debated and discussed what they had been reading. They rambled and picnicked on the South Downs and finished the day with pints of ale and pies in pubs. Marx later told her mother that each time 'he left me stronger and happier', but this worried Jenny because she saw that being accepted locally as engaged they could go about unchaperoned.

Marx was not qualified as a teacher but was popular with the girls and impressed her employers. There was one girl, said to be of inferior intellect, who had 'an immense interest in the Commune, the International etc'. Outrage on the part of the Misses Hall occurred when Jenny proposed that Eleanor should leave in order to accompany the Marx's housekeeper, Helene Demuth ('Lenchen'), who had had news of her sister's impending death, to Germany. But while Marx did not go along with her mother's plan, pressurised by mother and father she became stressed and anorexic. She saw out the school term and returned, nervously exhausted, to live with her parents in London.

A few months after her return she left a letter for her father on his desk (addressing him as 'Dear Moor' and signed 'Your Tussy'), asking him not to be angry but she wanted to know when she might see 'L' (Lissagaray) again: 'It is very hard never to see him. I have been doing my best to be patient, but it is difficult and I don't feel I could be much longer.' She does not expect her lover to be allowed to come to the house, 'but could I not, now and then, go for a little walk with him? . . . When I was so very ill in Brighton (during a time when I fainted two or three times a day), L. came to see me and each time left me stronger and happier [as she had told her mother], and more able to bear the heavy load left on my shoulders.' (Karl Marx knew nothing of these visits.)

But her pleas were to no avail. She threw herself into literary activity, felt liberated by her father's death in 1883 and the next year began to live openly with Edward Aveling, a married zoologist and socialist and serial philanderer. Continuing as a translator and trade union agitator, in 1897 Marx learned of Aveling's secret marriage and while she continued to live with him on and off, she committed suicide in her home in Sydenham in Kent in 1898.

Robin Maugham, 2nd Viscount Maugham (1916–1981)

NOVELIST AND PLAYWRIGHT
2 Brunswick Terrace, Hove
14 Bute Street
5 Clifton Road

Maugham is best known today for being the nephew of Somerset Maugham and author of the novella *The Servant*, adapted for the screen by Harold Pinter, directed by Joe Losey and starring Dirk Bogarde.

He came to Brighton in the 1950s, where he had a flat in Brunswick Terrace, and he later moved to the Bute Street house. Clifton Road was his final home. He could be snobbish and cruel, but he was also a generous and kind host and a brilliant raconteur when he entertained friends from out of town and locals like **Laurence Olivier** (*qv*) and his wife Joan Plowright, **Terence Rattigan** (*qv*), **Hector Bolitho** (*qv*) and **Gilbert Harding** (*qv*). He was particularly friendly with Harding, who was gay but inhibited, whereas Maugham was bisexual, sexually indiscreet and adventurous. They two men imbibed large amounts of alcohol together.

While he was a prolific author – he wrote more than 25 works of fiction and non-fiction, 14 plays, and plays for television and radio – Maugham had a taste for the louche life. At the end of his days his creativity was drying up and he relied much on his secretary, **Peter Burton** (*qv*). By then he was all but financially bankrupt. His partner William Lawrence said that Maugham came to realise that his work did not place him in the older establishment, but neither was he a member of the *avant-garde* of working class novelists. Maugham knew that his writing was no longer fashionable and that his reputation would be as an obscure writer from 'the dark and forgotten fifties'.

He died from an embolism in the Royal Sussex County Hospital, but his body was missing for two days. He was later buried with his parents – he had inherited his title from his father, a former Lord Chancellor – in Hartfield, Sussex.

Harriot Mellon, Duchess of St Albans (1777–1837)

ACTOR AND BANKER
Regency House (now Regency Restaurant, 131 Kings Road)
19 and 28 Brunswick Terrace, Hove

The Regency Restaurant, which has stood on the corner of Kings Road and Regency Square since the 1930s (and where, from earlier years of that century, there was a shop front), belies the grandeur of what had been one of the great places of fashion and entertainment 100 years before. In 1830 what was then called Regency House was taken permanently by the Duke and Duchess of St Albans. The house, which became St Albans House, had been designed in 1828 by **Amon Henry Wilds** (*qv*).

Born in Ireland as Harriot Mellon, the illegitimate daughter of a wardrobe keeper in a company of strolling players, she became an actor, but gave that up when she married the banker Thomas Coutts, 42 years her senior, in 1815. When he died at 82 he left her a partnership in the eponymous family bank and made her the richest woman in England. Mellon and the duke married in 1827 (he was 24 years her junior) and visited Brighton every year.

Before taking Regency House they had stayed at Brunswick Terrace and elsewhere for a few of seasons. When they were at 19 Brunswick Terrace in 1829–1830 **Sir Francis Burdett MP**, radical politician and reformer, whose wife was Mellon's stepdaughter through the latter's first marriage, stayed for three months at number 14.

The ducal couple's annual gatherings, to which hundreds of guests came to wine and dine, were referred to as 'omnium gatherums' by the duchess. A riding stable to the rear of the house only added to its attractions as a place of both residence and entertainment. 'An unrivalled establishment' opined the *Sussex Advertiser* in 1834. And well it might – the riding school attached to the stables was said to be the largest space in England save for Westminster Abbey, and the dome, unsupported by pillars, was inferior only to that of St Paul's. The duke was the hereditary Grand Falconer of England and during their stays he and his wife would often hold hawking parties on the Downs which would attract Brighton society.

But the duchess was not the spendthrift and frivolous wife of an aristocrat: she excelled as a businesswoman and banker, actively engaged in investment and management. However, jealousy and snobbery took their toll and she was often snubbed and hurt by rumours and stories about her. Her generosity to local charities had no effect in that regard. In March 1837 she vowed she would never return to Brighton and she died five months later at her London home in Piccadilly.

She left most of her estate of £1.8 million in trust to her first husband's youngest granddaughter, Angela, who, as Baroness Burdett-Coutts, was to become one of the greatest of the Victorian philanthropists.

Alan Melville (1910–1983)

TELEVISION AND RADIO PERSONALITY, WRITER AND LYRICIST
17 Clifton Terrace
28 Victoria Street

Melville lived in Clifton Terrace from 1951–1973, and then, until his death, in Victoria Street.

A prolific playwright, lyricist and revue author, who collaborated with Ivor Novello on his last show, *Gay's the Word*, Melville also became a familiar face on television and was also sometimes heard on radio's *Brains Trust*. Almost forgotten today, this may be due, in part, to the death of the once highly popular West End revue.

Prince Klemens von Metternich (1773–1859)

STATESMAN
42 Brunswick Terrace, Hove Ⓟ

The liberal revolutions which convulsed Europe in 1848 saw Metternich, the former Foreign Minister of the Holy Roman Empire and, later, the Austro-Hungarian Empire, in exile in London. When he found the city expensive, he rejected the alternatives of Torquay and Hastings as too remote from the capital, and he and his third and much younger wife, Melanie, chose Brighton.

Apart from convenience, they wished to follow the fashion for the seaside. They took a lease on this sea-front house in September 1848 and stayed here until April the next year. They read, made calls, played whist, walked up The Steine, observed the Royal Pavilion, and walked back to the emerging suburb of Hove.

News from home was not cheering: while Metternich was here there was a week-long siege in Vienna and the Minister of War was lynched. The prince found solace in his enjoyment of the changing pattern of the waves and the boats and ships plying up and down the Channel. When Lord Palmerston, the Foreign Secretary, and Benjamin Disraeli, MP and future prime minister, came to call Melanie was brusque to both. Disraeli wrote of his visit that it was 'divine talk … a masterly exposition of the present state of European affairs'. Metternich was witty, with a 'sunny sympathy with his shining thoughts'.

From November to February, Metternich was reunited and reconciled with his former lover princess Dorothea Lieven, who stayed at the Brunswick Hotel and whom he had not seen since 1822. She established a salon in Brighton. When Metternich gave a private reading of his memoirs, the princess, who was present, slumped back wearily in her chair and exclaimed: 'Oh, God! How boring all that is'. The Metternichs eventually moved to London seeking more accommodation for a visit from their daughter and grandchild. He later returned to Vienna.

Max Miller (1894–1963)

COMEDIAN

43 Hereford Street (gone)

160 Marine Parade P

25 Burlington Street P *

Max Miller is the most commemorated of all Brighton's memorable residents. Not only are there two plaques highlighting his Brighton connections, but a statute, unveiled in 2005, now stands in Pavilion Gardens. (There is also a plaque on his home in Shoreham-by-Sea.)

Known as Harry, Thomas Henry Sargent was born in Hereford Street on 21 November 1894, the second of five children of James Sargent, a labourer and Alice, a flower seller. His parents were very poor and often unable to pay the rent so were forced to move to other parts of the town and surrounding areas.

Miller worked successively as a labourer, milkman, a caddy at Brighton and Hove Golf Course, and sold fish and chips. Finally, he trained to be a motor mechanic in London.

In the army during the First World War, when he had been temporarily blinded, he started a troops' concert party. Back from service, and after a false start on the stage in London, he returned to his home town and joined Jack Sheppard's concert party in an alfresco theatre on Brighton beach as a 'light comedian' for the 1919 summer season. It was here that he met his future wife, sometime stage partner and his manager, Kathleen Marsh. Like Miller, she was a native of Brighton but from a middle class family. Her elder brother Ernest Marsh (1882–1958) was a Brighton alderman for 43 years and was mayor of Brighton from 1949 to 1950. Thus began Miller's highly successful career (in one week in 1943 he was paid £1,025) as 'Cheeky Chappie', a risqué comedian, wearing his trademark garish suit, plus-fours, kipper tie, trilby and co-respondent shoes.

His preference was for theatres in London or the South, so he could return to the town he so loved after a show, and his only overseas tour was to South Africa in 1932. From 1936 to 1946 he lived in Marine Parade, although he donated the house to St Dunstan's Hospital to use during the Second War. During this time, he owned and lived in Woodingdean Dean House (changing the name to 'Woodland Grange'), on which Ovingdean Close was later built. From 1945 to 1950 he lived at Ashcroft, Kingston Lane, Shoreham-by-Sea. He then moved to Burlington Street (pictured).

In September 1959, Miller suffered a heart attack and made his final stage appearance in Folkestone the following year. He never mastered television and apart from a few recording sessions, he had a rather solitary retirement and died in Burlington Street on 7 May 1963. He was cremated in the Downs Crematorium, Brighton. A memorial tablet is mounted on a wall in the Garden of Remembrance. His wife Kathleen died nine years later in a nursing home in Hove in 1972.

In 2009 a collection of Miller memorabilia was opened at Bardsley's fish and chip restaurant in Baker Street.

Miller's birth date is given a year later than it actually was (1894 not 1895) on this plaque put up by the British Music Hall Society.

David Mocatta (1806–1882)

ARCHITECT
Brighton Railway Station P
38–39 Devonshire Place P

Mocatta was the architect of Brighton railway station (1841) and, as architect for the London and Brighton Railway Company, designed stations in the Italianate or Doric style (the others were Croydon, Redhill, Reigate, Horley, Haywards Heath and Hassocks or Ditchling Gate).

Brighton Station was the railway company's headquarters, offices, and boardroom. It remains the only one of his stations still in use or not rebuilt, although extensions have since obscured some of the original building.

Mocatta had studied under Sir John Soane in London from 1821 to 1827. He was also responsible for the former Regency Synagogue (now apartments) in Devonshire Place, which was erected in 1836–8 and was replaced by Middle Street Synagogue in 1875. It is one of three synagogues that came from his drawing board, the others being Ramsgate Synagogue and West London Synagogue, of which he and his father, Moses, were also founding members.

He worked with the engineer of the London and Brighton Railway, John Urpeth Rastrick (1780–1856), on his greatest work, the Ouse Valley Viaduct, north of Haywards Heath. This has been described as an 'otherwise monotonous brick structure, 491 yards long and 96 feet high, and consisting of thirty-seven semicircular arches each spanning 30 feet, [. . .] ennobled by Mocatta's embellishments' and a design that is 'simple yet exuberant and triumphant'.

William Moon (1818–1894)

INVENTOR OF TYPOGRAPHY FOR BLIND PEOPLE
44 Kensington Place
104–109 Queen's Road (gone, now Queensberry House)*

When he was 22 Moon suffered total blindness. He had lost the sight in one eye through scarlet fever when he was four. The other eye was seriously affected and he underwent several operations. After being educated in London he moved to Brighton at the age of 18 to live with his widowed mother (his parents had moved to the town in his childhood but he had remained some time in his native Horsmonden, Kent, intending to study to enter the Church).

Familiar with different systems of type for blind people, Moon started a day school in Egremont Place to teach blind children and others without speech. After several years teaching he came to believe that systems using contractions were unnecessarily complicated, especially for older people, and in 1845 devised a system of simplified Roman lettering. He began a monthly magazine using the system and also published books, often devotional works (*The Last Hours of Cranmer* appeared in 1847). He prepared the entire *Bible*.

Moon sold his publications for below cost price, subsidising them with charitable donations. When his critics attacked him for the cost and bulk of his publications – in 1858 his *Bible* appeared in 60 volumes – he replied with a formal riposte, arguing that other systems' use of contractions complicated notation to render books so produced of no use to most blind people.

He extended his system to foreign languages and by the time of Moon's death either the Lord's Prayer or other scripture had been embossed in 476 languages and dialects.

Scripture was only part of his output: there were devotional works, scientific treatises, and selections from Shakespeare, Milton, Burns, Scott, Longfellow, and others. He also issued embossed diagrams for Euclid, music, and maps, and devised a book, *Pictures for the Blind*, to help blind people understand the shape of common objects by touch. He helped establish many home-teaching societies for blind people, while lending libraries of his books were common in his lifetime. He was made a fellow of the Royal Geographical Society in 1852, a fellow of the Society of Arts in 1859, and awarded an LLD by the University of Philadelphia in 1871. (One of his two children, Robert, became a doctor in Philadelphia.)

Moon's first wife, Mary, who died in 1864, was the daughter of a Brighton surgeon and the couple lived in Kensington Place.

In September 1856 the foundation stone was laid for the Moon Printing Works at 104 Queen's Road. Less than 20 years later the Moon Alphabet had been adopted as the national standard and, while superseded by Braille, is still in use. It was at Queen's Road that he died on 10 October 1894 and is buried in the **Extra-Mural Cemetery**. His daughter, Adelaide, took over the publishing work.

* The plaque, which was once in the entrance hall to Queensberry House, has been removed.

Terence Morgan (1921–2005)

ACTOR

13 Wyndham Street

Born in London, Morgan was a familiar face in supporting roles in films for many years but best known when he starred as Sir Francis Drake in the television series of the same name.

Invalided out of the army during the Second World War, he later joined the Old Vic and played Laertes in a film version of *Hamlet* by **Sir Laurence Oliver** (*qv*). Others of his 20 films included *Captain Hornblower* and *Mandy*. He came to specialise in roles as villains.

He lived at this address in the 1950s and later bought a small hotel in Hove before becoming a property developer.

David (DM) Murray (1888–1962)

NOVELIST AND NEWSPAPER EDITOR

Chichester House, Chichester Terrace

Born in London and educated at Harrow and Oxford, Murray worked for *The Times* and *The Times Literary Supplement*. He published many books, including 14 mainly historical novels. His first great success was *Regency*, the story of four generations of women in Brighton, the first of them a mistress of the Prince Regent. It came out in 1936, although Murray did not move here until 1938. His interest in history was such that he had at home an army of toy soldiers that he would move about on the carpet to simulate the battles he was writing about in his books.

Murray's years in Brighton almost exactly coincided with his years as editor of *The Times Literary Supplement*, which he took over in 1937 with the agreement that he need come to the office only three days a week to leave himself time for his books. He lightened the newspaper's tone, changed its direction, and its political stance became more favourable to socialism. None of this increased the circulation, however, and Murray left in 1945.

He moved from Brighton to London in 1944 and while his novel writing continued, it was less successful. Murray's wife, Leonora Eyles (1889–1960), also a novelist and journalist, died in 1960, and in August 1962 he committed suicide by taking poison.

Napoleon III (1808–1873)

PRESIDENT OF THE SECOND FRENCH REPUBLIC AND LAST FRENCH MONARCH

Bedford Hotel, Kings Road (now site of Holiday Inn)
Grand Hotel, Kings Road

In the early years of the reign of **Queen Victoria** (*qv*), Louis-Napoleon, the future Napoleon III, made several visits to Brighton.

His father, King Louis-Philippe, died in 1846, the same year that Louis-Napoleon had escaped from six years' imprisonment in the Chateau de Ham and went into exile in London. One of the first people he met there was Brighton-born Harriett Howard (1823–65), who would be his long-standing mistress and financial supporter, and who bore him two sons.

In October of that year he travelled from Bath to Brighton, then in the grip of gales. This did not prevent him leaving the Bedford Hotel for a walk along the front each day. He visited the Theatre Royal and often rode on the South Downs. He returned to London in November.

In 1848 he was elected President of the Second Republic but in 1851 he engineered a coup and declared himself emperor. In 1870 he was defeated at the Battle of Sedan, during the Franco-Prussian War, and was deposed. The empress and their son, the Prince Imperial, fled to Hampshire and exile where Napoleon joined them in 1871.

In August 1872, only five months before he died, the ex-emperor took his son Prince Eugene to Brighton where they stayed at the newly opened Grand Hotel (pictured) and visited the Aquarium. He had last been in the town in 1848 when he had sat on the Chain Pier and had had a wager with Princess Matilde, his cousin and one-time fiancée, that he would be emperor within four years. Now it was not the future that he contemplated, but exile and the loss of a throne.

Jacqueline Nearne (1916–1982)

OFFICER, SPECIAL OPERATIONS EXECUTIVE
32 West Hill Street

Nearne was born at this address, the eldest daughter of an English father and a French mother. The family moved to France in 1923. In 1940 she escaped to Britain, via Portugal and Gibraltar.

In 1942 Nearne and her sister, Eileen, were recruited into the First Aid Nursing Yeomanry, but their fluency in French led them to work for the Special Operations Executive's French Section. (Francis, one of her two brothers, was also recruited by the organisation). She was parachuted into occupied France in January 1943, her sister following in March 1944, where she worked as a courier. That April Nearne was airlifted out, having built up one of the most extensive and successful networks.

She later cared for her sister, who had suffered Nazi interrogation and incarceration in Ravensbruck concentration camp. Nearne also worked for the UN in New York, and returned to London to live with her sister. She died of bronchopneumonia.

Blessed John Henry Newman, Cardinal Newman (1801–1889)

PRIEST, THEOLOGIAN AND CARDINAL
11 Marine Square

John Henry Newman, then a young academic and an Anglican vicar of a year's standing, came to Brighton in 1826, seeking a home for his mother and sisters after his father's death.

In his search for a home, he found Worthing 'damp, low, relaxing and (I fear) in winter unwholesome'. Brighton was bracing and 'a beautiful place', which he preferred to Bath: 'It is magnifique – and the waves are breaking so soft, blue-green and white'. He also liked the new Regency buildings.

Marine Square was still under construction when the family took up residence in 1827. The house had two drawing rooms and communicating folding doors on the ground and first floors, and there were initial queries about what they would do for bedrooms. He questioned whether the sea could be seen from the upper end of the square in which the house stood. He planned that he would live there when not working as a tutor and examiner at Oriel College, Oxford.

In the summer of 1827 he stayed again when preparing for his first stint as an examiner for the BA degree.

At one time Newman returned to stay for two months due to a mysterious illness that struck in late 1827. He was there that Christmas but on the following 4 January Mary, his younger sister, was taken ill at the dinner table, retired to her room and died the following evening. She was 19. Though Newman saw God's providence in Mary's death, he confided to his journal: 'But I feel sick, I must cease writing'. Decades later he wrote: 'I have not even now got over my sister's death.'

In 1830, Newman rode on horseback down to Brighton to spend a fortnight with his family. But that year the family left the house and moved to Iffley, near Oxford, as his mother felt that she wanted to be near to her son. Newman would, however, return at least twice to Brighton to visit cousins, in one of whose albums he wrote verses on each visit. He was also there in August 1832, with his sister, to visit a friend in Lewes.

In 1833 Newman landed in Brighton from a memorable six-month journey, by boat and land, around southern Europe. He had travelled part of the way with his great friend, Richard Hurrell Froude, who had brought him into the Anglo-Catholic Oxford Movement. Newman returned with the manuscript of the prayer, Pillar of the Cloud, now better known as the hymn, 'Lead, Kindly Light', in his pocket, and the conviction that 'he had a work to do for England' in his heart.

Newman was received into the Roman Catholic Church in 1845, a decision that would send reverberations through Church life, and he would become the most influential figure in 19th century Christianity.

In 1846 Newman returned to the town to sail to Rome by way of France with his great friend, Ambrose St John. In 1861 he holidayed in Brighton in a hotel not far from Marine Square, and visited his sister's grave to lay flowers.

In July 1861, suffering from insomnia and strain, Newman went on a three-week holiday, with Fr William Neville, one of the priests at Newman's Birmingham Oratory, which he had founded in 1849. On this trip to visit places familiar from his early life, he visited Brighton.

His final visit to Brighton was on the afternoon of Saturday, 28 June 1879. He had returned to England from Rome, where he had received the cardinal's red hat. The next morning he said mass at the Church of St John the Baptist, Kemp Town, assisted by Fr Neville. That afternoon he was driven to several parishes to visit priests. The following Monday he left for London to return to Birmingham. On the way, he broke his journey and visited the Rev Dr John Bloxam, rector of Upper Beeding, Sussex, his former curate at Littlemore, Oxfordshire, walking to the village from Bramber Station.

Richard Henry Nibbs (1816–1893)

PAINTER AND BOOK ILLUSTRATOR
8 Howard Place
7 Buckingham Place

Born in Brighton, Nibbs was educated in Worthing. He lived in Brighton all his life, and trained as a musician, becoming a professional cellist with the Theatre Royal Orchestra.

As a painter he was self-taught, with a natural talent for detailed observation. He worked in both water colours and oils. In 1840 a substantial inheritance allowed him to devote himself full-time to art. He specialised in marine scenes and his work depicts the coasts of Sussex, France and Holland. He also painted buildings and landscapes. He moved to Buckingham Place in 1873.

Sir William Nicholson (1872–1949)

PAINTER
The Grange, The Green, Rottingdean (now The Grange Museum and Art Gallery)
North End House (now Aubrey House), The Green, Rottingdean

Nicholson came to the village to paint a portrait of **Rudyard Kipling** (*qv*) and liked it so much he bought The Grange, which had been built in 1740. Then called The Vicarage, he renamed it. (The museum and art gallery has a gallery named after him).

He called himself 'the painter of the Downs' and, indeed, much of his work features the landscape of Sussex, including his *Cliffs at Rottingdean* and *High Barn, Rottingdean*. He is also noted for his woodcuts and illustrations.

Nicholson's wife Mabel Pryde (1871–1918) was a noted artist and their children were the painters Ben Nicholson and Annie ('Nancy') Nicholson and the architect, Christopher ('Kit') Nicholson.

In 1920, Nicholson sold The Grange to the local solicitor Sir George Lewis, who had it extended by Sir Edwin Lutyens. Nicholson bought North End House, which he sold three years later to **Enid Bagnold** (*qv*) and her husband, Sir Roderick Jones.

Ray Noble (1903–1978)

BAND LEADER AND COMPOSER
1 Montpelier Terrace Ⓟ

Noble was born here, the son of a London neurologist. He began to play the piano when he was ten, and later studied at the Royal Academy of Music for five years. He was an accomplished player by the age of 15 and an LRAM at 16.

He left Brighton at an early age and was living and working in Streatham when he came to public attention in his early 20s. By his mid-20s he was working as an arranger and composer and featuring in radio.

He moved to New York in 1933 where his number 1 single hits included 'Love is the Sweetest Thing' and 'The Very Thought of You'.

Helena Normanton (1882–1957)

BARRISTER AND FEMINIST CAMPAIGNER

16 Cheltenham Place
4 Clifton Place
11 Hampton Place, Hove

Normanton was born in London; her father died in mysterious circumstances when she was four – he was found with a broken neck in a railway tunnel. Jane, her mother, moved to Brighton where she ran a small grocery store, and later turned the family home at Clifton Place into a modest boarding house.

In 1895, Normanton went to York Place Junior School, York Place, and in 1896 won a scholarship to York Place Science School (now Varndean School), which she left in July 1900 as a student teacher. After her mother's death she helped to run the boarding house. She then moved to Hampton Place, another boarding house run by her aunt. She left the town in 1903 to attend a teacher training college in Liverpool.

She decided to become a barrister at the age of 12 when she visited a lawyer with her mother. She had to fight to gain admission to the Middle Temple and was called to the Bar in 1922, the second woman to do so, but always emphasising that she was the first female barrister to practise.

When she married Gavin Bowman Clark her application to retain her maiden name attracted considerable public interest. She achieved many 'firsts': the first married British woman to be issued a passport in her maiden name (1924); the first woman to obtain a divorce for a client and to lead the prosecution in a murder trial (1948); the first female counsel in cases in the High Court of Justice (1922), the Old Bailey (1924), and the London sessions (1926). She achieved for a client the highest damages at that date achieved by a woman in a breach of promise case (£1,250 and costs); and was the first woman to conduct a case in the United States, appearing in the test case in which a married woman's right to retain her maiden name was confirmed (1925). In 1949, with Rose Heilbron, she became the first female King's Counsel in England and Wales.

She faced many challenges in her profession, where myths were fabricated that were damaging to her career, like charges of advertising (forbidden by legal etiquette); and the notoriety she had gained from her writing, public speaking, and feminist activities.

She fought for divorce law, the rights of women and children and financial security reform, and wrote several books, including a novel. She was also a pacifist, who, aged 70, publicly protested against the atomic bomb.

Normanton made the first £5 donation to the Sussex University appeal in 1956, followed by a gift of £45 and she bequeathed the capital of her trust to the university. She requested that part of the university be named after her 'because I was the first subscriber to the project and because I make this gift in gratitude for all that Brighton did to educate me when I was left an orphan'.

She died in a London nursing home and her ashes were buried with her husband in the churchyard of **St Wulfran's Church**, Greenways, Ovingdean.

TP O'Connor (1848–1929)

JOURNALIST AND MP

64 Lansdowne Place, Hove
6 Marine Drive, Rottingdean

Thomas Power O'Connor (usually known as TP O'Connor and nicknamed 'Tay Pay') entered the House of Commons in 1880 as a Home Rule MP, with the encouragement of **Charles Stewart Parnell** (*qv*). By then, though, he had well established himself in journalism.

He and his wife, Elisabeth, lived for most of their married life in their home in Chelsea. From about 1895 they also had their Brighton homes, first in Marine Drive. It is said that they then lived in Medina Terrace but I could find no record. They then lived in Lansdowne Place. O'Connor's biographer also says that he had 'a more permanent home' in The Drive, Blackrock from about 1903 but, again, I could find no record of this.

In 1888, O'Connor founded the *Star*, an evening journal noted both for its radicalism and for its inauguration of the 'new' journalism. Differences led the proprietor to buy O'Connor out, reportedly for £15,000. In 1891 O'Connor bought the *Sunday Sun* (later the *Weekly Sun*). In 1902, he created *T.P.'s Weekly*, a popular penny literary paper. Other publications and books followed.

O'Connor acted as mediator and ambassador for Irish nationalism. President of the Irish National League of Great Britain from 1883 to 1918, in 1917 he became the first president of the British Board of Film Censors.

Sir Laurence Olivier, later Baron Olivier (1907–1989)

ACTOR AND THEATRICAL DIRECTOR

4 Royal Crescent 🅿

The first time Laurence Olivier appeared in public (billed as 'Lawrence Oliver') was at the still standing but now empty Brighton Hippodrome, in Middle Street, in a charity gala in 1925, when he tripped on stage and fell flat on his face. But he seems to have absorbed enough of the town in later years to remark in 1944, following the stage production of *Richard III*: 'There is a phrase: "The sweet smell of success". And I can only tell you, I've had two experiences of that and it just smells like Brighton and oyster bars and things like that.'

In 1961, 36 years after that first appearance, knighted, rich and the most famous actor of his day, a star of stage and Hollywood, he returned to Brighton to make it his permanent home. He lived there, in one of the town's most attractive Regency addresses, until 1979. The deposit on the black-tiled house was paid for by the royalties from the eponymous cigarettes.

His arrival was fortuitous as he had at the same time accepted the directorship of the new Chichester Theatre and its festival, which were within easy commuting distance. It was also, in another way, a new chapter in life for Olivier: divorced the previous year from Vivien Leigh, in 1961 he had married the actor Joan Plowright (born in 1929).

This was to be their new home – they knew the town well for they had first become lovers here on 28 November 1957. Their three children were born in Brighton and later the Oliviers acquired number 5, where the children were to live, and joined the two houses together. It was the beginning of a period of stability and family life that had eluded Olivier so far. But grand though the house was, in 1972, the facade was declared to be unsafe and had to be rebuilt at great expense. That year, too, the Oliviers were twice burgled and, on the second occasion, he was coshed.

In the house he kept a small theatrical *musée*, which he would proudly show visitors. Among the exhibits: the earliest known stage wig; the dagger with which Henry Irving had killed himself in *Othello*; and a lace collar that had once belonged to Edmund Kean.

From Brighton Olivier travelled to London on 'that lovely *Brighton Belle*' – he had campaigned to have kippers restored to the breakfast menu – to his work as both actor and founder-director at the fledgling National Theatre in London. The Oliviers left the town in 1979 but when created a peer nine years before, he had taken the title of Baron Olivier of Brighton.

Cecil Parker (1897–1971)

ACTOR
1 Dyke Road Place

Born Cecil Schwabe in Hastings, Parker began a theatrical career in 1922 (which would later include the original West End production of *Blithe Spirit*) and played usually supporting, most often middle class, roles in 91 films from 1928 to 1969. The latter included *The Lady Vanishes, Under Capricorn, The Lady Killers, The Man in the White Suit, Heavens Above, Moll Flanders,* and *Oh, What a Lovely War*. He died in Brighton.

Charles Stewart Parnell (1846–1891)

IRISH NATIONALIST LEADER
8 Medina Villas, Hove*
10 Walsingham Terrace, Hove (now site of Dorset Court, Kingsway, Hove)

It was in Walsingham Terrace that Parnell died in his wife's arms on 9 October 1891, as crowds gathered on the seafront outside the house. He and the former **Mrs Katharine O'Shea** had been married for less than three months. She would have preferred that he had been buried in Brighton but the next day, in heavy rain, his polished oak coffin, surmounted with a medieval cross and covered with wreaths, travelled on a carriage, drawn by four black horses to Brighton Station. It was followed by carriages containing, among others, several Irish Members of Parliament. The cortège went at walking pace past pavements lined with onlookers, and 200 more people waited at the station. The 1.45 pm train took the mourners to Victoria and thence the eight-hour journey to Holyhead for the Irish boat, and burial in Dublin.

Parnell had begun his illicit relationship with the English Catholic O'Shea in 1880, when she was separated, but not divorced from her husband, Willie, a Home Rule Party MP (they had married in Brighton in 1867). She and Willie had lived in Brighton and in 1881 she records staying a month in rooms in Brighton with her children (she would eventually have six, three of whom were fathered by Parnell before their marriage) when Parnell, the Anglican leader of the Irish Parliamentary Party would stay. She says that his engineering interests gave him time to admire Brighton Station and he would spend 'hours, pacing the station, measuring distances, heights, depth of roof etc, etc' in order to build a cattle shed on the same lines at his country house in Ireland, as he was to do.

They lived together at various times before their marriage. In 1889 she had moved with her children permanently to Brighton, the divorce having been filed by her husband, and Parnell would live with her there when not in Ireland.

O'Shea's divorce in 1890 publicly exposed their relationship. This fatally weakened Parnell's political career (he lost three by-elections after the divorce) and split his party. His erstwhile political colleague, Tim Healey, dubbed Katharine 'the Brighton banshee'.

They married in Steyning Registry Office in 1891 and lived first at Medina Villas, but later moved to Walsingham Terrace. The house was spacious, with four storeys and a glassed-in balcony with iron decorations at the top and base. Katharine spoke of 'cornfields from one side of the house away up to Shoreham basin and harbour, a waste of hay at the back of the house, an excellent train service and sufficient distance from Brighton proper to enable us to avoid the crowd'. (That part of the terrace where Parnell and O'Shea had lived was damaged by bombs in 1943 and later demolished. The plaque on Dorset House says that in a house on this spot, Parnell died.)

Willie O'Shea died in Hove in 1905. A servant's memory of Katharine O'Shea in later years was of the short, plump old lady sometimes going for walks along the seashore at two o'clock in the morning. She died in Littlehampton in 1921 aged 76 and was buried there.

*A plaque has been placed on Parnell Court, Medina Place, which is off Medina Villas, dedicated to his memory.

Fred Perry (1909–1995)

LAWN TENNIS CHAMPION
24 Newlands Road, Rottingdean
1 Grange Close, Dean Court Road, Rottingdean
10 Little Crescent, Rottingdean

Perry, who won three championships both at Wimbledon and in theUSA, as well as French and Australian titles, had long retired from tennis when he came to live in Rottingdean. He and his business partner had sold their Fred Perry Sportswear Company, the clothing line for which he's probably as well known today, in 1961. Their initial investment had been £300 each. But Perry was already living in Rottingdean village when he found a second career (a third, if one counts his business ventures) as a pungent, ironic and informal commentator for the BBC during Wimbledon week.

In the winter months he and his fourth wife, Barbara (Bobby) Friedman, sister of the actor Patricia Roc, who survived him, lived in Florida and elsewhere in the USA.

In 1976 he sold many possessions from his career – cups, salvers, and gifts – because his wife said that it was no longer possible to take care of them in Rottingdean and they were anxious about burglary.

Perry had become a US citizen in 1938, but, upon his death, his daughter, Penny, said: 'He did not forget his roots. He felt he belonged here, though he was not here for much of his life'. Penny was so attached to Rottingdean – she had been educated privately in Brighton – that she returned from the USA to marry Dean Evert, brother of another tennis star, Chris Evert, at St Margaret's Church, Rottingdean.

Perry died in hospital in Australia after falling and breaking his ribs in his hotel. His funeral took place at St Margaret's Church and his ashes are buried at Wimbledon.

Roland Pertwee (1885–1963)

PLAYWRIGHT AND TELEVISION SCRIPTWRITER, DIRECTOR AND ACTOR
19 Denmark Villas, Hove

This was Pertwee's boyhood home, where his parents ran a school. He worked as a screenwriter and actor. In 1954 he and his son Michael created *The Grove Family*, the first television soap opera, which was watched by almost a quarter of all those who owned TV sets. (His other son Jon achieved fame as *Doctor Who*.)

Pertwee also wrote young people's adventure novels *The Islanders* (1950), *Rough Water* (1951), *An Actor's Life for Me* (1953), and *Operation Wild Goose* (1955), as well as short stories.

When *The Grove Family* was discontinued in 1957, Pertwee retired from writing.

His second cousin, **Bill Pertwee**, who found fame as air raid warden Hodges in *Dad's Army*, lived in Hove, in a house he named Pertwee Towers.

Wilfred Pickles (1904–1978)

BROADCASTER AND ACTOR
19 Courcles, Arundel Street

Pickles was one of the best-known radio broadcasters of his day, identified by his rich Yorkshire accent, his relaxed and homely manner and a variety of catch phrases.

Amateur drama in Halifax led him to a broadcasting debut in BBC's *Children's Hour*. His war-time role as a BBC newscaster made him the first to speak with a northern accent.

After a series of variety and pantomime seasons throughout England, in 1946 he became compère of a trailblazing new radio quiz show, *Have a Go*, with a jackpot £3 prize money. His wife, **Mabel Myerscough** (1906–89), was his partner on the show. ('Give 'em the money, Mabel' was his catch phrase.) The programme ran until 1967 with a peak audience of 26 million. When the show's appeal declined, Pickles developed a career as stage, television and film character actor.

His wife was with him when he died at their home of carcinoma of the lung and chronic emphysema, in this rather indifferent block where they lived for the last years of his life, on 27 March 1978.

Margaret Powell (1907–1984)

WRITER

10 Montgomery Street, Hove
222 Old Shoreham Road, Hove

Margaret Powell was born in Montgomery Street as Margaret Langley, one of seven children of a seasonally employed house painter and a char. Powell's grandmother also shared the three rooms. It was experiences like this and her own later life in service that brought her fame and fortune through best-selling memoirs like *Below Stairs* and *Climbing the Stairs*. When she died she left a not inconsiderable estate worth £77,000.

When she was 13 Powell won a grammar school scholarship, a first step in her ambition to becoming a teacher, but family poverty prevented her from taking it. She wrote: 'I remember once having to queue like Oliver Twist for watery gruel at the town [Hove] soup kitchen when I was seven. One winter, we'd even burnt all the shelves and banisters just to keep warm'. Instead, she went to work in a laundry until she was 15, while at the same time she was devouring Balzac and Dickens at the local library. Her life, she wrote, gave her two things: a great sense of inferiority and the ability to cook a seven-course meal. 'In the local parks, if any wealthy child wandered up to me, its nurse would say: "Come away this instant!"'

After the laundry she gained a position as a maid in the Regency home of a Rev Clydesdale and his family. For £24 a year, she began work at 5am, took on all manner of jobs, and had half a day a week off. Later she found work in grand houses in London. She escaped domestic service by marrying a milkman, but returned to work as a maid toward the end of the war, by which time she had three sons. She took evening classes and gained O'levels and in 1969 English at A'level.

She died on 25 April 1984 at the **Avenue Clinic, 14 New Church Road**, Hove.

Roger Quilter (1877–1953)

SONGWRITER AND COMPOSER
4 Brunswick Square

Quilter was born the fifth of the seven surviving children of wealthy parents in this house with its full complement of servants. His father Sir William Quilter (1841–1911) was the first baronet, a shrewd businessman, and a Liberal Unionist MP. The family had musical and artistic tastes (Sir William was a noted art collector). Although the family moved to Suffolk five years after his birth, these early years in Brighton gave Quilter a life-long love of southern England.

He was educated at prep school and Eton, and he then pursued his musical studies in Germany. He returned to London where he lived for the rest of his life. A chronic depressive, he wrote music for theatre, orchestral works, part songs and pieces for piano, but is best remembered for his songs.

Margaret (Peggy) Ramsay (1908–1991)

THEATRICAL AGENT

34 Kensington Place

This pleasant, otherwise unremarkable terrace house was a bolt-hole for Ramsay, the most famous and successful theatrical agent of her day. She had started her agency, Margaret Ramsay Ltd, with the help of friends when her recommendation of plays for West End managements was gaining her no commission. The agency had been going for a decade or so when she first came to Brighton and bought the house. Here she could retreat at weekends and separate her private life from her hectic professional one. She otherwise lived in London, but, as an Australian by birth who had grown up in South Africa, she did not like the city, which seemed cramped and without a sky.

One incursion by her into local life was her support for Bill Butler, owner of the Unicorn Bookshop. In 1968, he was prosecuted under the Obscene Publications Act, for publishing a satire by the novelist JG Ballard called *Why I Want to Fuck Ronald Reagan*. He was tried at Brighton Magistrates' Court, convicted and fined.

Among those she represented were the playwrights Joe Orton, David Hare, John Arden, Edward Bond, Howard Brenton, Caryl Churchill, Christopher Hampton, John Mortimer, David Mercer and Alan Ayckbourn; the novelists Iris Murdoch, Jean Rhys, James Baldwin, and Muriel Spark for original dramatic works and adaptations of their novels; the actor Simon Callow, who himself has written his own book about their relationship, *Love is Where it Falls*; the singer-songwriter John Lennon; and the film director David Lean.

In her final years physical ailments prevented her from leaving her London home and dementia took its toll.

In her will she bequeathed £1.5 million to set up the Peggy Ramsay Foundation, to assist playwrights. The foundation placed the plaque on the house, which was unveiled by Simon Callow.

Sir Terence Rattigan (1911–1977)

PLAYWRIGHT

Bedford House, 79 Marine Parade

When Rattigan bought this house in February 1961, he was one of the world's most famous playwrights. *After the Dance, The Winslow Boy, The Deep Blue Sea, Separate Tables, Ross,* and *The Browning Version*, and screenplays, such as *Brighton Rock*, had secured his reputation, great wealth and honours (he had received a CBE in 1958 and was to be knighted in 1971).

He had been living in a flat in Embassy Court, Hove, which he now made over to his lover Michael Franklin (Rattigan made a point of never sharing his homes with his many lovers), at whose suggestion he had bought this house. This would allow Franklin to get a large fee to design and decorate the house. Rattigan kept a bedroom free especially for his great friend, actor Margaret Leighton for whenever she wanted to use it.

Much of the time in the Brighton years Rattigan was away working but by 1962 Franklin's efforts at interior design were not appreciated. Rattigan had returned from abroad (where, among other things, he had been working on the script for the Burton–Taylor film, *The VIPs*), when he met the critic, his friend BA Young, walking along the seafront. 'I've just moved into my new house after waiting 18 months', he said 'and it's uninhabitable. There isn't a single room I can bear to sit in.' The heavy curtaining, provided by Franklin, did not allow sufficient light; the interior had been stripped away and the staircase replaced by one from a Chelsea antique shop; while the Regency facade had been flattened to look, as one visitor, Vivien Leigh, said, more like Belgravia than Brighton. He put the house on the market but, when *Man and Boy* opened at the Theatre Royal in August 1963, he told the local press that he was not selling after all. He explained he hadn't been too well that winter but had felt better when he returned to Brighton, adding: 'The view might not be as good as Ischia [in Italy, where he owned two villas], but the air is a damn sight better. Now I am taking walks along the seafront every day and I am taking up golf again.'

In 1964 a fan letter to new, lauded playwright Joe Orton about *Entertaining Mr Sloane* occasioned an invitation for Orton and his lover, Kenneth Halliwell, to spend a weekend in Brighton. Halliwell arrived wearing makeup, determined to push aside Orton, of whom he was jealous (he claimed to have written the play). Soon bored, Rattigan invited round his neighbours, **Laurence Olivier** (*qv*) and his wife, **Joan Plowright**, but Halliwell, as Rattigan put it, proceeded to bore the royal pants off them.

Apart from the Brighton house, Rattigan had a little-used mansion in Scotland (he also rented a flat in London's Eaton Square). He sold these in 1966 to live abroad for health and tax reasons, and for somewhere warmer in the winter. He divided his time between Hollywood, Ischia and an apartment in Paris. He returned for a short while to live in England but never again in Brighton. He died in Bermuda.

Rev Frederick Robertson (1816–1853)

CLERGYMAN

9 Montpelier Terrace **P**

60 Montpelier Road **P**

Holy Trinity Church, Ship Street **P**

Robertson, one of the greatest preachers of his time, came to the former Holy Trinity Church (now deconsecrated and serving as an art gallery) after being educated in Yorkshire, Oxford, Edinburgh, and Tours. His hopes of a military career were frustrated, having resisted his father's original hopes that he would seek ordination. He had had an unsatisfying spell in a solicitor's office in Suffolk, travelled abroad, and, after ordination, served in curacies in Cheltenham and Oxford, and married in 1841. And even then, despite an annual stipend of £150, he had to be persuaded to accept the position in Brighton. He preached his first sermon on15 August 1847.

But his six years in the town – first living in Montpelier Terrace (pictured) from 1847 until he moved to Montpelier Road in 1850 – saw him emerge as a leader of social reform, founding a working men's institute, known later as the Mechanics Institute, in 1848 and supporting the Early Closing Association on behalf of the shop assistants in his congregation. The plaque on Montpelier Road, where he died in 1853, refers to him as 'an elder brother among Christians'.

His writings offered popular theology but what made him influential and attracted followers were his sermons. Carriages would queue outside the church and crowds lined the streets on Sundays; people came down for the weekend to hear him; and visitors included Lord Shaftesbury and **Charles Dickens** (*qv*). The latter said that he was 'one of the greatest masters of elocution I ever knew. To hear Robertson read the church prayers was itself a liberal education'.

But Robertson's work caused his health to suffer. **Henry Wagner** (*qv*), vicar of Brighton, did not accept his choice of curate to assist him, and Robertson took this as a slight, probably suffering a nervous breakdown. He died on 15 August 1853 from what was described as 'brain fever'. (In fact, the cause of his death may have been occipital nerve neuralgia.) Thousands lined the four-mile funeral route to the **Extra-mural Cemetery** and the *Brighton Gazette* said his death caused 'a massive loss'. The city's working men paid for his grave's memorial.

However, it was only after his death that Robertson became most widely known through the publication of a biography and his sermons in 20 volumes. He had destroyed his sermons, describing how 'I do hate, detest and abhor … all speechifying and publicity', but they were collected by a Brighton woman who took them down in shorthand when delivered.

Marilyn Thomas Faulkenberg discovered a diary in code and a suitcase of papers six years after her biography of Robertson appeared in 2001. Her long-held suspicions of infidelity, which she had inferred from some opaque remarks that Robertson had made about his behaviour, proved to be correct. She published (as Marilyn Thomas) her exposé in 2008 showing that far from being the upright married father of two, Robertson had been unfaithful to his wife with Lady Augusta Fitzpatrick. There was a hint of other infidelities, and another lover may have been Lady Byron, widow of the poet and a great admirer of Robertson, and who was 24 years his senior.

Sir George Robey (1869–1954)

COMEDIAN
8 Rutland Court, New Church Road, Hove
The Lawns, Arundel Drive, Saltdean

George Edward Wade was born in South London, began his education at a dame-school, but from 11 to 16 was educated in Dresden and Leipzig.

Back in England he became bored with office life, took up football, at which he excelled, and started singing comic songs in smoking concerts and charity shows. When he started earning the occasional guinea from comedy, he saved his family embarrassment by changing his name to George Robey.

His professional debut was at the Oxford Music Hall, London, in July 1891. Soon he was sharing equal billing with established stars such as Dan Leno and Marie Lloyd, sometimes playing five music halls a night. His trademark costume was a bald-fronted wig, a red nose, heavy blacking of his naturally prominent eyebrows, while wearing a small flat bowler hat, a shapeless crumpled, collarless soutane, and carrying a short flexible cane. He specialised in the double entendre that later served **Max Miller** (*qv*) so well ('honest vulgarity', Robey called it). His best known song was 'If You Were the Only Girl in the World'. For 40 years he also played an outstanding pantomime dame. **Laurence Olivier** (*qv*), with whom he appeared as the dying Falstaff in the film of *Henry V*, referred admiringly to his 'whiplash diction'.

The 'Prime Minister of Mirth' was also a connoisseur and shrewd collector of Chinese porcelain, netsuke and Japanese antiquities, and took an interest in Egyptology, oriental art, and comparative religion. He was a watercolourist who exhibited at the Royal Academy and he also made violins. He made guest appearances for professional football teams, while once playing cricket with WG Grace.

Robey's marriage to Ethel Haydon, which produced two children, ended in divorce in 1938. That year he married Blanche Littler, 30 years his junior, with whom he had lived for eight years. With her better-known brothers, Prince and Emile, she was a theatrical impresario, and she managed Robey's affairs. After Robey's reluctant retirement in 1948, the couple lived at Rutland Court. He now opened bazaars and entertained at old people's clubs and even joined the Hove Civil Defence Corps. But he was never free of an admiring public and, seeking more privacy, the couple then moved to Grand Avenue and, finally, to Arundel Drive, Saltdean, where Lady Robey nursed him until his death. Lady Robey later moved back to Grand Avenue.

Dame Flora Robson (1902–1984)

ACTOR

14 Marine Gardens 🅿

7 Wykeham Terrace, Dyke Road 🅿

St Nicholas' Church, Church Street 🅿

Robson had visited Brighton in her distinguished theatrical career to perform at the Theatre Royal. When she retired, she moved from London and found the house in Marine Gardens. She had a small room built on the top which became known as the Lighthouse. She had planned to keep her grand piano there but the narrow stairway in the tall, thin house made that impossible. Her happy time in Marine Gardens was marred by a well-publicised burglary.

When the husband of her sister, Shela, died, she came to share the house with Robson, who cared for Shela when dementia set in. Her two other surviving sisters, Lila and Margaret, shared a house together in Hove. Upon Margaret's death the three sisters moved to Wykeham Terrace to live together, which became home from home for their large extended family (there were 30 at one time).

Robson was much involved in local life. St Nicholas' Church sits just above Wykeham Terrace and here Robson was so regular a worshipper that a commemorative plaque has been placed inside.

She supported efforts to open a new arts centre in the Old Market, as well as helping local amateur dramatic companies. When the Brighton Theatre Group presented Somerset Maugham's *Lady Audley's Secret*, in which she had appeared at the start of her career, she agreed to direct it. She acted as narrator for *Peter and the Wolf* at the Brighton Festival at a performance by the Brighton Youth Orchestra. This was the beginning of a long involvement with the orchestra, including fund raising and unpublicised financing for some members to go abroad.

When Bette Davis, the American film actor, made a personal appearance tour of the UK, she came to the Theatre Royal. 'I believe that there is another Queen Elizabeth in the audience', she said, referring to the fact that she and Robson had played the monarch on screen. Robson received an ovation.

Dame Anita Roddick (1942–2007)

BUSINESSWOMAN, ENVIRONMENTALIST AND HUMAN RIGHTS CAMPAIGNER
22 Kensington Gardens 🅿

Anita and Gordon Roddick had already tried their hand at running a hotel and a restaurant in their home town of Littlehampton, when, on 26 March 1976, she opened the first Body Shop at this address, then a dingy storefront in a bad state of repair. The name was chosen from a notice at a local garage specialising in panel beating, and when the local undertakers protested at the name, the shop gained free publicity. What became the Body Shop corporate green was first used to cover the mould spots on the walls. Early products, with exotic names, were made in Roddick's kitchen, and sold in recycled urine sample bottles to save money. However, she eventually found a herbalist in the telephone directory, who made 25 products.

Anxious about her new venture, she told her husband that she needed about £400 a week to make it work. Two months later she was employing a 16-year-old assistant. A second shop was opened that same year in Chichester, backed by a loan from the boyfriend of a friend, who owned a local garage. By 1984 the Roddicks were millionaires. As the century turned, there were 1,800 shops in 49 countries. In 2006 the company was sold to L'Oreal for £625 million, earning the Roddicks about £130 million.

J.H Round (1854–1928)

MEDIEVAL HISTORIAN AND GENEALOGIST
15 Brunswick Terrace, Hove 🅿

John Horace Round was born in this house to Laura, daughter of **Horace Smith** (*qv*) and John, the scion of a well-placed family of Essex landowners that included politicians, lawyers and civil servants among its members. The young Round said, on visiting the family farms: 'In Brighton I am asked nowhere and treated as nobody, while in Essex I am asked everywhere and treated with a consideration to which I am unused … it is a real mistake to wrap oneself in the fond illusion that our family occupies any position in Brighton'. Yet he lived and worked at this address for much of his life.

J.H.
ROUND
1854 - 1928
Historian
was born here

The house had been bought in 1827 for £7,000 by his other grandfather, John Round, an Essex man who had married well and had been a successful banker and MP. The house became his son's when he died in 1860. But Round's parents let the house immediately and the family went to live in Paris for four years. The death of Laura and the couple's nine-year-old daughter, also called Laura, both in 1864, caused John to return to Brunswick Terrace, with Round and his sister, Violet.

Young Round was educated at prep school and at home, and after Oxford, he returned to care for his father, who had sunk into depression and become emotionally dependent on his son. Violet, younger by two years, married in 1889, had no children and she and her brother rarely met in later life. Only after his father's death in 1887 did Round let Brunswick Terrace to live in London from 1888 to 1903. Sometimes he would return to stay with his Aunt Eliza Smith at **21 Sillwood Place** and he would often travel abroad.

He returned to Brunswick Terrace for good in 1903 but said that Brighton's climate never suited him and contributed to his ill-health. He was a lord of the manor in Essex with a fine (inherited) house and became Deputy Lord Lieutenant of that county with the patronage of his cousin, James, whom, as a very convinced Conservative, he had often assisted in his election as an Essex MP. He was active in Essex's archaeological society. Round never held regular, salaried employment but, among much other work, he contributed to the *Victoria County Histories* and the *Encyclopaedia Britannica*.

He never married – he said he did not have the means – but seems to have had relationships with women. On one occasion 'an Irish girl' with 'lovely eyes and complexion and masses of golden hair' stayed with him. He died at this house on 24 June 1928.

Arnold Ruge (1802–1880)

WRITER AND POLITICAL THINKER
7 Park Crescent

For a man who had been imprisoned for treasonous conspiracy and disputed with Karl Marx, being president of the Park Crescent Residents Association was, at the very least, somewhat different.

Ruge had been born on the Baltic island of Rugen and in 1824 was sentenced to 14 years' imprisonment for involvement in a student nationalist conspiracy. Freed in 1830, he published several books, married Charlotte Duffer and was left well off when widowed in 1832. He married his second wife, Agnes, in 1834.

A leading Hegelian and leader of political and religious liberalism, he had no time for Marx's socialism and was satirised by the latter. He lost his publishing business and money with the collapse of the 1848 revolution.

Ruge rented this house in Brighton in 1850 and bought it in 1867 (he always longed to be near the sea). He supported himself by teaching and writing. Agnes ran a daguerreotype business at 180 Western Road, which folded as technology advanced.

In Brighton Ruge kept in contact with a group of political émigrés in London. His lectures in Brighton, London and Birmingham came out as *New Germany* in 1854.

Critical as he was of Britain and bitter at being ignored, Ruge took up gardening and enjoyed seaside walks. Despite receiving a pension from the German government, when he died at Park Crescent he left less than £100.

Lord John Russell (1792–1878)

PRIME MINISTER
14 Sussex Square **P**

The short period in which he lived here marked the end of the happiest time of Russell's life. On 1 November 1838 Adelaide, his wife of three years, died giving birth to their second child, Victoria. His stepdaughter, Adelaide, remembered Russell's 'bitter weeping'. He and his wife had come here late that year also with their two-year-old daughter, Georgiana, and the four children of Adelaide's first marriage.

At that time Russell was Home Secretary and had previously been leader of the Whig opposition. In 1846 he would become Prime Minister. But now his first thought was resignation. His colleagues and friends counselled against such a move and while he was not in the best of health, he rested in Cassiobury, a country home in Hertfordshire, which he had been lent, and came back to his duties after a few weeks. What really impelled Russell to stay in post was his strong sense of duty.

However, in Brighton, he had helped John Nelson Goulty, a cousin of Lord Nelson and a well-known local nonconformist minister at the Union Chapel in The Lanes, to start the British School in Eastern Road.

Richard Russell (1687–1759)

PHYSICIAN
Royal Albion Hotel, Kings Road **P**

The son of an apothecary and born in Lewes, after training as a physician and surgeon and gaining a medical degree from the University of Leiden, Russell returned to England to set up a practice in his native town.

He had observed how people living on the coast drank sea water (iodine being the key element) to cure stomach disorders, and he developed a therapeutic regime of sea water bathing and drinking which he urged his patients to follow in Brighton, as this was judged superior to inland spas. However, Russell did create a small spa where he erected a basin at St Anne's Wells, Hove, in about 1750 and recommended its use to his patients. He was elected a fellow of the Royal Society in 1752 and awarded a medical degree from Cambridge University.

His 1753 treatise, *A Dissertation Concerning the Use of Sea Water in the Diseases of the Glands*, which he had published in Latin three years earlier, distilled his ideas. The curative effects of the water treatment were combined with diet and hygiene routines, and recovery was also aided by the attraction of being in Brighton.

The next year he moved to a substantial house, which he had built, where the Royal Albion Hotel now stands, for use by his patients, but it was also large enough to accommodate him and his family. He lived there until 1759.

His advocacy of curative water treatment and sending patients to Brighton increased its already developing popularity.

The statement on his commemorative tablet – 'If you seek his monument, look around' – may not be original, but it is very true.

Lady Sackville (1862–1936)

ARISTOCRAT

39/40/40a, Sussex Square
White Lodge, 40 The Cliff, Roedean

The marriage of Lord and Lady Sackville had once been happy but in May 1919 it collapsed when he told her that his mistress, Olive Rubens, and her complaisant husband, Walter, were coming to stay at the Sackville country home, Knole, in Kent. Lady Sackville threatened to leave if they came. The next day she packed her bags for Brighton, where she owned the Sussex Square house, and lived in the town for the rest of her life. The house was furnished with three vanloads of furniture bought from Knole.

Lord Sackville had attempted to ascertain his wife's likely reaction by sounding out their daughter, the novelist **Vita Sackville-West** (*qv*). 'She seems absolutely delighted with Brighton and very happy there', he told her.

However, unlike Vita Sackville-West's marriage to the writer Harold Nicolson, the Sackvilles' marriage lacked the life-long affection which prevailed despite both the Nicolsons' ambiguous sexuality and multiple affairs.

Lady Sackville bought three large adjoining houses in Sussex Square. She employed Sir Edwin Lutyens to knock the three into one and redesign the garden so that it might be reached by a tunnel under the road. It is likely that she and Lutyens were lovers; she called him 'McNed', he called her 'McSack'. She spent £50,000 on the work and lived there alone with servants. However, Lutyens' work could not disguise three main staircases, three ballrooms and three front halls.

An idea of the exotic interior of the house may be judged from the description by Sackville of the room where her daughter stayed: 'Her walls are of shiny emerald green paper, floor green; doors and furniture sapphire blue; ceiling apricot colour. Curtains blue and inside curtains yellowish. The decoration of the furniture is mainly beads of all colours painted on the blue ground; even the doorplates are treated the same. I have 6 bright orange pots on her green marble mantelpiece, and there are salmon and tomato-colour cushions and lampshades. Pictures by Bakst, George Plank, Rodin, and framed in *passe-partout* ribbons.'

When Sackville decided to leave Sussex Square, she did so at a loss of £45,000. But money was no object when she moved in 1923 to her last home, White Lodge. She held a seven-day sale, which included a

42-stone diamond necklace that had belonged to Queen Catherine Parr, and sculptures by Auguste Rodin and Jacob Epstein.

Designed by Sir John William Simpson, son of **Thomas Simpson** (*qv*), and built in 1903, her new home was also to be redesigned by Lutyens at great cost. The distinctive outline shape with prominent gables and tall, angular chimneys is Lutyens' work. He also created a large York stone terrace of herringbone-style vertically laid floor tiles, lawns and herbaceous borders, which led to a sunken garden, and which spanned much of the width of the plot. Today, the house comprises apartments, the original yew plantings have been replaced by euonymus bushes and the garden is mostly laid to lawn. However, the sunken garden survives. The original roof of the east wing has been replaced with garish blue-green tiles and the loggia is hidden behind an ugly brick extension.

Having quarrelled with all her friends, Sackville relied on her grandsons, Ben Nicolson (future art historian) and Nigel Nicolson (future writer, publisher and MP) for company. Despite their protests, they would be driven down to the town. 'Even in wintertime', Nigel wrote '[we] were made to sit for hours on her balcony huddled in her fur coats and with hot-water bottles on our knees, waiting for lunch at 5pm, when it would be served by the under gardener, the cook having given notice that morning. She [his grandmother] was always in trouble with servants and tradesmen, refusing to pay their wages and bills, and, with a jocularity that only she enjoyed, named her house the Writs Hotel.'

In 1933 Ben Nicolson wrote in his diary that he had gone to see his grandmother who had spent the whole time saying things against his parents – about his mother and women; his father and men; about his mother's lovers, Violet Trefusis and Virginia Woolf – to put him against them. She then told him not to tell his parents what she had said, but he did. His father, Harold, said Lady Sackville was Iago and that no one would ever believe such a person could exist; his mother, Vita, that she was a genius gone wrong. 'I don't think I understand', young Nicolson noted.

When she was old and bed-ridden, her grandsons would arrange that one or other of them would spend a day with Sackville every two months. However, they never knew what to expect upon arrival – abuse, wild generosity, lunch cooked by the gardener at their grandmother's bedside or served on an icy terrace at 3.30pm, a cheque for £10, or dismissal after a five-minute interview.

When Sackville died in 1936, Harold Nicolson used a motorboat to scatter her ashes three miles from the shore opposite White Lodge, as she had instructed. Nigel was bequeathed the house and many of its contents, including several portraits of his grandmother, one by John Singer Sargent. He sold White Lodge, and ultimately the funds helped finance the launch of Weidenfeld & Nicolson, publishers. With the proceeds he was also able to purchase The Shiants Isles, uninhabited islands in the Outer Hebrides.

Vita Sackville-West (1892–1962)

WRITER AND GARDENER
39/40/40a Sussex Square

In 1918, Vita Sackville-West, who had been married for five years to the writer and diplomat Harold Nicolson and had two small sons, Ben (future art historian) and Nigel (future writer, publisher, and MP), began what was to be a tempestuous, emotionally draining, but, at times, exhilarating relationship with Violet Keppel, the future novelist, Violet Trefusis. They had known each other since childhood but it was in this year that the relationship became sexual, and they ran away together several times, mostly to France.

In 1919 Sackville-West came to Brighton to seek refuge from her turmoil at the home of her mother, **Lady Sackville** (*qv*), in Sussex Square. However, she was there 'alone, in a great empty and dust-sheeted house', as she wrote, feeling 'absolutely miserable ... I used to wonder whether I wouldn't throw myself over the cliffs'. On the fifth day, her lover's engagement to Denys Trefusis, an officer in the Royal Horse Guards, was announced. While Sackville-West had been expecting this, she wrote that when she bought the newspaper carrying the story at Brighton Station, she nearly fainted; but it did not stop the relationship. She and Violet resumed their affair even during the Trefusises' honeymoon, when they met in Paris. At one time they went to see Lady Sackville in Brighton, while Sackville-West's sons were staying with their grandmother.

In 1921 Sackville-West and Trefusis went off once again to France for six weeks, but that year the affair ended, under the threat by Harold Nicolson to end their marriage. Sackville-West and Nicolson were, in their terms, reconciled – they spent the rest of their lives together, bound by affection but with infidelities on both sides, he often living in London and she at Sissinghurst Castle, Kent.

George Augustus Sala (1828–1895)

JOURNALIST AND WRITER
2 Eastern Terrace
59 Norton Road, Hove

Though Sala was born in London and spent much of his life reporting from around the world – Russia, America (during the Civil War), Africa, Australia and Europe – he and his family had a long-standing association with Brighton. While Sala died in the town, according to his autobiography, his putative father, a dancing master, may have died in a house on the Old Steine three weeks after Sala's birth. His eldest sister had died in Brighton, aged 14, in 1814.

Sala's widowed mother, Henrietta, supported herself and five surviving children by teaching singing and giving annual concerts in London and Brighton, where she lived for six months of the year. She mixed in literary and social circles, and her friend and patron was **Harriot Mellon, Duchess of St Albans** (*qv*). When he was 12 Sala and his mother attended 'a grand Twelve Night entertainment' at the duchess's house, St Alban's House.

Sala's earliest journalism was for *Household Words*, edited by **Charles Dickens** (*qv*), and at this time, too, he gained a long-standing reputation for drunkenness, quarrelsomeness, and financial and professional unreliability. He joined *The Daily Telegraph* in 1857 and wrote for it for the rest of his life.

Sala returned to Brighton at the end of his life in 1873–5 and was living in Eastern Terrace (pictured) when he wrote his autobiography, *The Life and Adventures of George Augustus Sala*. There, too, he made an unsuccessful attempt to start his own periodical, *Sala's Journal*. He claimed that at the peak of his career he was earning £2,000 a year but improvidence and bankruptcy – in 1858 he was imprisoned for debt – saw him selling possessions, including a large library. In the last year of his life he was existing on a civil pension.

However, he must have been well regarded in the town because he turned down an approach to stand as a Liberal candidate for the election of 1880.

Less salubriously, in 1882 he part wrote *The Mysteries of Verbena House, or Miss Bellasis Birched for Thieving*, a pornographic novel set in a Brighton girls' school. It is known that he liked flagellation and in this book he reveals a liking for ladies' underwear.

Sala published dozens of books, among which was *Brighton As I Have Known It* (1895). Although living at Eastern Terrace, he died at Norton Road and is buried in **Hove Cemetery, Old Shoreham Road**.

Henry Salt (1851–1939)

SOCIAL REFORMER, WRITER AND CLASSICAL SCHOLAR
19 Highdown Road
21 Cleveland Road
15 Sandgate Road

Born in India and educated at Cambridge, Salt grew disenchanted with teaching classics at Eton and moved to Surrey to live a simpler life. Here he advocated for animal rights, through books and pamphlets (he is said to be the first to write on this, as opposed to animal welfare), the case against capital punishment, vegetarianism (Gandhi told Salt that his writing had converted him to a non-meat diet), and a host of other humanitarian causes. In 1891 he founded the Humanitarian League to promote his ideas.

A socialist, Salt was a member of the Fabian Society, who also wrote books on nature and wildlife, as well as biographies of Henry David Thoreau, Tennyson, Shelley and Thomas De Quincey, while undertaking translations from Latin.

It was said by Salt's friend Bernard Shaw that his first wife, Catherine Leigh Joynes, herself an author, refused to sleep with her husband, while engaging in affairs with her women friends. She died in1919 and two years later Salt moved to Highdown Road. In 1927 he married Catherine Mandeville, 40 years his junior, who was born in Brighton. That year, too, his friend **Edward Carpenter** (*qv*) stayed with him on his last visit to his native Brighton. They went to the West Pier to hear the orchestra. Salt moved to Cleveland Road in 1932 and, at the time of his death, at **Brighton Municipal Hospital**, Elm Grove, on 19 April 1939, Salt was living at Sandgate Road.

John Saxby (1821–1913)

INVENTOR AND RAILWAY ENGINEER
15 Oxford Street
20 Buckingham Street
Brighton Station Ⓟ

Born in Oxford Street, Saxby began his working life at 13 as a carpenter's apprentice and in that same trade was later employed by the London Brighton and South Coast Railway (LB&SCR). He became interested in railway safety after a series of accidents, and invented the signal interlocking points and signals system, which

should make it impossible to set up conflicting routes whereby trains become derailed or crash into each other. As a result of the success of his system, he started his own business in Haywards Heath, West Sussex, and later went into partnership with John Farmer as the firm Saxby and Farmer, the sole signalling contractors to the LB&SCR and the London and North Western Railway. In 1871 they introduced the 'rocker & grid' interlocking frame.

In 1878 works were established at Creil near Paris, managed by Saxby's son John. The partnership with Farmer ended in 1888 and the following year the French works became part of John Saxby Ltd. The firm later became part of the former Westinghouse Brake and Signal Company, which, when founded in 1935, had 'Saxby' in its title.

Saxby died in Hassocks, West Sussex on 22 April 1913.

Tom Sayers (1826–1865)

ENGLISH BARE-KNUCKLE CHAMPION BOXER
Titchborne Street **P** *

Sayers was born in Titchborne Street in the slum district of Pimlico in the North Laine area on 25 May 1826, and was baptised in St Nicholas' Church, Church Street. His father was a shoemaker but, after attending Middle Street School until he was nine, Sayers became a bricklayer, working at first for the Brighton and Lewes Railway, and in 1848 on the London and North Western Railway in Camden Town. Only 5 feet 8½ inches tall, and weighing between 10 stone 2lb to 10 stone 12lb, Sayers was known as 'the Brighton Boy' in his boxing career. He was noted for his extraordinarily muscular neck and shoulders and his tremendous hitting power.

Sayers was nearly 23 when his pugilistic career began and having been beaten only once, he retired in 1860 as the undefeated champion of England. His last fight was that year when he went 37 rounds in two hours and six minutes for £200 a side, with the American, John C Heenan. The fight was declared a draw. Public subscription raised £3,000 and Sayers was given the interest on the condition that he gave up fighting.

* The plaque is on the Guitar, Amp and Keyboard Centre, 79–80 North Road.

Sir Paul Scofield (1922–2008)

ACTOR
Varndean School for Boys, Surrenden Road (now Varndean School, Balfour Road)

Born in Birmingham, Paul Scofield moved with his family to Hurstpierpoint, Sussex, where his father was headmaster of the village elementary school, which he attended until he was 12. There he was noted for his delivery of Portia's 'quality of mercy speech' from *The Merchant of Venice*, and more dramatic opportunities occurred when he moved to Varndean School, to which he travelled each day by bicycle and train. While at the school Scofield first appeared on stage, aged 15, as one of the crowd in *The Only Way* at the Theatre Royal. Scofield left the school in 1938, during his final term, and, helped by his headmaster and the manager of the Theatre Royal, gained a scholarship to the Croydon Repertory Theatre School and the London Mask School.

He made his professional debut with a walk-on part in 1940. After touring he joined the Shakespeare Memorial Theatre in 1946. His first London starring role was in *Adventure Story* by **Terence Rattigan** (*qv*) in 1949, which was written for him.

Scofield established a reputation for performing works from playwrights from Shakespeare to Beckett, Chekhov to Christopher Hampton. His screen debut was in *That Lady* (1955) and his widest fame came with *A Man for All Seasons* (1966), in which he revived the role of Thomas More, which he had played to acclaim on the stage in 1961.

From 1951 he lived in Balcombe, West Sussex, and died of leukaemia at the **Royal Sussex County Hospital**, Brighton on 19 March 2008.

Ronald Searle (1920–2011)

CARTOONIST AND ARTIST
8 Arundel Terrace

Searle, creator of St Trinian's School, lived in an apartment in this house from 1958 until 1964 and they were significant years for him. He had spent more than three years as a prisoner of war of the Japanese, where he drew and hid sketches of the brutal conditions. After the Second World War, he acted as official artist at the Nuremberg Trials. In 1948 he married the journalist Kay Webb and they had twins, a boy and a girl. His move to Brighton would seem to have been part of the breakup of the marriage because in 1961 (the year, coincidentally, that Webb became the highly successful editor of the children's imprint Puffin Books) he moved to Paris. Records show, though, that he kept the apartment on for another three years. The couple divorced in 1967 and Searle married Monica Koenig, a painter and jewellery and theatre designer. He lived in France for the rest of his life.

Walter Sickert (1860–1942)

PAINTER
21 Bear Road
7 Old Steine
5b Lewes Crescent

Sickert was a frequent visitor to Brighton, and painted the seafront in pencil and watercolours. Time at the open-air Pierrot Theatre on the beach resulted in one of his most famous works, *Brighton Pierrots*. This focused again on the popular entertainments, as immortalised in his paintings of the music hall.

In 1913, he was the guest speaker when an exhibition on English Post-Impressionists was opened at the Brighton Museum and Art Gallery. With the outbreak of the First World War, he came to the town when he could not visit his favoured Dieppe. In 1914 he visited when convalescing from illness, and in 1915 he stayed with his friend, painter, art collector and fellow member of the Camden Town Group of artists, Walter Taylor (1860–1943), at his home at Bear Road, when he visited the Aquarium and went swimming. On the latter occasion he was given 'the run of the Pavilion' to study its treasures at leisure.

When Sickert married his third wife, the painter Therese Lessore (1884–1945), in 1926 they spent some of their honeymoon in a flat on the Old Steine. For his health, he took a daily swim at Brill's Baths and browsed second-hand bookshops. In his 'fine studio' in Lewes Crescent, which he had in the 1930s, he may have painted *Lazarus Before his Fast*.

Thomas Simpson (1825–1908)

ARCHITECT

16 Ship Street
Connaught Road School (now an annex of the West Hove Infants School)

London-born Simpson travelled in Italy and Germany before settling in Brighton when he was articled to his uncle, James Charnock Simpson, with whom he lodged for a time in a house off the Old Steine. He went into practice in 1856 in the town in succession to his uncle, and some time in 1863–4 he set up his office in Ship Street, where it remained until his death. It was also where he died.

Much of his early work in Brighton was on dissenting chapels and churches. His Belgrave Street Chapel and School (1862) still stand and are listed, although converted into apartments.

In 1871 he was appointed architect and surveyor to the Brighton (later Brighton and Preston) School Board and held the same post with the Hove School Board from 1876. During his career he designed all but one (Richmond Street) of Brighton's board schools and others in Hove, Portslade and Seaford.

Simpson's other buildings include the Renaissance Revival-style Clarendon Mission, Clarendon Villas, Hove; Preston Road School (1880), York Place Higher Grade School (1884)* and the School for Afflicted Children and Cookery School (1898), the last three now part of City College; Finsbury Road Schools (1881), Central National Infants' School, Upper Gardner Street (1887), both now flats; Ditchling Road School (1890), now Downs Junior School; Elm Grove School (1893); Stanford Road Board Schools (1894); and St Luke's School (1903). Six of his buildings are Grade II listed.

His son, **Sir John William Simpson** (1858–1933), was articled to his father and worked with him on the Elm Grove and Stanford Road Schools. He went on to design Roedean School, the Royal Sussex Regiment Memorial Regency Square, the war memorial, Old Steine, and other public buildings elsewhere in the UK. Simpson's other son, also a noted architect, **Gilbert Murray Simpson** (1869–1954), became a partner with his father and also worked with him on the Elm Grove School. After Simpson's death Gilbert continued the practice, retained his father's school board appointment and became architect to the Brighton education committee, which succeeded the board.

The Queen Anne Revival Connaught Road School was the last of Simpson's buildings to be listed.

At the time of writing, York Place (now known as the York Building) is threatened with demolition under plans proposed by the City College.

Sir C (Charles) Aubrey Smith (1863–1948)

STAGE AND FILM ACTOR, SUSSEX AND ENGLAND CRICKETER

27 Selbourne Road, Hove
19 Albany Villas, Hove

One part of Smith's unique dual career began when the family moved to Hove, when he was seven. At the Crescent House Academy, Marine Parade, a teacher introduced him to cricket.

At 12 he was sent to board at Charterhouse, and there his cricketing abilities began to blossom, so much so that Sussex County Cricket Club in Hove gave him professional instruction and allowed him to play in a few local matches before he left for Cambridge University. At university, while intending to follow his father into medicine, he became involved in St John's College's theatrical group, and continued to play cricket in the summer months.

After Cambridge, Smith worked for a while as a maths teacher and captained Sussex in 1886, and subsequently captained England on tour in Australia and South Africa. When he came back he lived at his parents' home in Selbourne Road (Albany Villas is pictured). He made his first professional stage appearance in Hastings in 1892 and three years later appeared on the West End stage and in 1911 on the New York stage for the first time. Between 1900 and 1930, there was not a year when he did not appear in a new production in either London or New York.

Smith's first silent film was in 1911, the first of 100 films. With the coming of talkies in the 1920s, he became better known for his film work than that on the stage. Tall, assured, erect, handsome, distinguished, if not a great actor, or even a film star in the classic sense, he was possessed of charm. He played supporting character parts, specialising in upper class English gentlemen. His films included *Lives of a Bengal Lancer, Clive of India* and *Little Women*. Making his home in the USA, in 1932 Smith founded the Hollywood Cricket Club, which raised money for charities.

When he attended a benefit cricket match at Hove in 1947, he needed police protection from being mobbed.

He died in California and nine months his ashes were interred in the churchyard of **St Leonard's Church, New Church Road**, Hove.

George Smith (1864–1959)

CINEMA PIONEER AND FILMMAKER
Caburn House, 15 Caburn Road, Hove
Rosedene, 7 Melville Road, Hove
Laboratory Lodge (now The Cottage), 10 Roman Crescent, Southwick
18 Chanctonbury Road, Hove **P**

George Smith's family moved to Brighton from London soon after the death of the father, Charles, and Mrs Smith ran a boarding house in Grand Parade. Well known in the town from 1882 as a hypnotist and telepathist, after leaving a job with the Society for Psychical Research, George Smith took a lease on St Ann's Well Gardens in 1892 and turned it into a popular pleasure garden and also the site for his filmmaking work. In 1892 he acquired his first camera, having seen the first Lumière programme in London, and probably the films of cinematographer Robert Paul in Brighton.

Like **James Williamson** (*qv*), the friend whom he influenced, he worked on continuity over multiple shots. His first films were all made in 1900: *As Seen through the Telescope, Grandma's Reading Glass, The House that Jack Built*, and *Let me Dream Again*. They offered interpolated close-ups, subjective and objective point-of-view shots, the creation of dream-time, and the use of 'reversing' (when action appears to happen backwards). Smith and his first wife, an actor, **Laura Bayley** (1864–1938), lived in Caburn Road. She played in his films – *Let me Dream Again* and *Mary Jane's Mishap* (1903) – and helped him understand visual comedy and the tastes of seaside audiences. She played in more British films than any other female actor at this time. They later moved to Melville Road, where she died in 1938.

One of Smith's collaborators was Edward Grun, who lived at The Hall, 49 The Green, Southwick. A surgeon and apothecary and medical officer of the Steyning Union, in 1901 Grun received the patent for a 'liquid lens', which would allow films to be shown at normal theatrical lighting levels. The image was inferior, but working with Smith, Grun used his lens to experiment with colour. However, the liquid lens did not catch on.

The pump house at St Ann's Well Gardens was turned into a developing and printing space, and Smith also built a glasshouse film studio. Smith developed a successful commercial film production and processing business before the turn of the century. Through his connection with his largest customer, the Warwick Trading Company, he became part of the company and developed a long partnership with its managing director, American-born film producer, **Charles Urban** (1867–1942), who lived in Brighton and died in a nursing home at Dyke Road (now site of Homelees House, 61–67 Dyke Road).

At his home in Roman Crescent, to which he moved after selling St Ann's Well Gardens, Smith developed Kinemacolor, a two-colour additive process, which was presented in Paris in 1908 to a group of scientists and the cinema pioneers, the Lumière brothers. (The first English demonstration took place later that year.) Urban created the Natural Colour Kinematograph Company, which from 1910 to 1913, produced over 100 short features from its studios in Hove and Nice. However, the system was not taken up by the industry and it collapsed after a patent action by **William Friese-Greene** (*qv*) in 1914. It was the end of Smith's life in the film world. In later life Smith spent much time using his telescope through his seafront arch.

He resided, at the time of his death in **Brighton General Hospital** on 17 May 1959, in Chanctonbury Road, and was cremated at the Downs Crematorium.

Horatio (Horace) Smith (1779–1849)

WRITER AND HUMORIST
10 Hanover Crescent
12 Cavendish Place Ⓟ

Smith's affection for his adopted home town (he was born in London) can be seen by his describing Brighton as 'the Queen of watering places'.

Smith had become wealthy as a stockbroker, making enough money to devote himself to writing novels and poetry. He and his wife and daughters had been living in Versailles for four years and came to England in 1825. After a brief stay in Tunbridge Wells, they came the next year to Brighton, living first in Hanover Crescent and from 1838 in Cavendish Place (pictured).

'If I mount my little white nag, and ride from Kemp Town to Brunswick Terrace I am sure of half-a-dozen invitations to dinner', he wrote. 'This I call enjoying life.' He gave as good as he got in that respect because his homes were the hub of literary and social life. Guests, like the actor Charles Kean, the historian Thomas Macaulay, and the novelists **Charles Dickens** (*qv*), **William Harrison Ainsworth** (*qv*), and

William Makepeace Thackeray (*qv*), could be found at the table. Smith was also a friend of Richard Cobden, the great advocate of free trade, and also of the poet Percy Bysshe Shelley.

Perhaps unsurprisingly, Smith was generous, hospitable, happy and well liked. The journalist and poet James Leigh Hunt referred to him as 'delicious' with a figure that was 'good and manly, inclining to the robust; and his countenance extremely frank and cordial; sweet without weakness'. Smith was also public spirited. He supported Brighton's Mechanics' Institute, the Literary Society, the Mantellian Institution and Phillips' School of Science.

In Smith's Brighton years, 15 novels and five long tales came from his pen, and he also published three volumes of collected essays and comic tales, as well as compilations. Like his friend Ainsworth, he would often write historical novels. He also wrote comic and occasional verse and prose.

However, a severe attack of laryngitis in 1841 caused him to cut back on his work and he announced that he was retiring as a novelist. In 1849 the family moved to Tunbridge Wells, where Smith died that July from heart problems.

Henry Solomon (1794–1844)

CHIEF OFFICER OF POLICE
27 Kensington Gardens
Town Hall, Bartholomew Square

Solomon became the town's second chief officer (now the post of chief constable) in 1832, at an annual salary of £120, having held the job jointly with William Pilbeam. It was a notable appointment then as he was a Jew. Solomon had a force of 30 officers (two superintendents, three inspectors, 24 constables and a night constable) for a population in 1831 of 40,634.

Solomon had moved to the town in 1821 to work for the town commissioners and the next year became inspector of nuisances and collector of post-horse duty (this was a fee for the use of horses kept for the use of travellers and post-chaise carriages). In 1823 he became superintendent of Hackney carriages, bathing machines and pleasure boats at £25 a year. Three years later he was superintendent of watering the road and inspector of nuisances, adding inspector of gas lights a year later. He was also an elder of the town's synagogue, a trustee and then its vice president.

During his tenure, there were several scandals, two of which (1836 and 1838) involved sacking most of the force and replacing them with new constables and inspectors.

Solomon was interviewing John Lawrence, aged 23, in the police station, which was in the basement of the town hall, about the theft of a roll of carpet. The prisoner became agitated and struck Solomon with a poker. He was taken to his home in Princes Street to be treated, but died. Solomon is believed to be the only chief constable ever to be murdered on duty. An appeal, to which Queen Victoria contributed £50, raised £500 to support his widow and children. He is buried in the **Florence Place Jewish Cemetery** (closed to the public), where he was joined 14 years later by his brother-in-law **Emmanuel Hyam Cohen** (*qv*), social reformer and founder of the radical *Brighton Guardian*. Lawrence was tried, found guilty and hanged at Horsham Gaol, the last person to be executed there.

* *Solomon's office is not the present Old Police Cells Museum, situated today in the basement of the town hall, as might be reasonably assumed, as the museum is, in fact, a former police station. However, in Solomon's day the police office was just to the south of the current west entrance of the town hall. There was a doorway which was later replaced with a window (which remains there).*

Nancy Spain (1917–1964)

JOURNALIST, WRITER AND TELEVISION PERSONALITY

10 Wentworth Street

With her unconventional, flamboyant, gay lifestyle, it might seem that Spain would have been a natural resident of Brighton. Great niece of Mrs Beeton, the champion of household management, and the granddaughter of the Victorian advocate of self-improvement Samuel Smiles, it was, after all, at Roedean School (which she hated) where Spain first began donning the 'mannish' clothes with which she was to become so associated. This was at a time when dress sense was still very conventional.

In later life she often visited the home in Montpelier Villas of her friend **Gilbert Harding** (*qv*), whom she met in 1952, but she lived at Wentworth Street from only the end of 1957 to early the following year. Spain had taken the house furnished to write a novel. That this never appeared is hardly surprising as she recalled 'a few crazy evenings. Champagne until 11pm, brandy thereafter, and endless telling of tales'.

At this time she was at the height of her fame: a columnist on the *Daily Express* (she caused that paper to be sued twice by the novelist Evelyn Waugh), a frequent guest on radio and television programmes, and the author of a series of camp detective novels. There was a long-running story that she and Harding, with whom she appeared on the panel of *What's My Line?*, were to marry, but given their respective sexual preferences this was, at very least, unlikely.

When she wasn't in Brighton Spain was living with her long-time lover Joan Laurie; Sheila Van Damm, the racing driver; Laurie's son, Nicholas; and Thomas, who masqueraded as Laurie's youngest child but who was, in fact, the offspring of a brief affair that Spain had had with the husband of the crime writer Margery Allingham. Laurie and Spain died in a light aircraft accident in 1964.

Herbert Spencer (1820–1903)

PHILOSOPHER, SOCIAL THEORIST AND SOCIOLOGIST

5 Percival Terrace 🅿

When he moved to Percival Terrace in early 1898, Spencer wrote: 'I think I shall get on with my work very well here, and I hope to benefit in all respects.' However, in this house Spencer was to spend the sorriest and saddest last years of an otherwise distinguished and publicly acclaimed life.

He was a polymath, who wrote on subjects as varied as religion and economics, anthropology and political theory, ethics and biology, and sociology and psychology. His authority was supreme within the English-speaking academic world. For him evolution offered an all-embracing understanding of how the physical world, biological organisms, the human mind, and human culture and societies progressively developed. (It was Spencer who coined the phrase 'the survival of the fittest' after reading Darwin.)

But, after 1900, there was a sharp decline in influence for the man who, it has been said, was 'the single most famous European intellectual in the closing decades of the 19th century'. This situation was aggravated by disillusionment and loneliness (he had never married) and his long-standing hypochondria. An author who had enjoyed mass sales, his readers were deserting him, his old friends were dying, his faith in progress – the central tenet of his outlook – diminished, and his political views became increasingly conservative.

Thus, in the in the last 15 years of his life, Spencer was afflicted with what he called much 'mental misery' and social isolation. When the arrangement he had enjoyed of sharing a London house with two unmarried sisters ended, he was obliged to seek a series of temporary lodgings until he moved to Brighton. He knew the town well: he had lived here for two years in the 1850s, had stayed here for his health, visited for other reasons and wintered here in 1886–1887. At Percival Terrace his staff were Miss Key, whom he engaged especially to play the piano several times a day, and Miss Killick, his housekeeper.

Beatrice Webb, Fabian socialist theorist, visited him regularly in the town and said that he was 'living a living death'. He was, she noted, 'poisoned by morphia and self-absorption'. His only companions were calculating sycophants. Spencer was reduced to a 'strangely crude vision of all human life as a series of hard bargains', in which 'even illness and death seem a nasty fraud perpetrated by nature'. Webb believed him to be obsessed with the idea that his life's work was a delusion, yet he still clung to the belief that the Synthetic Philosophy, which he had formulated, could reveal the truth. But this was also a man whose domestic staff were later to write warmly of the fun and good humour of the household.

Peter Spencer, later 2nd Viscount Churchill (1890–1973)

JOURNALIST, ACTOR AND PLAYWRIGHT
5 Arundel Terrace

Born Victor Alexander Spencer, cousin of **Sir Winston Churchill** (*qv*), godson of **Queen Victoria** (*qv*), and son of the wealthy Ist Viscount Churchill, Spencer was a page of honour at the coronation of **Edward VII** (*qv*). His father disinherited him when he was 16 and they never spoke again. He succeeded to the title in 1934.

Spencer served, as a major, on the Western Front at Ypres in the First World War. He later worked as a journalist and actor in London and New York, and also wrote plays. In his early forties he converted to socialism and, with the outbreak of the Spanish Civil War, was one of those who formed the Medical Aid Committee for Spain, and also went to Spain.

After Spain, Spencer went to the USA to work as a journalist and, with the coming of war, served as a staff sergeant in the US Air Force.

His first wife, Katherine Beaven, died in 1943. He married Joan Black in 1949 and they lived for a while in California. She died in England in 1957.

In Brighton Spencer lived in Arundel Terrace. He continued to work as a journalist, including a foray into Morocco with a Brighton *Evening Argus* reporter, Roger Ward, and photographer Dave McEnery. On his return it seems he moved to Chichester Place.

Count Eric Stenbock (1860–1895)

POET AND SHORT STORY WRITER
Withdean Hall, The Approach, London Road

Stenbock was born in Cheltenham to a German aristocratic father and the daughter of a German cotton importer. When he was 14 his father died, his mother remarried a man whom Stenbock hated and the family moved to this address in what was then the village of Withdean.

He had a brief schooling in Wiesbaden, then private instruction and spent four terms at Balliol College. He had been baptised Eric Magnus Andreas Harry and raised as a Lutheran. When he converted to Catholicism at Oxford, he took the name Stanislaus, and, said one writer, 'evolved a religion of his own, compounded of Buddhism, Catholicism and idolatry'.

By his early twenties Stenbock had published two slim volumes of poetry. A photographer, for whom he was a subject, wrote of him: 'He had on a magnificent blood red silk robe embroidered in gold and silver. He was swinging a silver censer before an altar covered with lilies, myrtles, lighted candles and a sanctuary lamp burning with scented oil'.

In 1885 Stenbock's grandfather died, leaving him the family's vast Estonian estate. Two years later he came back to London where he established a reputation for a *fin de siècle* legend of self-destruction but also became friends with many writers and artists, including **Aubrey Beardsley** (*qv*) and WB Yeats. The latter referred to him as a 'scholar, connoisseur, drunkard, poet, pervert, most charming of men'. His work often involved the Gothic, death, the occult and homoeroticism.

Stenbock became addicted to alcohol and opium and came back to live at Withdean Hall. He suffered *delirium tremens*. He died there of cirrhosis of the liver on the same day that, drunk, he tried to hit his stepfather with a poker. He was buried in the Catholic section of the **Extra-Mural Cemetery**.

John Francis (Jack) Strachey (1894–1972)

POPULAR COMPOSER
Flat J, 14 Marine Gate, Marine Drive

Strachey, who wrote, 'These Foolish Things (Remind Me of You)', was born Jack Strachey Parsons in Brighton and first started writing songs for theatre productions (including 'Lady Luck' in 1927) and musical revues. 'These Foolish Things', written in collaboration with Eric Maschwitz and Harry Link, had five Top Ten cover versions alone.

He later moved to solo composition, specialising in light orchestral works. His 1944 piece, 'In Party Mood', became the theme song for BBC radio's long-running *Housewives' Choice*. He and Alan Shranks penned The Ink Spots' British hit 'No Orchids for My Lady'. Strachey moved back to Brighton in 1958, married in 1965, and died in the town on 27 May 1972.

Robert Smith (RS) Surtees (1805–1864)

NOVELIST

Mutton's Hotel, 80 Kings Road (now the site of the Brighton Centre)

Surtees, creator of the fox-hunting, vulgar, good-natured cockney grocer, Jorrocks, first came to Brighton in 1828 soon after being admitted to Chancery (although he probably never practised). Feeling at a loose end, he was determined to enjoy his time. This town and other places offered him settings for his novels, while also providing a parade of colourful characters, who ended up, with little disguise, in his books. One of the most notable was Baron Gablenz of Saxony, who prowled Brighton in search of an eligible heiress.

Surtees' own life of travelling to Brighton and Paris, racing at Newmarket and boating on the Thames is also reflected in the novels. With Elizabeth, his wife, he would also visit Brighton from his home on the family estate at Hamsterley, County Durham, when the weather was too bad for hunting and he sought a more equable climate. The winter of 1864 was particularly severe and soon after checking into Mutton's Hotel, he awoke with a heart pain and ten minutes later was dead.

Rabindrath Tagore (1861–1941)

POET, MUSICIAN, NOVELIST, PAINTER, EDUCATIONIST AND NOBEL LAUREATE

43 Medina Villas, Hove

Tagore was born the eighth son and fourteenth surviving child to a prominent, cultured and wealthy family in Calcutta. When his parents wished that he become a barrister, they sent him to study at school in Brighton in October 1878 and he lived for several months at Medina Villas, a house which the family owned.

What he found surprised him. He wrote: 'When I heard in London that I am going to live at Medina Villas I lavishly imagined so many things about the house such as it had a garden, trees, field, pond nearby etc. After arriving [at] the villas I looked around and saw there were houses, streets, carriages. . .'. He also wrote: 'Here there is a pub on every corner but bookshops are rare'.

For the first time he met his six-year-old nephew, Suren, and five-year-old niece, Indira, children of his brother Satyendranath when he went to live with them at Medina Villas. A few days after his arrival he was admitted to the Brighton Proprietary School, 7 Ship Street (gone). He was in Brighton up until the end of December and then went to London, where he enrolled at University College London but never completed his degree. He left England a year later. However, his stay in England affected his composing, with his ability to meld Western music with Bengali musical traditions and create new forms of music, poetry and drama.

He travelled extensively throughout the world, lecturing and introducing aspects of Indian culture to the West and vice versa. He spoke in favour of Indian independence, and as a protest against the Massacre of Amritsar, he returned the knighthood he had received in 1915. He founded an experimental school in Bengal, which, in 1921, became Vishva-Bharati University, where he sought to blend Eastern and Western philosophies. In 1913 he was awarded the Nobel Prize for Literature.

Charles-Maurice de Talleyrand-Périgord (1754–1838)

DIPLOMAT
9 Old Steine Ⓟ

Talleyrand (as he was usually known) stayed here in 1831 during the second of his four years as French ambassador, under King Louis-Philippe. Most of that time he spent in London, where he was famous for his extravagant entertaining and complaining about the English weather.

Thomas Tanner (1824–1871)

DOCTOR
12 Royal Crescent

Tanner was one of the most prominent doctors of his day, and his energetic approach to his work so taxed his strength that he was forced to leave a large and successful practice in London and move to Brighton with his wife, Mary.

He worked at various London hospitals, was a member of the Royal Colleges of Surgeons and of Physicians, and began a consulting practice. He specialised in gynaecology, but also lectured on forensic medicine. He was one of the founders of the Obstetrical Society of London and its secretary from 1859 to 1863.

He wrote a large number of books, including ones on diseases in infancy and pregnancy, which sold in both England and the USA.

He died at his home on 7 July 1871.

Maurice Tate (1895–1956)

SUSSEX AND ENGLAND CRICKETER
28 Warleigh Road Ⓟ

Tate was born at this address on 30 May 1895, the eldest of the three sons and seven daughters of Frederick Tate (1867–1943), a professional Test cricketer. The family moved when he was young and his father took over the Burrell Arms, Haywards Heath, Sussex, and Tate was educated in that town. He was not good enough to play for the school XI, but with his father's encouragement he had a trial for Sussex at 15. He made his debut at 17.

One of cricket's leading all-rounders, Tate made his name as a bowler. He played 525 matches for Sussex and took 2,211 wickets at an average cost of 17.41 runs, while scoring just over 17,000 runs from 1912 to 1937 (apart from army service in France). He achieved the double of 100 wickets and 1,000 runs seven times for Sussex alone. He earned 39 caps for England.

His first-class career ended in 1937 after which he played professional league cricket for Walsall for a while. He died suddenly from a blood clot at the Greyhound Hotel, Wadhurst, Sussex, where he was landlord.

William Makepeace Thackeray (1811–1863)

NOVELIST

62 East Street
Royal York Hotel (now Youth Hostel),
Old Steine
Old Ship, Kings Road

Thackeray enjoyed Brighton, finding it recuperative when he so often needed boosting physically or emotionally. Like his friend **Charles Dickens** (*qv*), he sometimes stayed at the Bedford Hotel (now the site of the Holiday Inn) and he also stayed at Pegg's Hotel, Mutton's Hotel (where the Brighton Centre, Kings Road, now stands), and took a house for himself and his family in Marine Square.

The Royal York Hotel opened in 1819 and became the town's most fashionable establishment. It was where Thackeray would stay when he achieved fame. He lodged at the Old Ship (pictured) when writing *Vanity Fair* where he places his characters, George and Amelia, in the first few days of their marriage. The novel also tells us that: 'A comfortable inn in Brighton is better than a sponging-house [where debtors were detained] in Chancery Lane.'

Thackeray attended the literary parties at 21 Sillwood Place, put on by Eliza and Rosalind Smith, the unmarried daughters of **Horace Smith** (*qv*), as he had when Smith had held them.

In August, 1845, with a sprained ankle, a bag of books and William, a manservant, Thackeray went to Brighton to be joined by William Brookfield, his old Cambridge friend, a clergyman who became a schools inspector. They stayed at lodgings in **54 Grand Parade** (gone). They lounged on the beach while the novelist sketched and dined at the Star and Garter Inn (now Dr Brighton's, Little East Street). A fortnight later Thackeray wrote to his mother that, as ever, the town 'agrees with me excellently'. He was trying to finish *Cornhill to Cairo* but his mind was occupied by missing his daughters, and the illness of his wife Isabella, who was seriously and chronically mentally ill.

Thackeray was in Brighton again in September 1848 intending that his family should join him but he cancelled, complaining of a 'pile of bills' to pay. An old flame, Virginia Pattle, was there, 'lovely, interesting and unwell', but she failed to reignite his feelings.

The following July he returned to holiday in Brighton, shaken by the news of the pregnancy of Brookfield's wife, Jane, with whom he was deeply in love and whom he imagined to be in a sexless marriage. 'Why is a day's Brighton the best of Doctors?' he wrote to Jane. Then Brookfield arrived, on an inspection, and he accompanied Thackeray to the National School. They also dined with two dragoon officers whom Thackeray knew (Brookfield liked to sample the bachelor life) accompanied by 'the wickedest weed and the wickeder distillations'.

In January 1851 Thackeray gave his lectures on 'The Four Georges' at the town hall. These had been intended for republican American audiences. However, he did not give the one on **George IV** (*qv*), in which he had said that he had searched George's whole life and found nothing but 'a bow and a grin' and trying to take George to pieces found nothing but clothing and wigs reeking of oil. He saw Geroge 'reeling into chapel to be married ... hiccupping out his vows of fidelity'. A local historian, Henry Martin, asked Thackeray why he had not delivered this rebuke in the Royal Pavilion to be told he 'did not like to abuse a man in his own house'.

In October 1854 he wrote to Mark Lemon, the magazine editor and playwright, from Brighton, that he had been 'dreadfully seedy & glum yesterday looking for another attack of my complaint this morning, but a walk by the sounding sea has done me good'. However, his illnesses – the effects of malaria, an inflamed urethra, and what may have been Crohn's disease – and substances, like laudanum and calomel, weakened him, laid him low and depressed, and made him wish to avoid company. Three years later he returned to the town again to recuperate and did so sufficiently to start on *The Virginians*.

Sir Wilfred Thesiger (1910–2003)

EXPLORER
St Aubyns School (now closed), 76 High Street, Rottingdean

Thesiger was born within the mud walls of the British Legation in Addis Ababa, Abyssinia, where his father was consul-general and minister at the court of Emperor Menelik.

His first seven years in Abyssinia were vastly different from the unhappy years at St Aubyns School, where he went, with his brother Brian, in 1919. He left in 1923 to go to Eton.

The spectacular sights Thesiger had observed in his early years gave him his life-long craving for adventure. At two, he saw the arrival at the British Legation of Crown Prince Lij Yasu's 1,000-strong war band, resplendent in their scarlet cloaks trimmed with lions' manes. At six, he witnessed the victory parade, with wave after wave of glinting spear points and captives in chains, of Ras Tafari, who had triumphed over Lij Yasu in a civil war. The next year, his uncle, the viceroy, took him on a tiger shoot in India.

The years at Rottingdean were made worse by Thesiger's father's sudden death. His parents had taken lodgings in Brighton to be near their sons and now his mother was not only devastated at her loss, but without a home and short of money.

Of the school, Thesiger wrote: 'Suddenly ... we found ourselves in a crowd of seventy boys, nearly all older. There was no privacy anywhere; we were always among others, whether in classrooms, dining room or gymnasium, on the playing fields or in the dormitory at night.'

Those who defaulted on the regular parades conducted by a retired sergeant living in the village had to run endlessly around the asphalt yard. 'On a hot summer's day', recalled Thesiger, 'this was a punishment more suited to the Foreign Legion than to an English preparatory school'.

Thesiger recalled that his headmaster, RCV Lang was 'a sadist' and he and his brother were victims of Lang's savagery. This only stopped when he revealed all to Arnold Hodson, once consul in Southern Abyssinia, who was staying with the family in the holidays. He had visited the school and threatened Lang with court action if he persisted in his punishments.

Thesiger's stories of his former exotic life did not endear him to his fellow pupils. He retreated within himself and regarded overtures of friendship with distrust. Boys, he wrote, are conventional and gang up on those who do not, in some way, conform: 'With our extraordinary background, Brian and I lacked the ability to cope with our contemporaries; as English boys who had barely heard of cricket we were natural targets.' His comfort was to recall the sights and scenery of Abyssinia.

Angela Thirkell (1890–1960)

NOVELIST

North End House (now Aubrey House), The Green, Rottingdean

Angela Mackail (as she then was) and her brother and sister spent their summer holidays, and often Christmases, here at the home of their maternal grandfather, **Sir Edward Burne-Jones** (*qv*), the painter, and his wife, Georgiana.

Lady Burne-Jones, who wrote her husband's biography, was a widow for most of the time that her granddaughter knew her (her husband had died in 1898) and always, in Thirkell's memory, wore the same clothes: long black gowns of velvet or satin with a little lace and a lace head dress. A large watch set, a present from Sir Edward, was always pinned at her waist.

The children would arrive at Brighton Station and then take an omnibus, rather like the ones in London, which **John Leech** (*qv*) had drawn in *Punch*, with the coachman blowing his horn. This vehicle was allowed along the sea front; the other buses went by the back streets. The sight of the black sails of the Rottingdean windmill signalled the journey's end. There was another bus, which they didn't use as it was drawn by four, scraggy horses, but a third, which they sometimes did use, was drawn by two stout greys.

Burne-Jones would often paint the walls in the house and Thirkell describes how once, when he found his granddaughter facing the wall in the nursery for some infraction, he painted a cat, a kitten playing with its mother's tail, and a flight of birds 'so that I would never be unhappy or without company in my corner again'.

Thirkell complained that in both their houses her grandparents had only one comfortable item of furniture: a sofa in London. But there would often be many guests for lunch or dinner.

She remembered visits to the Palace Pier to spend pennies and having lunch at the Metropole Hotel, Brighton, with 'Uncle Phil' (**Sir Philip Burne-Jones**), also a painter, who sometimes stayed at the house. Or the children would play with their cousins, Josephine, Elsie and John, who were close in age, the children of 'Cousin Ruddy', **Rudyard Kipling** (*qv*), who lived in the village, and sometimes those of Stanley Baldwin, the future prime minister, who would visit with his family. They would lie in a haystack on the Downs, play Roundheads and Cavaliers in the garden, or bathe in the sea using 'Trunky' Thomas's bathing machines.

Kipling would try out the *Just So Stories* on his nursery audience, and he would also give his young cousin a sheet of his autographs for her to swap at school for stamps and other items.

In 1899 Kipling's daughter Josephine died in New York and Thirkell later wrote: 'Much of the beloved Cousin Ruddy of our childhood died with Josephine and I feel that I have never seen him as a real person since that year'.

It was in Rottingdean that Thirkell and her brother, the future novelist **Denis Mackail** (1892–1971), and sister saw their first telephone – it was one of their treats to be allowed to hear a neighbour phoning to Brighton – and motor car (which was Kipling's).

And while Thirkell's life was to lead her far away from Rottingdean (at one time she lived in Australia), she is buried in the churchyard of **St Margaret's Church** in the village, below a curious, poorly maintained wooden memorial.

Sir Charles Thomas-Stanford (1858–1932)

POLITICIAN

Preston Manor, Preston Drove

Sir Charles was born in Hove and held the Brighton seat for the Conservatives from 1914, when he was elected unopposed, to 1922, when he stood down. He was three times mayor of the town.

When he married the heiress, Ellen Stanford, he added her name to his. She inherited Preston Manor, which, upon their deaths, they left to Brighton Corporation. It opened in 1933 as the museum it remains today.

Vesta Tilley (1864–1952)

MUSIC HALL ARTISTE

8 St Aubyns Mansions, Kings Esplanade, Hove **P**

The most famous male impersonator of her day was born Matilda Powles in Worcester to working class parents, the second of 12 children. She gained great fame and wealth – in 1906 she was earning £300 a week – playing soldiers, sailors and policemen, and often took the part of principal boy in pantomimes. 'Following in Father's Footsteps', 'After the Ball', and 'Come into the Garden, Maud' are only some of the many songs – often with risqué lyrics – associated with her.

Tilley appeared frequently at the Hippodrome Music Hall in Middle Street during her 50 year career, which began in 1869. (Her husband, Walter de Frece, who was later knighted, built a chain of music halls, set up touring companies and was her manager.)

She retired from her profession in 1919, breaking off a farewell tour that lasted more than a year to help her husband's successful bid for Parliament as a Conservative in Ashton-under-Lyne (he later also represented Blackpool).

Sir Walter died in 1935 in Monte Carlo, where they had gone to live in 1932 for his health. TIlley bought the flat in Hove in 1947. The world she lived in was changing and certainly the one in which she had found fame was gone, but every year Covent Garden flower sellers would send her a bunch of violets, a sign of the regard in which she was held long after her working life was past. She lived here until moving to London before her death in 1952. She left £10,000 in her will to each of her brothers and sisters.

Doreen Valiente (1922–1999)

MOTHER OF MODERN WITCHCRAFT, POET AND AUTHOR

6 Tyson Place, Grosvenor Street ℗

Born in South London, Valiente's interest in magic began as a teenager. She walked out of her convent school at 15 and took up factory and office work. Her interest in the occult continued and in 1953 she was initiated into witchcraft in Hampshire.

Valiente had taken exception to the works of the occultist Aleister Crowley and reconstructed and embellished his work, excising much and adding her own poetry to create what was regarded by its followers as a practical, logical and workable system of magic and religion. This came to be known as Wicca and led years later to the revival of paganism. She later founded her own coven.

She was living in Tyson Place in 1992 when her second husband Casimiro Valiente, whom she married in 1944, died. (Her first husband, a merchant seaman, had died at sea in 1941.) Through the local residents association Valiente met Ron ('Cookie') Cooke who was to become her partner until he died in 1997.

Ralph Vaughan Williams (1872–1958)

COMPOSER

Field House School (later St Aubyns School, now closed), 76 High Street, Rottingdean*

Vaughan Williams was living at his family home at Leith Hill House, Surrey, when in September 1883 he joined his brother Hervey at this school. The school had begun its life in The Vicarage, later The Grange, The Green, whose then headmaster, **Rev Thomas Redman Hooker** (*qv*), moved the expanding school to the High Street. It became Field House in the 1860s under the headmaster, a Mr Hewitt, who still reigned in Vaughan Williams' day.

Life at the school was far tougher than the relaxed atmosphere of the Vaughan Williams' home, with the boys rising at 6.30am for half an hour's prep. This was followed by music practice and those who played an instrument were excused prayers.

Vaughan Williams performed in school concerts but also attended concerts and at one, in Brighton, he first heard Wagner. A consequence of this was his playing the violin after hours with the boys dancing in their nightshirts.

At Field House, Vaughan Williams became aware of class consciousness and engaged in conversations which shaped his democratic and egalitarian views.

* *In different premises in Rottingdean the school became St Aubyns and closed in 2013.*

Victoria (1819–1901)

MONARCH

Royal Pavilion, Old Steine

Victoria had visited Brighton when her uncle, **William IV** (*qv*), was on the throne, but never took to the town. When Victoria succeeded William in 1837 she inherited the Royal Pavilion and made her first visit there that year, where a great triumphal arch was erected at the North Gate.

Her distaste for Brighton was unchanged, although she was ambivalent about the palace, where she stayed four times. Mindful of the extravagance of her other uncle, **George IV** (*qv*), her stays were marked by financial stringency.

Victoria wrote that the palace was 'a strange, odd Chinese looking thing, both inside and outside; most rooms low'. Her room was over the entrance and she asked what was the good of living in the town 'and I only see a little morsel of the sea from one of my sitting room windows. . . .'. However, the next day she wrote that her sitting room was 'pretty & cheerful' and the 'little morsel' had become 'a nice little peep of the sea'.

John Creevey, the diarist, met her at the Pavilion and heard her loud, uninhibited laughter. **Prince Albert** (1819–1861) was less ambivalent: he liked the palace, particularly the music room and banqueting room.

Some visitors' views of the palace were uncompromising. The Prince de Joinville, French admiral and son of Louis Philippe, Duke of Orleans, later King of the French, who had been in France with Victoria and Albert accompanied them back to Brighton for a couple of nights in 1843. (The Brighton Museum and Art Gallery has a painting by **Richard Henry Nibbs** (*qv*) of the royal yacht arriving at the Chain Pier.) The prince called the Pavilion 'hideous'. It was 'where nobody could move about or open a window without being exposed to the fire of all the opera glasses in the houses opposite'. He mistakenly believed in later years that 'this masterpiece of bad taste' had been turned into a casino – 'the one thing it was fitted to be'.

Victoria found the Pavilion was too small for her growing family. She also disliked the fact that living in the centre of town afforded her no privacy. What happened on her last visit in 1845 showed this all too well. As the royal family walked on the Chain Pier, she wrote in her journal, 'we were mobbed by all the shopboys in the town, who ran and looked under my bonnet, treating us as they do the Band, when it goes to the Parade! We walked home as fast as we could'.

Thus, she planned to sell the palace in order to buy Osborne House on the Isle of Wight, where she said she could obtain privacy and quiet. In the belief that the palace would be demolished, she began stripping the Pavilion in 1846, and in the following two years 143 vans removed 40 fireplaces, fittings and furnishings to Buckingham Palace. In 1847 there was a sale of porcelain, furniture, and *objets d'art* and the next year there was another sale on the lawns. On 7 June 1848 the doors were locked and the keys sent to the Lord Chamberlain.

In 1849 27,563 people came through the doors in one week to view the empty rooms. It was claimed that **Thomas Cubitt** (*qv*) offered £100,000 to buy the site for development but in 1850 Victoria sold the palace to Brighton Corporation for £53,000. The queen began to return some of the goods in 1864, and while more has come back from her successors, some Chinese interiors can still be seen at Buckingham Palace.

Magnus Volk (1851–1937)

ELECTRICAL ENGINEER AND INVENTOR

40 (now 35) Western Road, Hove
51 Preston Street
40 Preston Road
17 Gloucester Place
128 Dyke Road* **P**

Born in Western Road, the only son out of the seven children of a German clockmaker, Volk was partly educated at home and at Philip Capon's local proprietary school. His father died in 1869, two years after he had moved his shop and home to Preston Street. Volk helped his mother, Sarah, with the business.

Keen on new technology, Volk designed and produced an electric telegraph instrument for household use in the 1870s and he was described, in 1877, as a 'telegraph apparatus manufacturer'.

In 1879 Volk married Anna Banfield, daughter of a Brighton merchant, and they lived in Preston Road. He then worked for the London Ordnance Works. His inventiveness led him to create a short telephone line (Brighton's first) from his home to that of a friend in Springfield Road, and to install electric lighting in his home in Preston Road in 1880 using a dynamo. (The public system did not begin for another 13 years.) In 1881 he successfully demonstrated a fire alarm system and that year opened a new and larger workshop at 25 Ditchling Rise.

He became agent to the United Telephone Company, which opened an exchange in Brighton in 1882 and for which Volk supplied equipment. He brought electricity to the Royal Pavilion in 1883 and the following year to the Dome, the museum and the art gallery, the library and the Pavilion's grounds.

Electric traction had been demonstrated in Berlin in 1879, and on 4 August 1883 the two-feet-gauge Volk's Electric Railway opened to run along Madeira Road, the first permanent electric railway in Great Britain. (The line had to be re-laid, as a two-feet-eight-and-a-half-inches gauge, a year later after storm damage.) In 1883 the family moved to Gloucester Place and Volk also had business premises at 8 Gloucester Street as well as in Ditchling Rise. Two years later he had premises in 106 Church Road, Hove.

In 1887 he invented an electric dog-cart, with an order from the Sultan of Turkey, said to be the first export order for a British motor car.

Financial troubles caused Volk to sell his house and rent **31 Kings Road**, and the next year **71 Queen's Park Road.** He was declared bankrupt in January 1888, but was discharged in 1891. He moved to London to work but returned to Brighton in 1892.

Volk's next venture fared less well than the Electric Railway: the Brighton and Rottingdean Seashore Electric Tramroad, which was a car mounted on four stilts running on a pair of tracks laid on the seabed. It was said to be 'a sea voyage on wheels' and it opened in November 1896, but closed in 1901.

Volk's eldest son, Herman, took over management of the railway and in 1913 set up a seaplane station near the line, against his father's disapproval. Volk moved to Hassocks in 1903 and back to Brighton to Dyke Road in 1914, when he managed the railway while his son was on active service during the First World War.

* No 38 is the number stated in the glass above the door, even though the number is 128 Dyke Road.

Volk died at his home in Dyke Road on 20 May 1937, having taken part in the opening of the rebuilt railway terminus at Black Rock two weeks previously. He was buried in the churchyard of **St Wulfran's, Greenways**, Ovingdean.

Rev Henry Wagner (1792–1870)

CLERGYMAN AND CHURCH BUILDER
The Old Vicarage, Temple Gardens **P**

Rev Arthur Wagner (1824–1902)

CLERGYMAN AND PHILANTHROPIST
The Old Vicarage, Temple Gardens **P**
Belvedere, Temple Gardens (now site of Park Royal apartments, Montpelier Road)

When Henry Wagner became vicar of Brighton and West Blatchington in 1824, having been tutor to the sons of the Duke of Wellington, there were 5,000 free pews for a population of 20,000 people. He had six churches built, of which St John's and St Paul's survive.

A controversial figure – for his church appointments, his Toryism in a Whig-dominated vestry and his assault of a seven-year-old boy who had ridiculed him (which cost him a £2 fine) – nevertheless, at his death, all the churches were hung in black and crowds watched his funeral procession to the **Extra-Mural Cemetery**.

Wagner's son Arthur was ordained in 1849 and was appointed as perpetual curate to St Paul's in 1850. Unlike his father, Arthur was an Eton-educated ritualist and Tractarian. His was Brighton's first church to adopt advanced ritual, which eventually included the use of vestments and incense. St Paul's practices, popularly known as 'London, Brighton, and South Coast Religion', were illegal, but Wagner was never prosecuted. He become St Paul's first vicar when a parish was created in 1873 and he remained there for the rest of his life.

Five years after taking over, Wagner instituted the Community of the Blessed Virgin Mary at 3–4 Queen's Square. That year, too, he took over St Mary's Home for Female Penitents (prostitutes) on the death of his cousin, Rev George Wagner, who had started it. Wagner moved the home from Lewes Road to Wykeham Terrace, Church Road.

A decade later, **Constance Kent**, who was living at the home as a paying lodger (some say as a nurse), was tried for the murder of her half-brother. She had sacramentally confessed the crime to Wagner and then, at Wagner's urging, voluntarily told the police. However, when Wagner refused to answer questions about the confession at her trial, public protest meetings were organised in Brighton, and a sister (the female care staff were members of a sisterhood) of the home was attacked. Wagner himself was assaulted in the street, once by a man who fired a pistol at him. However, when his assailants were sent to prison he supported their families. (The case is the subject of Kate Summerscale's best-selling book, *The Suspicions of Mr Witcher*.)

Wagner never married and lived at the Old Vicarage (now the sixth form of Brighton and Hove High School) until his father's death in 1870, when he moved into the neighbouring house, Belvedere, which was left to him by his aunt, Mary Ann Wagner in 1868, and where he died. (This was later a school and then, in 1933, the Park Royal Hotel, which was demolished in 1975 to be replaced by the Park Royal apartments.)

Wagner's wealth enabled him to build four churches in Brighton: St Mary Magdalene (1862), the Annunciation (1864), St Bartholomew (1874), and St Martin (1875), and even one in Buxted, Sussex. He spent an estimated £70,000 funding churches, schools, and housing – he had 400 houses constructed in the Islingwood Road district and built the Round Hill Estate between the Lewes and Upper Lewes Roads for his poorer parishioners.

Wagner's only luxury was the purchase of books, and after his death on 14 January 1902, the sale of his library of 12,000 books took three days. He was buried at **Lewes Road Cemetery**, clothed in full eucharistic vestments. Three thousand people attended the interment. His considerable estate of £49,907, 15s 6d provided endowments for the churches and the sisterhood.

Keith Waterhouse (1929–2009)

NOVELIST, PLAYWRIGHT, AND NEWSPAPER COLUMNIST
91 Embassy Court, 95 Kings Road

Waterhouse is famously said to have compared Brighton to 'a town that is helping the police with their enquiries'. He moved to this address probably in 1983 and left in 1992, and fully embraced the atmosphere he implies in his Brighton novel, *Palace Pier*, published in 2001.

The novel evokes the seediness of the town's 'pocket size pubs with the interior of drinking barracks' and the low life characters who drink there, and takes in everywhere from the Theatre Royal to the Metropole Hotel to the Palace Pier.

His central character, a writer, 61-year-old Chris Duffy, sets 'the Woolworth alarm clock . . . Never later than ten thirty, which is opening time down here in Brighton'. Embittered by the failure of his second novel and too inebriated to attempt a third, Duffy drinks and makes money from a bric-a-brac stall in North Laine market that he subcontracts to a friend named Eggo, while alternately sleeping with his landlady, Maureen, and burgling her flat.

Irritated by the wealthy, Duffy is also put out by what he sees as the pretensions of those who attend the Brighton Literary [*sic*] Festival. Ironically, he is asked to stand in for an absentee speaker to interview a 'corduroy-clad bearded bugger' about his new book.

A prodigious drinker who never missed a deadline, Waterhouse produced not only millions of words for newspapers and magazines, but also plays, film scripts, novels and collections, several of which appeared during his Brighton years.

It is claimed that he compared Embassy Court to an East End slum when he lived there with Jean Leyland, his secretary and lover, before and after his divorce from his second wife. At that time, the block had seen better days and its condition was no doubt one of the reasons why Waterhouse left.

Sir William Watson (1858–1936)

POET AND LITERARY CRITIC

The Poet's House, 17 Marine Drive, Rottingdean*
Arlington Cottage, 33 High Street, Rottingdean

Watson is forgotten today and news of his death surprised many who had not realised that he had survived so long. It had not always been so. In 1895, after Oscar Wilde's arrest, Watson led the fight to remove **Aubrey Beardsley** (*qv*) as art editor of *The Yellow Book*.

He enjoyed eminence but periods of creative inactivity, bouts of mental illness and producing poetry that was out of step with Modernism ('the last vestige of rhetoric-ridden Victorianism', said one writer) caused his decline. He was aware of this long before the turn of the century but his last poems appeared a decade before his death. His political views were outspoken: he favoured the British Empire but he had also a seemingly contradictory belief in national self-determination.

In his last years Watson was so impoverished that Lord Brotherton, manufacturer, former Tory MP and uncle of Watson's friend, the poet and writer Dorothy Una Ratcliffe, gave him a home locally, though he was not particularly grateful. In 1930 fellow writers, like John Masefield, Sir James Barrie, John Galsworthy and Rudyard Kipling, as well as Lloyd George, signed a public appeal to raise money to support him. A similar appeal was made in the USA. The fund raised £4,000 and he had an annual civil pension of £200 but he died leaving only £733 7s 5d. The money had gone on extravagances: among other things, he moved to what the *Brighton and Hove Herald* called 'the quaint Arlington Cottage in Rottingdean High Street'. In 1931 his heart problems were worse and he was difficult to manage. His wife, Maureen, 22 years his junior, eventually had him admitted to a nursing home at Ditchling Common, where he died two weeks later.

* *A plaque, once attached to The Poet's House, has disappeared.*

Charlie Webb (1886–1973)

FOOTBALLER AND TEAM MANAGER
15 Frith Road, Hove Ⓟ

Webb was born in Ireland, where his father, a Scottish soldier, was stationed. The family moved to Worthing and at 16 Webb played for the first team of Worthing FC. In 1904, he joined the Army and played for his regimental team.

On leave, in January 1909, he played for Brighton and Hove Albion, which led to their being fined and him being banned from regimental football for 12 months. He bought himself out of the Army and signed for Albion as an amateur. A few days later he became the first Albion player to play internationally when he turned out for Ireland against Scotland. A week later he played against Wales and the next year earned his third and last cap, again against Scotland. He never scored and Ireland never won in any of the matches. In his Albion career, he went on to hold the club record for the most number of goals scored (64) in the Southern League.

In the First World War, he served on the Western front, attained the rank of captain and was a prisoner of war. He returned in 1919 to take over as Albion manager and led the club into the Third Division of the Football League. While there were very public clashes with the Albion board, Webb was well known for his sound judgement of players and the acuteness of his transfer deals. Such was his standing that he was given two testimonial matches.

Webb's daughter, Joyce Watts, unveiling the memorial plaque in 2003, remembered: 'On match days all the gate money used to come to Frith Road and we used to store it in our larder in a safe because the banks weren't open. For Cup ties we even sold tickets from the house!'

Webb lived in Frith Road until shortly before his death in a nursing home in Hove.

Sir George Augustus Westphal (1785–1875)

NAVAL OFFICER
2 Brunswick Square 🅿

Westphal came to live in this elegant house in 1834, when he was invalided out of active service, having entered the Navy at the age of 13 to work on a frigate in North America. He lived here for 40 years. Severely wounded, as a 20-year-old midshipman, at the Battle of Trafalgar, he lay next to Nelson on *HMS Victory*, with the admiral's coat under his head as a pillow.

In 1807 he was returning to England from the West Indies on a merchant ship when he was captured by a French privateer, severely wounded and taken to Guadeloupe. He managed to escape and was picked up at sea by an American schooner, ultimately returning to England.

Westphal served in more than 100 actions,, including in the invasion of Martinique, the defence of Cadiz, in the Gulf of Mexico (as commander to which he was promoted in 1813), and in New Orleans in the War of 1812. After other expeditions, he was promoted to captain in 1819 and knighted in 1824.

He served as a magistrate of Brighton and Hove, but seldom sat. He was appointed naval aide-de-camp to the Queen in 1846, rear-admiral in 1851, vice-admiral in 1857, and admiral in 1863. He died at his home on 11 January 1875, and is buried in a vault in **St Andrew's Church, Church Road**, Hove.

Eddie Whaley (1877–1960)

COMEDIAN
124 Marine Parade
13 Royal Crescent
27A Bear Road

Whaley, who was born in the USA, took a six-week engagement in England in 1909, with his partner Harry Scott, and the two of them stayed for the rest of their lives. Whaley eventually became a British citizen and, after his retirement, ran a hotel in Brighton.

The pair were African-American music hall and radio comedians, with Whaley playing the straight man, Cuthbert, to Scott's clown, Pussyfoot. They were the first black performers to star in a British film (*Kentucky Minstrels* in 1934), recreating the roles they had popularised in their long-running BBC radio series.

Whaley moved to Brighton in the 1930s. His home in Marine Parade, to which he moved in 1941, was not far from that of **Max Miller** (*qv*), with whom Scott and Whaley shared theatrical billing. The house was used as a lodging place for leading black artistes in the 1940s and 1950s. However, Whaley wasn't very good with money – he was bankrupted twice (in 1920 and 1930) despite his earnings being estimated at £200 a week in 1920.

Whaley married Emily Duncan in 1937, a year after his divorce from American-born Belle Davis (c. 1874–unknown), herself a performer. Whaley and Emily had a son, **Eddie Whaley Jr** (1939–date) born in Brighton and who made his professional debut on BBC radio with his father as a three-year-old. Aged eight, he appeared in the film *Black Narcissus*. He had a show business career and was tenor of the Deep River Boys, an American Gospel singing group from 1969–71. Whaley's other son, Duncan (1928–2000), whose mother is unknown, was a well-known professional ice-skating clown in *Holiday on Ice*. He was born during his father's marriage to Davis. Whaley had at least one other child, Annie Solomon, with Dora Federman.

Whaley senior lived in various addresses in Brighton – in 1936 he lived in London Road and two years later came to Royal Crescent, and then in Bear Road, the home of his former wife, Emily Duncan, where he died. He was cremated at Woodvale Crematorium.

Sir Herbert Wilcox (1890–1977)

FILM PRODUCER AND DIRECTOR
18 Lewes Crescent Ⓟ

Dame Anna Neagle (1904–1986)

ACTOR AND FILM PRODUCER
18 Lewes Crescent Ⓟ

Neagle and Wilcox lived at this house in Lewes Crescent from 1953 until 1969. Wilcox's family had moved from London to Brighton for his mother's health when he was eight, the fourth of five children. Irish Catholics, the family attended mass at St John the Baptist Church, Bristol Road, Kemp Town. Because of the move, Wilcox's father had had to leave his job and circumstances were straitened. Wilcox later wrote that 'my predominant recollection of Brighton in those days is of hunger'. But one day, with a shilling, he went to Harris's cook shop in West Street and treated himself to its famous 'S.O.P.' – sausage, onions and potatoes. This, he wrote in his 60s, was his abiding recollection of memorable food, though by then he had eaten in the best hotels and restaurants in the world.

He was educated at the Convent of the Sacred Heart, Dyke Road, as a day scholar. One day he witnessed the Prince of Wales, the future **Edward VII** (*qv*), strolling along the seafront at Hove. At this time, too, Wilcox added five shillings (25p) to the weekly family kitty by making his debut at the Brighton Hippodrome, as a member of a boys' chorus. However, the domestic financial situation remained precarious and on one occasion the piano had been taken away as instalments had not been paid.

Soon after his mother died at the age of 42 the family disintegrated and only Wilcox and his father remained at home. At 14 he was working as a pageboy in the former Harley House Hotel, Marine Parade. Soon after this his father died and Wilcox left for London, where he had been offered a job and room as a billiards professional.

While his and Neagle's names are inseparable (they married in 1943), Wilcox had, in fact, been married twice before. The first marriage, which lasted only a year, took place at St Luke's Church, Queen's Park Road, and both marriages ended in divorce.

Wilcox directed Neagle in her first big hit, the musical *Goodnight Vienna* in 1932 and from that year, with one exception, she was exclusively under his direction in 32 films, including *Nell Gwynne, Victoria the Great, They Flew Alone, Spring in Park Lane, Odette* and *Lady with the Lamp*. He went bankrupt in 1964, while living at Lewes Crescent, but Neagle revived their fortunes when she returned to the stage the next year, for six years and more than 2,000 performances in the musical *Charlie Girl*.

Amon Henry Wilds (baptised 1790–1857)

ARCHITECT
Western Pavilion, 9 Western Terrace, Hove Ⓟ

Wilds built this flamboyant, two-storey house as a home for himself but it stands as a monument to his genius and to the extraordinary legacy he left the town through his work on his own and in his partnerships with **CA Busby** (*qv*) and his father, **Amon Wilds** (1762–1833), a carpenter and builder.

The Wildses established their firm in 1806 in Lewes and moved to Brighton, where there was much development, in 1815 and then permanently from 1820. Before the initial move the younger Wilds had had significant responsibility for the speculative development of Richmond Terrace and Waterloo Place. (The elder Wilds lived at **9 Richmond Terrace,** which he built for himself and where he died).

In 1818, Wilds junior submitted a design for a new road to connect Middle Street and West Street, but the project grew and by 1821 he was supervising the construction of a raised promenade and seawall to stretch from West Street to East Street, which would offer a direct link across the town from east to west via the seafront. It was opened as Kings Road by George IV in 1822, and quickly became a fashionable place for carriages and horse riders.

The Wildses, father and son, built Holy Trinity church (now deconsecrated and used as a gallery), Ship Street, for **Thomas Read Kemp** (*qv*), MP and speculative builder, in 1817 and Kemp's house, The Temple, Montpelier Road (now Brighton and Hove High School), in 1819. They also created the 350-capacity Unitarian Chapel (then called Christ Church) in New Road the following year.

There is not sufficient documentary evidence to show which work belongs to Wilds and which to Busby but Egyptian details, ammonite Ionic capitals, bold scallop shells recessed over windows and Italianate designs are characteristic of Wilds. The two built Kemp Town and both are credited with the Gothic House, Western Terrace (later known as The Priory or Priory Lodge) (c.1822–5), with its turrets and spires, but this may well have been largely Wilds' creation.

Wilds' own work continued while he was in partnership with both his father and Busby, and his projects included what are judged to be Wilds' most important works: the sequences of linked villas at Hanover Crescent (1822–7), Montpelier Crescent (1843–7), and Park Crescent (1849–55) in Brighton, and Park

Crescent, Worthing (1825–9). He was also responsible for Oriental Place and Sillwood Place, the Royal Newburgh Assembly Rooms, 1 St Margaret's Place, and the Royal Albion Hotel. Oriental Place and Sillwood Place are what remain of an ambitious scheme that never materialised because the sponsor's money ran out. This would have comprised an Oriental-style garden with a tall, steam-heated glasshouse, a library, museum and school, all surrounded by high-class houses.

Unlike the comparatively short-lived partnership between Wilds and Busby, which ended acrimoniously – Wilds pulled out of the Brunswick Town development on the very day that the building agreement was signed in November 1824 – the partnership between Wilds father and son lasted from about 1806 to 1823. Wilds continued to work in Brighton and elsewhere. His last work in Brighton was the Victoria Fountain, Old Steine, in 1845.

Wilds' recreational activity was archery, and later in his life he experimented in other areas: he invented a new way of cleaning chimneys and proposed a breakwater to protect Brighton's coastline. In 1831 he became high commissioner of Hove and helped prepare the local petition in favour of the Reform Bill. He also served as a Brighton commissioner from 1845 to 1848 (as his father had been earlier). The commissioners asked him to plant elm trees along the road to Brighton Race Course, which became Elm Grove. He moved to Shoreham, where he died.

William IV (1765–1837)

MONARCH

58 Marine Parade
Royal Pavilion, Old Steine
Royal York Hotel (now Youth Hostel), Old Steine **P**

Although his relationship with the actor Mrs Dorothy Jordan produced ten children (none of his children with **Queen Adelaide** survived infancy), William lived comparatively moderately for one of his station, even if he found the £18,000 a year income he enjoyed in 1806 insufficient. He had a strong head and confined his bouts of drinking to visits to his brother **George IV** (*qv*) at the Royal Pavilion ('as usual after dinner, a little lively and unsteady on his legs', as he was said to have been at the palace). On one occasion at the Pavilion the diarist Thomas Creevey had passed out with the Duke of Norfolk and they awoke to find the two brothers 'in a very animated discussion as to the particular shape and make of the wig worn by George II'. Mrs Jordan seems not quite to have believed her lover when she reported that when he returned from Brighton in August 1810 he had complained that he had been 'on very hard duty as to drinking'. When he was king, William took wine at one dinner in Brighton with each of his 30 guests in turn.

William often fell asleep after dinner and then had an occasional propensity to make long speeches, which was allowed full rein when he became king. At one time he called the King of France 'an infamous scoundrel'. At a dinner for the diplomatic corps he spoke in French, proposing a vulgar toast. However, when William and Adelaide entertained at the Pavilion, the style was more informal and less glamorous and extravagant than it had been in the days of George.

The Duke and Duchess of Clarence (as William and Adelaide were styled before he came to the throne) were unaccustomed to rich food and self-indulgence, and a visit to the Pavilion in 1823 left Adelaide with stomach pains and William with gout. As the Clarences, they lived in Marine Parade (in a house which, in 1901, was combined with 14 Grafton Street and then named Clarence Lodge), and they also stayed at the Royal York Hotel.

Adelaide attended St George's Church, St George's Road, Kemp Town, to which she made gifts of plate.

William first went to Brighton as king in August 1830 (the year he acceded to the throne), and was observed in the grounds of the Pavilion the following morning sketching out plans in the gravel with the architect John Nash. The Royal Pavilion had been built for George IV, who effectively lived a bachelor existence. But when William married Adelaide (he was 53 and she 26) the palace proved too small for their two households and so additions were made for servants' quarters and the like.

William's major changes to the Pavilion were the erection of a North and South Lodge (the former now the North Gate, the latter demolished). A popular and affable monarch, William, with the queen stayed in the town every year during his reign, usually from mid-November to mid-February. They would take their daily 'carriage airings', often to Kemp Town and sometimes further on to Rottingdean.

William was unimpressed by his late brother's art collection in the Royal Pavilion, which he then called 'nick knackery'. He had no interest in the subject: 'Ah, seems pretty, I dare say it is', he said when shown one painting.

Three months after succeeding to the throne in June 1830 he paid his respects to Lady Nelson, widow of the victor of Trafalgar, at the Sea House Hotel.

In 1832 William's niece **Princess (later Queen) Victoria** (*qv*) came to Brighton with her mother, the Duchess of Kent. William was put out that the duchess had arranged a progress through England for her daughter although this was the year of the Great Reform Bill. But, to his further chagrin, Victoria was warmly greeted by those who came to see her, something in contrast to popular feelings about the king, due to his refusal to create enough new peers to force through the bill and his attempt to restore the reactionary Duke of Wellington as prime minister.

James Williamson (1855–1933)

CINEMATIC INNOVATOR, INVENTOR AND FILMMAKER
144 (now 156) Church Road, Hove Ⓟ
55 Western Road, Hove
Cambridge House, Cambridge Grove, off Wilbury Villas, Hove Ⓟ

Scots-born Williamson moved from Kent to Church Road in 1886 where he continued his pharmacy practice and lived with Betsy, his wife, and their seven children. Lantern photography was a hobby and he encountered cinematography through friends and neighbours such as **William Friese-Greene** (*qv*), the pioneering cinematographers **George Smith** (*qv*) and **(Arthur) Esme Collings** (1859–1936), and the machinist and engineer Alfred Darling.

In 1896 he introduced X-ray photography to Sussex and took apparatus to the Royal County Hospital. But in 1894 he had begun experiments in cinematography, producing first viable films in 1897, where he joined family and friends as the dramatic troupe. He introduced his first programme of films to the Hove Camera Club at Hove Town Hall. His film catalogue, published 1899, listed 60 films.

Williamson pioneered film narrative, with faked news items like *Attack on a China Mission* (1901). In this film he was the first filmmaker to cut from one shot to another for dramatic effect. The same year *Stop Thief* introduced the movie chase of more than one shot, while *Fire!*, also in that year, with a family saved by a fire crew, was shot on location in Hove. This is the earliest film in which the story is progressed by the logical sequence of cutting from shot to shot. Continuous action through multiple shots established the grammar of film. Films on the hardship of war, melodrama and Dickensian-like social awareness followed.

In 1898 Williamson moved his chemist's shop to Western Road, and the size of the premises and nearness to Smith's 'film factory' at St Ann's Well Gardens enabled him to concentrate on film processing and film production.

In1902 the Williamson Kinematographic Company had a purpose-built film production studio and film processing works in Cambridge Grove, whilst Williamson was living nearby in Cambridge House with his wife and children in a large detached family house. His family were part of the team, creating scenarios, making sets and costumes, and acting in small and major acting roles. Alan, the eldest son, would open the company's New York office in 1907.

Williamson also devoted time to exhibiting shows in institutions and private houses throughout Sussex. In 1908 he advertised an invention of his, a device with which exhibitors could make their own intertitles. In 1910, he turned his attention to manufacturing film equipment and patented a projector which could intersperse slide titles into the films it showed.

In 1908 he switched his production work to colleagues and the next year dropped commercial film production and then his exhibition service. Williamson then started making information films on science and nature, but when this failed he sold his Hove properties in 1910 and went to work in London.

He met with success with film processing and film equipment work, where he invented the Williamson camera, which was widely used in the film industry, as well as a variety of specialist cameras.

He died at his home in Mortlake, Surrey.

Godfrey Winn (1908–1971)

JOURNALIST AND WRITER

The Mill House, Mill Street, Falmer

Born in Birmingham – he gives his birth date in *Who's Who* as 1908, two years later than many other sources – Winn lived here toward the end of his life, when he was rich enough also to own a home in London's Belgravia.

Starting out as a boy actor (he also later in life appeared in *Billy Liar* and other films), Winn published his first novel at the age of 20 and went on to become a columnist for the *Daily Mirror* and the *Sunday Express*. By 1938 he claimed to be the most highly paid journalist in Fleet Street. He served both as a war correspondent (he was the first British journalist to cross the Maginot Line) and as an ordinary seaman in the Royal Navy. An accomplished bridge player, he was much associated with writing for women's magazines, like *Woman* and *Woman and Home*, with articles like 'Do we understand our parents?' and 'The girl that I marry'. The latter was somewhat ironic (but necessary in the days when homosexual activity was illegal) as he was the one-time lover of the writers JR Ackerley and Somerset Maugham.

It is reckoned that the second volume of Winn's autobiography, *The Positive Hour* (1970), sold far better than its predecessor, *The Infirm Glory* (1967), because of the editing by his friend, **Francis King** (*qv*), who called him 'Winifred God'.

John Wisden (1826–1884)

CRICKETER AND ALMANAC EDITOR
2 and 26 (later 32) (latter gone) Crown Street

Wisden was born in Crown Street (although where is not known), where William, his father, was supervising builder for the street's construction. While he was doing that job, the family probably lived at number 2; William's business was probably at number 25 and John's long-term home was at number 26 (later 32). Wisden attended Middle Street School.

At 12 he was working for Tom Box, a well-known wicketkeeper, and began earning pennies as a longstop on the Montpelier ground, and in 1838 he played for Eleven Youths of Brighton against Lewes.

Wisden's first significant match was for Sussex against Kent, and when the All-England XI, the most famous and reputable of exhibition teams, was formed in 1846, he became a member. He would later form a rival team, the United England XI. He played 86 county matches for Sussex, taking 578 wickets, but he also played one match for Kent and three times for Middlesex. He organised the first English overseas tour to the USA and Canada, thus opening cricket's 'oceanic stage'.

Known as the 'Little Wonder' due to his diminutive size (he was 5 feet 4 inches and weighed seven stone), Wisden took 681 wickets in first-class cricket, including all ten in an innings – all were clean bowled – for the North against the South in 1850.

He coached cricket at Harrow School from 1852 to 1855, and was secretary of the Cricketers' Fund Friendly Society from 1857 to his death. Nicknamed the Cardinal, Wisden retired in 1863.

In 1855 he had opened a cricketing and cigar business in London, from which he published in 1864 the *Wisden Cricketer's Almanack*, which eventually saw off its rivals. He also owned The Cricketers pub at Duncton, near Petworth, Sussex, and in 1866 published *Cricket and How to Play It*.

He died in London in 1884.

Sir Kingsley Wood (1881–1943)

POLITICIAN
3 Lewes Crescent

A Conservative, Wood served in the National Government as its first Postmaster-General in 1931 and entered the Cabinet as Minister of Health in 1935. In this job he created the full-time, salaried midwifery service. Three years later Wood took over as Air Minister, speaking in the Commons as the Secretary of State, Lord Swinton, was in the Lords. He later served as Lord Privy Seal and war-time Chancellor of the Exchequer. He had this flat in the 1920s.

Grace Eyre Woodhead (1864–1936)

PHILANTHROPIST AND SOCIAL REFORMER
12 Norfolk Terrace
30 Compton Avenue

Woodhead was born to a prosperous family in Norfolk Terrace, the tenth of 11 children, and went, with her sister, Hilda, to Cambridge. In 1898 she was providing holiday homes in Heathfield, Sussex, for underprivileged London children and those who were 'physically and mentally defective'. By 1900 the headquarters had moved to London, with a permanent base for people to stay.

When the Mental Deficiency Act of 1913 sought compulsory institutionalisation and the separation of the sexes, Woodhead was one of those who founded, in Brighton, the Guardianship Society to allow for the fostering of 'mental and physical defectives' with families. Standards of accommodation were laid down, medical treatment was provided, training and employment offered, and an interest taken in the moral and material welfare of the disabled people, who, where they could, contributed to their own upkeep and received pocket money. Woodhead received no salary but other staff were paid, and money came from charitable donations and local authority grants. The charity started off at **4 Richmond Terrace** and remained there until 1917.

Respite care was developed and in 1926 an out-patient clinic for early nervous disorders and after-care was opened at the society's offices in **82 Grand Parade** (gone), where they were based from 1919 to 1928, having moved from **7 St George's Place**, where they had been from 1917. They were at **2 Old Steine** (gone) for a month in 1928 and then moved back to **Grand Parade** to **number 8** that July, where they remained until 1937.

There were also two (eventually three) farms, run by married couples, to create a homely atmosphere for boys, who after two to three years would be placed in work with local farmers. By 1931 there were six occupational centres in the Brighton area, which both boys and girls attended. But work spread beyond the town to all parts of Britain. Woodhead oversaw all aspects of the work, and all staff and volunteers were accountable to her.

Woodhead lived at Compton Avenue and worked until the last months of her life. She died on 5 April 1936 in a nursing home at **12 Dyke Road**, Brighton, and is buried in the **Extra-Mural Cemetery**.

Her organisation was renamed Grace Eyre and now works with learning disabled adults, providing day centres and offering support for health, sport, housing and employment.

Ten things you (probably) didn't know about Brighton people and places

1. As a child, the future sculptor and artist **Eric Gill** attended a school run by the daughters of **Hablot Browne**, Dickens' illustrator.

2. **Francis King**, the writer and critic, had to sell his house when he libelled his neighbour, **Thomas Skeffington Lodge**, a pompous former Labour MP.

3. **C Aubrey Smith** was a stage and Hollywood film actor, who also played cricket for Sussex and England.

4. **Ivy Compton-Burnett**, whose subjects often concerned the upper middle classes, could, as a child, have passed the mother of **Margaret Powell**, another future novelist and writer, who wrote about life below stairs, as she went about her work as a maid in the same road where the Compton-Burnetts lived.

5. **Victoria Lidiard** (1889–1992), the last surviving suffragette, lived and died in Brighton, as did **Henry Allingham** (1896–2009), the longest-lived veteran of the First World and Britain's oldest man ever.

6. Of all the many actors associated with Brighton, **Dame Flora Robson** (1902–1984) is the one with three commemorative plaques: on her homes at 14 Marine Gardens and 7 Wykeham Terrace, Dyke Road, as well as in St Nicholas' Church, Church Street, where she worshipped.

7. **Anita Roddick** opened the first Body Shop at 22 Kensington Gardens on 26 March 1976. It was a dingy storefront in a bad state of repair. The name was chosen from a notice at a local garage specialising in panel-beating and when the local undertakers protested at the name, the shop gained free publicity. What became the Body Shop corporate green was first used to cover the mould spots on the walls.

8. The popular songs 'Love is the Sweetest Thing' and 'The Very Thought of You' were written by **Peter Noble**, who was born in Brighton, as was **Jack Strachey**, who wrote 'Those Foolish Things'; while 'Come into the Garden, Maud' and 'Following in Father's Footsteps' were popularised by **Vesta Tilley**, who lived in Brighton.

9. **The Blessed John Henry Newman** first visited Brighton as a young Anglican clergyman but became a Catholic convert. Years later, on his return from receiving the red hat in Rome, his first mass in England as a cardinal was said in Brighton.

10. Two Nobel Prize winners for literature spent their early years in Brighton. **Sir Winston Churchill** attended prep school in Hove before going to Harrow, while **Rabindrath Tagore** came from Calcutta as a teenager to attend school in the town.

List of **subjects** and associated **addresses** by category

Architecture and construction

Sir Samuel Brown (1776–1852), Civil engineer, naval officer and builder of the Brighton Chain Pier, 48 Marine Parade **P**

CA Busby (1786–1834), Architect, 11 Waterloo Place; 1 Stanhope Place (2 Lansdowne Place, Hove) **P**

Thomas Cubitt (1788–1855), Builder, 13 Lewes Crescent **P**

Ken Fines (1923–2008), Planning officer, 74 Northease Drive, Hove; 23 North Road **P**

William Holford, later Baron Holford (1907–1975), Architect and town planner, 133 Marine Parade

Thomas Read Kemp (1782–1844), Property speculator, The Temple (now Brighton and Hove High School), Montpelier Road **P**; 22 Sussex Square **P**

Sir James Knowles (1831–1908), Architect and journal editor, 3 Percival Terrace **P**

David Mocatta (1806–1882), Architect, Brighton Railway Station **P**; 38–39 Devonshire Place **P**

Thomas Simpson (1825–1908), Architect, 16 Ship Street; Connaught Road School (now an annex of the West Hove Infants School) **P**

Amon Henry Wilds (baptised 1790–1857), Architect, Western Pavilion, 9 Western Terrace, Hove **P**

Art and illustration

Aubrey Beardsley (1872–1898), Artist and illustrator, 31 (then 12) Buckingham Road **P** (around the corner in West Hill Place); 21 Lower Rock Gardens

Robert Bevan (1865–1925), Artist, 17 Brunswick Square, Hove **P**

Hablot Browne (1815–1882), Illustrator, 8 Clarendon Villas, Hove **P**

Sir Edward Burne-Jones (1833–1898), Painter, North End House (now Aubrey House), The Green, Rottingdean **P**

John Constable (1776–1837), Painter, 11 Sillwood Road **P**

Eric Gill (1882–1940), Sculptor, typographer and wood engraver, 32 Hamilton Road **P**; 2 Prestonville Road; 17 Clifton Road; Preston View, Highcroft Villas

Sir Edwin Landseer (1802–1873), Animal painter and sculptor, 65–66 Regency Square **P**

John Leech (1817–1864), Illustrator, 16 Lansdowne Place, Hove **P**; Bedford Hotel (now the site of the Holiday Inn), Kings Road

Richard Henry Nibbs (1816–1893), Painter and book illustrator, 8 Howard Place; 7 Buckingham Place

Sir William Nicholson (1872–1949), Painter, The Grange (now The Grange Museum and Art Gallery), The Green, Rottingdean; North End House (now Aubrey House), The Green, Rottingdean

Ronald Searle (1920–2011), Cartoonist and artist, 8 Arundel Terrace

Walter Sickert (1860–1942), Painter, 21 Bear Road; 7 Old Steine; 5b Lewes Crescent

Business

William Waldorf Astor, later lst Viscount Astor (1848–1919), Newspaper proprietor and property owner, Western House, 155 Kings Road (now site of Embassy Court)

Sake Dean Mahomed (1759–1851), Entrepreneur, traveller and writer, 2 Black Lion Street (gone); 32 Grand Parade

Dame Anita Roddick (1942–2007), Businesswoman, environmentalist and human rights campaigner, 22 Kensington Gardens **P**

Diplomacy

Gerald de Gaury MC (1897–1984), Diplomat, explorer, writer, soldier and Arabist, Flat 3, 18 Sussex Square

Charles-Maurice de Talleyrand-Périgord (1754–1838), Diplomat, 9 Old Steine **P**

Education

Marcus Cunliffe (1922–1990), Academic, 8 Lewes Crescent

Rev Thomas Redman Hooker (1762–1838), Clergyman and headmaster, The Vicarage (later The Grange, now The Grange Museum and Art Gallery), The Green, Rottingdean

Penelope Lawrence (1856–1932), Dorothy Lawrence (1860–1933), and Millicent Lawrence (1863–1925), Founders of Roedean School, 25 Lewes Crescent **P**; 3 Arundel Terrace; 37 Chesham Road; 35–37 Sussex Square

E.J Marshall (1832–1899), Headmaster, 79 Buckingham Road **P**

Exploration

Edward Bransfield (c. 1785–1852), Antarctic explorer, 11 Clifton Street, 61 London Road (now The World's End pub)

Sir Wilfred Thesiger (1910–2003), Explorer, St Aubyns School (now closed), 76 High Street, Rottingdean

Invention

William Henry Fox Talbot (1800–1877), Pioneer of photography The Vicarage (later The Grange, now The Grange Museum and Art Gallery),The Green, Rottingdean

William Friese-Greene (1855–1921), Developer of the cinematograph, 20 Middle Street 🅿; 9 Worcester Villas, Portslade 🅿

Sir Rowland Hill (1795–1879), Inventor of the penny post and reformer of the London–Brighton Railway, 11 Hanover Crescent 🅿

William Moon (1818–1894), Inventor of typography for blind people, 44 Kensington Place; 104–109 Queen's Road (gone, now Queensbury House)

John Saxby (1821–1913), Inventor and railway engineer, 15 Oxford Street; 20 Buckingham Street; Brighton Station 🅿

George Smith (1864–1959), Cinema pioneer and filmmaker, Laboratory Lodge (now The Cottage), 10 Roman Crescent, Southwick; Caburn House, 15 Caburn Road, Hove; Rosedene, 7 Melville Road, Hove; 18 Chanctonbury Road, Hove 🅿

Magnus Volk (1851–1937), Electrical engineer and inventor, 40 (now 35) Western Road, Hove; 51 Preston Street; 40 Preston Road; 17 Gloucester Place; 128 Dyke Road 🅿

James Williamson (1855–1933), Cinematic innovator, inventor and filmmaker, 144 (now 156) Church Road, Hove 🅿; 55 Western Road, Hove; Rose Cottage, Cambridge Avenue, Hove 🅿

Journalism

Peter Burton (1945–2011), Journalist, publisher, editor and author, 5 Arundel Terrace, 33 Bristol Gardens

Levy Emanuel Cohen (1796–1860), Newspaper editor and owner and social reformer, 2 Clarence Square; 34 North Street (gone)

TP O'Connor (1848–1929), Journalist and MP, 64 Lansdowne Place, Hove; 6 Marine Drive, Rottingdean

George Augustus Sala (1828-1895), Journalist and writer, 2 Eastern Terrace; 59 Norton Road, Hove

Nancy Spain (1917–1964), Journalist, writer and television personality, 10 Wentworth Street

Peter Spencer, later 2nd Viscount Churchill (1890–1973), Journalist, actor and playwright, 5 Arundel Terrace

Godfrey Winn (1908–1971), Journalist and writer, The Mill House, Mill Street, Falmer

Law

Thomas Hayter Chase (1814–1874), Chief Officer of Police, 37 Duke Street

Edward Vaughan Kenealy (1818–1880), Barrister, 163 Wellington Road, Portslade (gone)

Sir Edward Marshall Hall (1858–1927), Barrister and MP, 30 Old Steine 🅿

Helena Normanton (1882–1957), Barrister and feminist campaigner, 16 Cheltenham Place; 4 Clifton Place; 11 Hampton Place, Hove

Henry Solomon (1794–1844), Chief Officer of Police, 27 Kensington Gardens; Town Hall, Bartholomew Square **P**

Literature

William Harrison Ainsworth (1805–1882), Novelist, 38 Brunswick Terrace, Hove; 6 Brunswick Square, Hove; 5 Arundel Terrace **P**

Enid Bagnold (1889–1981), Novelist and playwright, North End House (now Aubrey House), The Green, Rottingdean **P**

Maurice Baring (1874–1945), Novelist and poet, Half Way House, Steyning Road, Rottingdean (now site of Highbury House Care Home)

Ada Ellen Bayly (1857–1903), Novelist (writing as Edna Lyall), 5 Montpelier Villas

Arnold Bennett (1867–1931), Novelist, Royal York Hotel (now a Youth Hostel), Old Steine

Hector Bolitho (1897–1974), Writer, 1 St Nicholas Road

Dion Boucicault (1820–1890), Dramatist and actor-manager, 6 Cavendish Place **P**

Mary Elizabeth Braddon (1835–1915), Author and actor, 26 and 34 New Road (26 is now Mrs Fitzherbert's pub)

Edward Bulwer-Lytton, later 1st Baron Knebworth, (1803–1873), Writer and politician, The Vicarage (later The Grange, now The Grange Museum and Art Gallery), The Green, Rottingdean

Anthony Burgess (1917–1993), Novelist, critic and composer, 78 Tisbury Road, Hove

Lewis Carroll (1832–1898), Writer, mathematician and photographer, 11 Sussex Square **P**; 4 Park Crescent

Dame Ivy Compton-Burnett (1884–1969), Novelist, 20 The Drive, Hove **P**

Alfred Edgar (AE) Coppard (1878–1957), Short-story writer and poet, 25 Gladstone Place

Antony Dale (1912–1993), Historian and conservationist, 46 Sussex Square **P**

Kay Dick (1915–2001), Writer and editor, Flat 5, 9 Arundel Terrace

Charles Dickens (1812–1870), Novelist, Bedford Hotel (now Holiday Inn), Kings Road **P**; 16 Lansdowne Place, Hove **P**; 148 Kings Road; Old Ship Hotel, Kings Road

Lord Alfred Douglas (1870–1945), Poet and lover of Oscar Wilde, 28 Brunswick Square, Hove; 35 Fourth Avenue, Hove; Flat 1, St Anne's Court, Nizells Avenue, Hove **P**

Constance Garnett (1861–1946), Translator, 58 Ship Street (now a restaurant); 40 Buckingham Place

Graham Greene (1904–1991), Novelist, Hotel Metropole, Kings Road; Royal Albion Hotel, 35 Old Steine

James Orchard Halliwell-Phillipps (1820–1889), Antiquary and literary scholar, Hollingbury Copse (the street of the same name stands on the site)

Patrick Hamilton (1904–1962), Novelist and playwright, 12 First Avenue **P**

Richard Jefferies (1848–1887), Writer, novelist and mystic, 3 and 8 (now 87) Lorna Road

Samuel Johnson (1709–1784), Writer and lexicographer, and Hester Thrale (1741–1821), Writer, 77 West Street **P**; St Nicholas' Church, Church Street **P**

Francis King (1923–2011), Novelist and critic, 17 Montpelier Villas

Rudyard Kipling (1865–1936), Writer and poet, The Elms, The Green, Rottingdean **P**

Edward Knoblock (1874–1945), Playwright and novelist, 20 Clifton Terrace

Robin Maugham, 2nd Viscount Maugham (1916–1981), Novelist and playwright, 2 Brunswick Terrace, Hove; 14 Bute Street; 5 Clifton Road

David (DM) Murray (1888–1962), Novelist and newspaper editor, Chichester House, Chichester Terrace

JH Round (1854–1928), Medieval historian and genealogist, 15 Brunswick Terrace, Hove **P**

Vita Sackville-West (1892–1962), Writer and gardener, 39/40/40a Sussex Square

Horatio (Horace) Smith (1779–1849), Writer and humorist, 10 Hanover Crescent; 12 Cavendish Place **P**

Count Eric Stenbock (1860–1895), Poet and short story writer, Withdean Hall, The Approach, London Road

Robert Smith (RS) Surtees (1805–1864), Novelist, Mutton's Hotel, 80 Kings Road (now site of the Brighton Centre)

Rabindrath Tagore (1861–1941), Poet, musician, novelist, painter, educationist and Nobel Laureate, 43 Medina Villas, Hove

William Makepeace Thackeray (1811–1863), Novelist, 62 East Street; Royal York Hotel, Old Steine (now Youth Hostel); Old Ship, Kings Road

Angela Thirkell (1890–1960), Novelist, North End House (now Aubrey House), The Green, Rottingdean **P**

Keith Waterhouse (1929–2009), Novelist, playwright, and newspaper columnist, 91 Embassy Court, 95 Kings Road

Sir William Watson (1858–1936), Poet and literary critic, The Poet's House, 17 Marine Drive, Rottingdean; Arlington Cottage, 33 High Street, Rottingdean

Medicine

Sophia Jex-Blake (1840–1912), Doctor and campaigner for women's rights, 13 Sussex Square

Frederick Henry Horatio Akbar Mahomed (1849–1884), Doctor, 2 Black Lion Street (gone); 32 Grand Parade

Gideon Mantell (1790–1852), Surgeon and geologist, 20 Old Steine **P**

Louisa Martindale (1872–1966), Gynaecologist and feminist, 2 Lancaster Road; 11 Adelaide Crescent, Hove; Windlesham House (now site of York Mansions East), Windlesham Road, Hove

Richard Russell (1687–1759), Physician, Royal Albion Hotel **P**

Thomas Tanner (1824–1871), Doctor, 12 Royal Crescent

Military

Henry Allingham (1896–2009), Longest-lived veteran of the First World War and Britain's oldest man ever, St Dunstan's Centre, Greenways, Ovingdean

Earl of Cardigan (1797–1868), Soldier and commander of the Light Brigade, 45 Brunswick Square, Hove

Sir Edward Codrington (1770–1851), Naval officer, commander of combined fleets at the Battle of Navarino and MP, Hampton Lodge, 140 Western Road, Hove **P**

Sir John Hindmarsh (1785–1860), Admiral and founding Governor, State of South Australia, 30 Albany Villas, Hove **P**

Jacqueline Nearne (1916–1982), Officer, Special Operations Executive, 32 West Hill Street

Sir George Augustus Westphal (1785–1875), Naval officer, 2 Brunswick Square, Hove **P**

Miscellaneous

Jane Elizabeth Digby, Lady Ellenborough (1807–1881), Aristocrat and adventuress, Norfolk Arms, Kings Road (site now the Mercure Brighton Seafront Hotel), 149 Kings Road

Christiana Edmunds (1828–1907), Murderer, 16 Gloucester Place (gone)

Henry Fauntleroy (1784–1824), Banker and forger, Hampton Lodge, Western Road, Hove (gone but part was on land now at the corner of Hampton Place and Western Road; the porch is at Hampton Lodge, 140 Western Road)

Edward Fitzgerald, 7th Duke of Leinster (1892–1976), Gambler and bankrupt, 6 Arundel Terrace

Martha Gunn (1726–1815), 'Queen of the dippers', 36 East Street **P** (now a restaurant)

Lady Sackville (1862–1936), Aristocrat, 39/40/40a Sussex Square; White Lodge, 40, The Cliff, Roedean

Doreen Valiente (1922–1999), Mother of modern witchcraft, poet and author, 6 Tyson Place, Grosvenor Street **P**

Music

Richard Addinsell (1904–1977), Composer, 5 Chichester Terrace **P**

Dame Clara Butt (1872–1936), Singer, 27 Adur Terrace, Southwick; 4 St Aubyns Mansions, Kings Esplanade, Hove **P**

Bob Copper (1915–2004), Traditional folk singer, collector of folk songs and writer, 1 Challoner's Cottages, Falmer Road, Rottingdean **P**

Sir Hamilton Harty (1870–1941), Composer, song writer and arranger, 33 Brunswick Square, Hove **P**

Ralph Vaughan Williams (1872–1958), Composer, Field House School (later St Aubyns School, now closed), 76 High Street, Rottingdean

Politics

Alma Lillian Birk, later Baroness Birk (1917–1996), Politician and journalist, 10 Belgrave Place

Margaret Bondfield (1873–1953), First woman Cabinet minister, 14 Church Road, Hove

Frederick Hervey, 1st Marquess of Bristol and 5th Earl of Bristol (1768–1859), Politician, landowner and philanthropist, 19–20 Sussex Square

RA ('Rab') Butler, later Baron Butler (1902–1982), Politician, The Wick, The Wick School, Furze Hill (now the site of Furze Croft apartments. St Ann's Well Gardens), Hove

George Canning (1770–1827), Prime minister, Marine Parade (now Royal Crescent Mansions)

Sir Herbert Carden (1867–1941), Local politician and mayor of Brighton, 19 West Hill Road; 103 Marine Parade

Sir Edward Carson (1854–1935), Irish Unionist politician and lawyer, Northgate House, Bazehill Road, Rottingdean (now the site of Northgate close)

Sir Winston Churchill (1874–1965), Prime minister, writer and Nobel Laureate, Lansworth House, 29–30 Brunswick Road, Hove (also in Lansdowne Road)

Lewis Cohen, later Baron Cohen (1897–1966), Local politician, philanthropist and businessman, 55 Dyke Road Avenue

William George Spencer Cavendish, 6th Duke of Devonshire (1790–1858), Whig grandee and connoisseur of the arts, 1 Lewes Crescent (now Fife House)

Sir Elwyn Jones, later Lord Elwyn-Jones (1909–1989), Politician and lawyer, 17 Lewes Crescent

William Ewart Gladstone (1809–1898), Prime minister, 20 Brunswick Square, Hove; Lion Mansion Hotel (now west wing of Royal Albion Hotel), Kings Road

Alan Lennox-Boyd, Ist Viscount Merton (1904–1983), Politician, 36 Brunswick Terrace, Hove

Prince Klemens von Metternich (1773–1859), Statesman, 42 Brunswick Terrace, Hove

Charles Stewart Parnell (1846–1891), Irish Nationalist leader, 8 Medina Villas, Hove; 10 Walsingham Terrace, Hove (now site of Dorset Court, Kingsway, Hove)

Lord John Russell (1792–1878), Prime minister, 14 Sussex Square

Sir Charles Thomas-Stanford (1858–1932), Politician, Preston Manor, Preston Drove

Sir Kingsley Wood (1881–1943), Politician, 3 Lewes Crescent

Popular entertainment

Chesney Allen (1893–1982), Comedian, 21 Park Crescent Place

Douglas Byng (1893–1987), Comic singer and songwriter, Flat 2, 6 Arundel Terrace

Clarissa Dickson Wright (1946–2014), Broadcaster, cook, barrister, writer and bookshop owner, Convent of the Sacred Heart School, The Upper Drive, Hove (now site of Cardinal Newman School)

Gilbert Harding (1907–1960), Television personality, 20 Montpelier Villas

Alan Melville (1910–1983), Television and radio personality, writer and lyricist, 17 Clifton Terrace; 28 Victoria Street

Max Miller (1894–1963), Comedian, 43 Hereford Street (gone); 160 Marine Parade; 25 Burlington Street

Ray Noble (1903–1978), Band leader and composer, 1 Montpelier Terrace ℗

Roland Pertwee (1885–1963), Playwright and television scriptwriter, director and actor, 19 Denmark Villas, Hove

Wilfred Pickles (1904–1978), Broadcaster and actor, 19 Courcles, Arundel Street

Sir George Robey (1869–1954), Comedian, 8 Rutland Court, New Church Road, Hove; The Lawns, Arundel Drive, Saltdean

John Francis (Jack) Strachey (1894–1972). Popular composer, Flat J, 14 Marine Gate, Marine Drive

Vesta Tilley (1864–1952), Music hall artiste, 8 St Aubyns Mansions, Kings Esplanade, Hove ℗

Eddie Whaley (1877–1960), Comedian, 124 Marine Parade; 13 Royal Crescent; 27A Bear Road

Religion

Deryk Carver (c. 1505–1555), Protestant martyr, Black Lion Pub, 14 Black Lion Street ℗

Rev Richard Enraght (1837–1898), Clergyman and controversialist, 36 Russell Square; 5 Station Road (formerly 5 Courtney Terrace), Portslade

Selina, Countess of Huntingdon (1707–1791), Religious reformer, North Street (now the site of Huntingdon House, 20 North Street)

Blessed John Henry Newman, Cardinal Newman (1801–1889), Priest, theologian and cardinal, 11 Marine Square

Rev Frederick Robertson (1816–1853), Clergyman, 9 Montpelier Terrace; 60 Montpelier Road ; Holy Trinity Church, Ship Street ℗

Rev Arthur Wagner (1824–1902), Clergyman and philanthropist, The Old Vicarage, Temple Gardens ℗; Belvedere, Temple Gardens (now site of Park Royal apartments, Montpelier Road)

Rev Henry Wagner (1792–1870), Clergyman and church builder, The Old Vicarage, Temple Gardens

Royalty

Augusta Sophia (1768–1840), Daughter of George III, North Gate House, Church Street

Sara Forbes Bonetta (c. 1843–1880), West African princess, 17 Clifton Hill

Edward VII (1841–1910), Monarch, 8 Kings Gardens, Hove ℗; Fife House, 1 Lewes Crescent

Maria Fitzherbert (1756–1837), Morganatic wife of George IV, 55 Old Steine (now Youth Hostel) ℗; Church of St John the Baptist, Bristol Road

George IV (1762–1830), Monarch, Royal Pavilion, Old Steine; Marlborough House, Old Steine

Victoria Ka'iulani Kalaninuiahilapalapa Kawekiu i Lunalilo Cleghorn, Crown Princess Ka'iuni (1875–1899), Heir to the throne of Hawaii, 7 Cambridge Road, Hove

Manuel II (1889–1932), Deposed king of Portugal, Eastern House, 9 Eastern Terrace

Napoleon III (1808–1873), President of the Second French Republic and last French monarch, Bedford Hotel (now site of Holiday Inn), Kings Road; Grand Hotel, Kings Road

Victoria (1819–1901), Monarch, Royal Pavilion, Old Steine

William IV (1765–1837), Monarch, 58 Marine Parade; Royal Pavilion, Old Steine; Royal York Hotel (now Youth Hostel), Old Steine **P**

Social reform

Dame Henrietta Barnett (1851–1936), Social reformer, 45 Wish Road, Hove **P**

Edward Carpenter (1844–1929), Campaigner for gay equality and socialist writer, 45 Brunswick Square, Hove **P**

George Jacob Holyoake (1817–1906), Secularist, journalist, trade unionist and Co-operative pioneer, 36 Camelford Street **P**

Dr William King (1786–1865), Social reformer, Co-operative pioneer, physician and mathematician, 2 Regency Square **P**; 23 Montpelier Road

Peter Kropotkin (1842–1921), Anarchist, scientist and writer, 9 Chesham Street

Victoria Lidiard (1889–1992), Suffragette, Flat 1, 14 Palmeira Avenue, Hove **P**

Louisa Martindale (1839–1914), Suffragist and feminist, 2 Lancaster Road

Eleanor Marx (1855–1898), Socialist revolutionary, 2 Manchester Street; 6 Vernon Terrace **P**

Arnold Ruge (1802–1880), Writer and political thinker, 7 Park Crescent

Henry Salt (1851–1939), Social reformer, writer and classical scholar, 19 Highdown Road; 21 Cleveland Road; 15 Sandgate Road

Herbert Spencer (1820–1903), Philosopher, social theorist and sociologist, 5 Percival Terrace **P**

Grace Eyre Woodhead (1864–1936), Philanthropist and social reformer, 12 Norfolk Terrace; 30 Compton Avenue

Sport

Sir John Berry ('Jack') Hobbs (1882–1963), Surrey and England cricketer, 13 Palmeira Avenue, Hove **P**; 32 Furze Croft, St Ann's Well Gardens, Hove

Fred Perry (1909–1995), Lawn tennis champion, 24 Newlands Road, Rottingdean; 1 Grange Close, Dean Court Road, Rottingdean; 10 Little Crescent, Rottingdean

Tom Sayers (1826–1865), English bare-knuckle champion boxer, Titchborne Street **P**

Maurice Tate (1895–1956), Sussex and England cricketer, 28 Warleigh Road **P**

Charlie Webb (1886–1973), Footballer and team manager, 15 Frith Road, Hove **P**

John Wisden (1826–1884), Cricketer and almanac editor, 2 and 26 (later 32) (latter gone) Crown Street

Stage and screen

Elizabeth Allan (1910–1990), Actor, 7 Arundel Terrace; Courtenay Tye, Courtney Terrace, Hove

Hermione Baddeley (1906–1986), Actor, 5 Arundel Terrace

Edna Best (1900–1974), Actor, Redcliff, Pembroke Crescent, Hove; 2 St Albyns (now Kingsway Hotel), Hove

Clive Brook (1887–1974), Actor, Garden House, 13 Clifton Place (gone)

Dora Bryan (1923–2014), Actor and comedienne, 108 Crescent Place, Clarges Hotel, 115–119, Marine Parade (now apartments); Springfields Nursing Home, 11 Langdale Road, Hove

Jack Buchanan (1891–1957), Actor and theatre manager, 19 Lewes Crescent **P**

Sir John Clements (1910–1988), Actor and theatre manager, 7 Royal Crescent

Sir Charles (CB) Cochran (1872–1951), Theatrical impresario, 15 Prestonville Road

Robert Flemyng (1912–1995), Actor, Flat 4, 6 Arundel Terrace

Kay Hammond (1909 –1980), Actor, 7 Royal Crescent

Sir Michael Hordern (1911–1995), Actor, Brighton College, Eastern Road

Evelyn Laye (1900–1996), Actor and singer, 20 Egremont Place; York Place School (now Varndean School, Balfour Road)

Oscar Lewenstein (1917–1997), Theatre and film producer, 9 and 11 Hove Seaside Villas (now Western Esplanade), Hove

Harriot Mellon, Duchess of St Albans (1777–1837), Actor and banker, 131 Kings Road; 19 and 28 Brunswick Terrace, Hove

Terence Morgan (1921–2005), Actor, 13 Wyndham Street

Dame Anna Neagle (1904–1986), Actor and film producer, 18 Lewes Crescent **P**

Sir Laurence Olivier, later Baron Olivier (1907–1989), Actor and theatrical director, 4 Royal Crescent **P**

Cecil Parker (1897–1971), Actor, 1 Dyke Road Place

Roland Pertwee (1885–1963), Playwright and television scriptwriter, director and actor, 19 Denmark Villas, Hove

Margaret (Peggy) Ramsay (1908–1991), Theatrical agent, 34 Kensington Place **P**

Sir Terence Rattigan (1911–1977), Playwright, Bedford House, 79 Marine Parade **P**

Dame Flora Robson (1902–1984), Actor, 14 Marine Gardens **P**; 7 Wykeham Terrace, Dyke Road **P**; St Nicholas' Church, Church Street **P**

Sir Paul Scofield (1922–2008), Actor, Varndean School for Boys, Surrenden Road (now Varndean School, Balfour Road)

Sir C Aubrey Smith (1863–1948), Stage and film actor, and Sussex and England cricketer, 27 Selbourne Road, Hove; 19 Albany Villas, Hove

Sir Herbert Wilcox (1890–1977), Film producer and director, 18 Lewes Crescent

Places and people

Adelaide Crescent, Hove

11 — Louisa Martindale (1872–1966), Gynaecologist and feminist (see also Lancaster Road and Windlesham Road, Hove)

Adur Terrace, Southwick

27 — Dame Clara Butt (1872–1936), Singer (see also Kings Esplanade)

Albany Villas, Hove

19 **P** — Sir C Aubrey Smith (1863–1948), Stage and film actor and Sussex and England cricketer (see also 27 Selbourne Road, Hove)

30 **P** — Sir John Hindmarsh (1785–1860), Admiral and founding Governor, State of South Australia

Arundel Drive, Saltdean

The Lawns — Sir George Robey (1869–1954), Comedian (see also New Church Road, Hove)

Arundel Street

19 Courcles — Wilfred Pickles (1904–1978), Broadcaster and actor

Arundel Terrace

3 — Penelope Lawrence (1856–1932), Dorothy Lawrence (1860–1933) and Millicent Lawrence (1863–1925), Founders of Roedean School (see also Chesham Road, Lewes Crescent and Sussex Square)

Flat 5, 9 — Kay Dick (1915–2001), Writer and editor

5 **P** — William Harrison Ainsworth (1805–1882), Novelist (see also Brunswick Square, Hove and Brunswick Terrace, Hove)

5 — Hermione Baddeley (1906–1986), Actor

5 — Peter Burton (1945–2011), Journalist, publisher, editor and author (see also Bristol Gardens)

5 — Peter Spencer, later 2nd Viscount Churchill (1890–1973), Journalist, actor and playwright

Flat 2, 6 — Douglas Byng (1893–1987), Comic singer and songwriter

Flat 4, 6 — Robert Flemyng (1912–1995), Actor

6 — Edward Fitzgerald, 7th Duke of Leinster (1892–1976), Gambler and bankrupt

7 — Elizabeth Allan (1910–1990), Actor (see Courtenay Terrace, Hove)

8 — Ronald Searle (1920–2011), Cartoonist and artist

Bartholomew Square

Town Hall **P** — Henry Solomon (1794–1844), Chief Officer of Police (see also Kensington Gardens)

Bazehill Road, Rottingdean
Northgate House (now site of
Northgate Close)

Sir Edward Carson (1854–1935), Irish Unionist politician and
lawyer

Bear Road
21

Walter Sickert (1860–1942), Painter (see also Old Steine and
Lewes Crescent)

27A

Eddie Whaley (1877–1960), Comedian (see also Marine Parade
and Royal Crescent)

Belgrave Place
10

Alma Lillian Birk, later Baroness Birk (1917–1996), Politician and
journalist

Black Lion Street
2 (gone)

Sake Dean Mahomed (1759–1851), Entrepreneur, traveller and
writer (see also Grand Parade)

2 (gone)

Frederick Henry Horatio Akbar Mahomed (1849–1884), Doctor
(see also Grand Parade)

Black Lion Pub, 14 🅟

Deryk Carver (c. 1505–1555), Protestant martyr

Brighton Railway Station

David Mocatta (1806–1882), Architect 🅟 (see also
Devonshire Place)
John Saxby (1821–1913), Inventor and railway engineer 🅟
(see also Buckingham Street and Oxford Street)

Bristol Gardens
33

Peter Burton (1945–2011), Journalist, publisher, editor and
author (see also Arundel Terrace)

Bristol Road
Church of St John the Baptist 🅟

Maria Fitzherbert (1756–1837), Morganatic wife of George IV
(see also Old Steine)

Brunswick Road, Hove
Lansworth House, 29–30 🅟 🅟

Sir Winston Churchill (1874–1965), Prime minister, writer and
Nobel Laureate

Brunswick Square, Hove
2 🅟
6

Sir George Augustus Westphal (1785–1875), Naval officer
William Harrison Ainsworth (1805–1882), Novelist (see also
Arundel Terrace and Brunswick Terrace, Hove)

17 🅟
20

Robert Bevan (1865–1925), Artist
William Ewart Gladstone (1809-1898), Prime minister (see also
Kings Road)

28

Lord Alfred Douglas (1870–1945), Poet and lover of Oscar Wilde
(see also Fourth Avenue, Hove and Nizells Avenue, Hove)

33 **℗**	Sir Hamilton Harty (1870–1941), Composer, song writer and arranger
45	Earl of Cardigan (1797–1868), Soldier and commander of the Light Brigade
45 **℗**	Edward Carpenter (1844–1929), Campaigner for gay equality and socialist writer

Brunswick Terrace, Hove
2	Robin Maugham, 2nd Viscount Maugham (1916–1981), Novelist and playwright (see also Bute Street and Clifton Road)
15	JH Round (1854–1928), Medieval historian and genealogist
19 and 28	Harriot Mellon, Duchess of St Albans (1777–1837), Actor and banker (see also Kings Road)
36	Alan Lennox-Boyd, later lst Viscount Merton (1904–1983), Politician
38	William Harrison Ainsworth (1805–1882), Novelist (see also Arundel Terrace and Brunswick Square, Hove)
42 **℗**	Prince Klemens von Metternich (1773–1859), Statesman

Buckingham Place
7	Richard Henry Nibbs (1816–1893), Painter and book illustrator (see also Howard Place)
40	Constance Garnett (1861–1946), Translator (see also Ship Street)

Buckingham Road
31 (then 12) **℗** (around the corner in West Hill Place)	Aubrey Beardsley (1872–1898), Artist and illustrator (see also Lower Rock Gardens)
79 **℗**	EJ Marshall (1832–1899), Headmaster

Buckingham Street
20	John Saxby (1821–1913), Inventor and railway engineer (see also Brighton Railway Station and Oxford Street)

Burlington Street
25 **℗**	Max Miller (1894–1963), Comedian (see also Hereford Street and Marine Parade)

Bute Street
14	Robin Maugham, 2nd Viscount Maugham (1916–1981), Novelist and playwright (see also Brunswick Terrace, Hove and Clifton Road)

Caburn Road, Hove
Caburn House, 15	George Smith (1864–1959), Cinema pioneer and filmmaker (see also Roman Crescent, Southwick; Melville Road, Hove; and Chanctonbury Road, Hove)

Cambridge Grove, Hove

Cambridge House **P** — James Williamson (1855–1933), Cinematic innovator, inventor and filmmaker (see also Church Road and Western Road, Hove)

Cambridge Road, Hove

7 — Victoria Ka'iulani Kalaninuiahilapalapa Kawekiu i Lunalilo Cleghorn, Crown Princess Ka'iuni (1875–1899), Heir to the throne of Hawaii

Camelford Street

36 **P** — George Jacob Holyoake (1817–1906), Secularist, journalist, trade unionist and Co-operative pioneer

Cavendish Place

6 **P** — Dion Boucicault (1820–1890), Dramatist and actor-manager

12 **P** — Horatio (Horace) Smith (1779–1849), Writer and humorist

Chanctonbury Road, Hove

18 **P** — George Smith (1864–1959), Cinema pioneer and filmmaker (see also Roman Crescent, Southwick; Caburn Road, Hove; and Melville Road, Hove)

Cheltenham Place

16 — Helena Normanton (1882–1957), Barrister and feminist campaigner (see also Clifton Place and Hampton Place)

Chesham Road

37 — Penelope Lawrence (1856–1932), Dorothy Lawrence (1860–1933), and Millicent Lawrence (1863–1925), Founders of Roedean School (see also Arundel Terrace and Sussex Square)

Chesham Street

9 — Peter Kropotkin (1842–1921), Anarchist, scientist and writer

Chichester Terrace

Chichester House — David (DM) Murray (1888–1962), Novelist and newspaper editor

5 **P** — Richard Addinsell (1904–1977), Composer

Church Road, Hove

14 — Margaret Bondfield (1873–1953), First woman Cabinet minister

144 (now 156) **P** — James Williamson (1855–1933), Cinematic innovator, inventor and filmmaker (see also Cambridge Grove and Western Road, Hove)

Church Street

St Nicholas' Church **P** — Samuel Johnson (1709–1784), Writer and lexicographer (see also West Street)

St Nicholas' Church **P** — Dame Flora Robson (1902–1984), Actor (see also Marine Gardens)

| North Gate House | Augusta Sophia (1768–1840), Daughter of George III |

Clarence Square

| 2 | Levy Emanuel Cohen (1796–1860), Newspaper editor and owner and social reformer (see also North Street) |

Clarendon Villas, Hove

| 8 🅟 | Hablot Browne (1815–1882), Illustrator |

Cleveland Road

| 21 | Henry Salt (1851–1939), Social reformer, writer and classical scholar (see also Highdown Road and Sandgate Road) |

Clifton Hill

| 17 | Sara Forbes Bonetta (c. 1843–1880), West African princess |

Clifton Place

| 4 | Helena Normanton (1882–1957), Barrister and feminist campaigner (see also Cheltenham Place and Hampton Place) |
| Garden House, 13 (gone) | Clive Brook (1887–1974), Actor |

Clifton Road

| 5 | Robin Maugham, 2nd Viscount Maugham (1916–1981), Novelist and playwright (see also Brunswick Terrace, Hove and Bute Street) |
| 17 | Eric Gill (1882–1940), Sculptor, typographer and wood engraver |

Clifton Street

| 11 | Edward Bransfield (c. 1785–1852), Antarctic explorer (see also London Road) |

Clifton Terrace

| 17 | Alan Melville (1910–1983), Television and radio personality, writer and lyricist (see also Victoria Street) |
| 20 | Edward Knoblock (1874–1945), Playwright and novelist |

Compton Avenue

| 30 | Grace Eyre Woodhead (1864–1936), Philanthropist and social reformer (see also Norfolk Terrace) |

Connaught Road

| Connaught Road School (now an annex of the West Hove Infants School) 🅟 | Thomas Simpson (1825–1908), Architect (see also Ship Street) |

Courtenay Terrace, Hove

| Courtenay Tye 🅟 | Elizabeth Allan (1910–1990), Actor (see also Arundel Terrace) |

Crescent Place

| 108 | Dora Bryan (1923–2014), Actor and comedienne (see also Langdale Road, Hove and Marine Parade) |

Crown Street
2 and 26 (later 32) (latter gone)   John Wisden (1826–1884), Cricketer and almanac editor

Dean Court Road, Rottingdean
1 Grange Close   Fred Perry (1909–1995), Lawn tennis champion (see also Newlands Road, Rottingdean and Little Crescent, Rottingdean)

Denmark Villas, Hove
19   Roland Pertwee (1885–1963), Playwright and television scriptwriter, director and actor

Devonshire Place
38–39 🅿   David Mocatta (1806–1882), Architect (see also Brighton Railway Station)

Duke Street
37   Thomas Hayter Chase (1814–1874), Chief Officer of Police

Dyke Road
7 Wykeham Terrace 🅿   Dame Flora Robson (1902–1984), Actor (see also Church Street and Marine Gardens)
128 🅿   Magnus Volk (1851–1937), Electrical engineer and inventor (see also Western Road, Hove; Preston Street; and Gloucester Place)

Dyke Road Avenue
55   Lewis Cohen, later Baron Cohen (1897–1966), Local politician, philanthropist and businessman

Dyke Road Place
1   Cecil Parker (1897–1971), Actor

East Street
36 🅿   Martha Gunn (1726–1815), 'Queen of the dippers'
62   William Makepeace Thackeray (1811–1863), Novelist (see also Kings Road and Old Steine)

Eastern Road
Brighton College   Sir Michael Hordern (1911–1995), Actor

Eastern Terrace
Eastern House, 9   Manuel II (1889–1932), Deposed king of Portugal
2   George Augustus Sala (1828–1895), Journalist and writer (see also Norton Road, Hove)

Egremont Place
20   Evelyn Laye (1900–1996), Actor and singer (see also York Place)

Falmer Road, Rottingdean
1 Challoner's Cottages 🅿   Bob Copper (1915–2004), Traditional folk singer, collector of folk songs and writer

First Avenue
12 **℗**   Patrick Hamilton (1904–1962), Novelist and playwright

Fourth Avenue, Hove
35   Lord Alfred Douglas (1870–1945), Poet and lover of Oscar Wilde
                                              (see also Brunswick Square, Hove and Nizells Avenue)

Frith Road, Hove
15 **℗**   Charlie Webb (1886–1973), Footballer and team manager

Furze Hill, Hove
The Wick, Wick House, Furze Hill   RA ('Rab') Butler, later Baron Butler (1902–1982), Politician
(now site of Furze Croft apartments,
St Ann's Well Gardens)

Gladstone Place
25   Alfred Edgar (AE) Coppard (1878–1957), Short story writer and
                                              poet

Gloucester Place
16 (gone)   Christiana Edmunds (1828–1907), Murderer
17   Magnus Volk (1851–1937), Electrical engineer and inventor (see
                                              also Western Road, Hove; Preston Street; and Dyke Road)

Grand Parade
32   Sake Dean Mahomed (1759-1851), Entrepreneur, traveller and
                                              writer (see also Black Lion Street)
32   Frederick Henry Horatio Akbar Mahomed (1849–1884), Doctor
                                              (see also Black Lion Street)

Greenways, Ovingdean
St Dunstan's Centre   Henry Allingham (1896–2009), Longest-lived veteran of the First
                                              World War and Britain's oldest man ever

Grosvenor Street
6 Tyson Place **℗**   Doreen Valiente (1922–1999), Mother of modern witchcraft, poet
                                              and author

Hamilton Road
32 **℗**   Eric Gill (1882–1940), Sculptor, typographer and wood engraver
                                              (see also Clifton Road, Prestonville Road and Highcroft Villas)

Hampton Place, Hove
11   Helena Normanton (1882–1957), Barrister and feminist
                                              campaigner (see also Cheltenham Place and Clifton Place)

Hanover Crescent
10   Horatio (Horace) Smith (1779–1849), Writer and humorist

11 **℗**	Sir Rowland Hill (1795–1879), Inventor of the penny post and reformer of the London–Brighton Railway

Hereford Street

43 (gone)	Max Miller (1894–1963), Comedian (see also Marine Parade and Burlington Street)

Highcroft Villas

Preston View	Eric Gill (1882–1940), Sculptor, typographe and wood engraver (see also Clifton Road, Hamilton Road and Prestonville Road)

Highdown Road

19	Henry Salt (1851–1939), Social reformer, writer and classical scholar (see also Cleveland Road and Sandgate Road)

High Street, Rottingdean

Field House School (later St Aubyns School, now closed), 76	Ralph Vaughan Williams (1872–1958), Composer
St Aubyns School (now closed), 76	Sir Wilfred Thesiger (1910–2003), Explorer
Arlington Cottage	Sir William Watson (1858–1936), Poet and literary critic (see also Marine Drive, Rottingdean)

Hollingbury Copse (the street of the same name stands on the site)	James Orchard Halliwell-Phillipps (1820–1889), Antiquary and literary scholar

Hove Seaside Villas (now Western Esplanade)

9 and 11	Oscar Lewenstein (1917–1997), Theatre and film producer

Howard Place

8	Richard Henry Nibbs (1816–1893), Painter and book illustrator (see also Buckingham Place)

Kensington Gardens

22 **℗**	Dame Anita Roddick (1942–2007), Businesswoman, environmentalist and human rights campaigner
27	Henry Solomon (1794–1844), Chief Officer of Police (see also Bartholomew Square)

Kensington Place

34 **℗**	Margaret (Peggy) Ramsay (1908–1991), Theatrical agent
44	William Moon (1818–1894), Inventor of typography for blind people (see also Queen's Road)

Kings Esplanade

4 St Aubyns Mansions **℗**	Dame Clara Butt (1872–1936), Singer (see also Adur Terrace, Southwick)
8 St Aubyns Mansions **℗**	Vesta Tilley (1864–1952), Music hall artiste

Kings Gardens, Hove

8   Edward VII (1841–1910), Monarch (see also Lewes Crescent)

Kings Road

Hotel Metropole	Graham Greene (1904–1991), Novelist (see also Old Steine)
Bedford Hotel (now site of Holiday Inn) **P**	Charles Dickens (1812–1870), Novelist (see also Lansdowne Place, Hove and Kings Road)
Bedford Hotel (now site of Holiday Inn)	John Leech (1817–1864), Illustrator (see also Lansdowne Place, Hove)
Bedford Hotel (now site of Holiday Inn) and Grand Hotel	Napoleon III (1808–1873), President of the Second French Republic and last French monarch
Old Ship Hotel	William Makepeace Thackeray (1811–1863), Novelist (see also East Street and Old Steine)
	Charles Dickens (1812–1870), Novelist (see also Lansdowne Road, Hove)
80 (now site of the Brighton Centre)	Robert Smith (RS) Surtees (1805–1864), Novelist
Lion Mansion Hotel (now west wing of Royal Albion Hotel, Old Steine) **P**	William Ewart Gladstone (1809–1898), Prime minister (see also Brunswick Square, Hove)
Norfolk Arms (site now the Mercure Brighton Seafront Hotel), 149 Kings Road),	Jane Elizabeth Digby, Lady Ellenborough (1807–1881), Aristocrat and adventuress
91 Embassy Court	Keith Waterhouse (1929–2009), Novelist, playwright and newspaper columnist
Regency House (now Regency Restaurant, 131)	Harriot Mellon, Duchess of St Albans (1777–1837), Actor and banker (see also Brunswick Terrace, Hove)
148	Charles Dickens (1812–1870), Novelist (see also Lansdowne Place, Hove)
Western House, 155 (now site of Embassy Court)	William Waldorf Astor, later Ist Viscount Astor (1848–1919), Newspaper proprietor and property owner

Lancaster Road

2	Louisa Martindale (1839–1914), Suffragist and feminist
	Louisa Martindale (1872–1966), Gynaecologist and feminist (see also Adelaide Crescent, Hove and Windlesham Road, Hove)

Lansdowne Place, Hove

2 **P**	CA Busby (1786–1834), Architect (see also Waterloo Place)
16 **P**	John Leech (1817–1864), Illustrator (see also Kings Road)
16 **P**	Charles Dickens (1812–1870), Novelist (see also Kings Road)
64	TP O'Connor (1848–1929), Journalist and MP (see also Marine Drive, Rottingdean)

Langdale Road, Hove

Springfields Nursing Home, 11	Dora Bryan (1923–2014), Actor and comedienne (see also Crescent Place and Marine Parade)

Lewes Crescent

1 (now Fife House)	William George Spencer Cavendish, 6th Duke of Devonshire (1790–1858), Whig grandee and connoisseur of the arts
	Edward VII (1841–1910), Monarch (see also Kings Gardens, Hove)
3	Sir Kingsley Wood (1881–1943), Politician
5b	Walter Sickert (1860–1942), Painter (see also Old Steine and Bear Road)
8	Marcus Cunliffe (1922–1990), Academic
13 **P**	Thomas Cubitt (1788–1855), Builder
17 **P**	Sir Elwyn Jones, later Baron Elwyn-Jones (1909–1989), Politician and lawyer
18 **P**	Sir Herbert Wilcox (1890–1977), Film producer and director and Dame Anna Neagle (1904–1986), Actor and film producer
19 **P**	Jack Buchanan (1891–1957), Actor and theatre manager
25 **P**	Penelope Lawrence (1856–1932), Dorothy Lawrence (1860–1933), and Millicent Lawrence (1863–1925), Founders of Roedean School (see also Arundel Terrace, Chesham Road and Sussex Square)

Little Crescent, Rottingdean

10	Fred Perry (1909–1995), Lawn tennis champion (see also Dean Court Road, Rottingdean and Newlands Road, Rottingdean)

London Road

61 (now The World's End pub)	Edward Bransfield (c. 1785–1852), Antarctic explorer (see also Clifton Street)
Withdean Hall, The Approach	Count Eric Stenbock (1860–1895), Poet and short story writer

Lorna Road

3 and 8 (now 87)	Richard Jefferies (1848–1887), Writer, novelist and mystic

Lower Rock Gardens

21	Aubrey Beardsley (1872–1898), Artist and illustrator (see also Buckingham Road)

Manchester Street

2	Eleanor Marx (1855–1898), Socialist revolutionary (see also Vernon Terrace)

Marine Drive, Rottingdean

6	TP O'Connor (1848–1929), Journalist and MP (see also Lansdowne Place, Hove)
Flat J, 14 Marine Gate	John Francis (Jack) Strachey (1894–1972), Popular composer
The Poet's House, 17	Sir William Watson (1858–1936), Poet and literary critic (see also High Street, Rottingdean)

Marine Gardens

14 **P** — Dame Flora Robson (1902–1984), Actor (see also Church Street and Dyke Road)

Marine Parade

Royal Crescent Mansions **P** — George Canning (1770–1827), Prime minister

48 **P** — Sir Samuel Brown (1776–1852), Civil engineer, naval officer and builder of the Brighton Chain Pier

58 — William IV (1765–1837), Monarch (see also Old Steine)

Bedford House, 79 **P** — Sir Terence Rattigan (1911–1977), Playwright

103 **P** — Sir Herbert Carden (1867–1941), Local politician and mayor of Brighton (see also West Hill Road)

Clarges Hotel, 115–119 (now apartments) — Dora Bryan (1923–2014), Actor and comedienne (see also Crescent Place and Langdale Road, Hove)

124 — Eddie Whaley (1877–1960), Comedian (see also Bear Road and Royal Crescent)

133 — William Holford, later Baron Holford (1907–1975), Architect and town planner

160 **P** — Max Miller (1894–1963), Comedian (see also Burlington Street and Herford Street)

Marine Square

11 — Blessed John Henry Newman, Cardinal Newman (1801–1889), Priest, theologian and cardinal

Medina Villas, Hove

8 — Charles Stewart Parnell (1846–1891), Irish Nationalist leader (see also Walsingham Terrace)

43 — Rabindrath Tagore (1861–1941), Poet, musician, novelist, painter, educationist and Nobel Laureate

Melville Road, Hove

'Rosedene', 7 — George Smith (1864–1959), Cinema pioneer and filmmaker (see also Roman Crescent, Southwick; Caburn Road, Hove; and Chanctonbury Road, Hove)

Middle Street

20 **P** — William Friese-Greene (1855–1921), Developer of the cinematograph (see also Worcester Villas, Portslade)

Mill Street, Falmer

The Mill House — Godfrey Winn (1908–1971), Journalist and writer

Montpelier Road

23 — Dr William King (1786–1865), Social reformer, Co-operative pioneer, physician and mathematician (see also Regency Square)

| 60 🅟 | Rev Frederick Robertson (1816–1853), Clergyman (see also Montpelier Terrace and Ship Street) |
| The Temple (now Brighton and Hove High School) 🅟 | Thomas Read Kemp (1782–1844), Property speculator (see also Sussex Square) |

Montpelier Terrace

| 1 🅟 | Ray Noble (1903–1978), Band leader and composer |
| 9 🅟 | Rev Frederick Robertson (1816–1853), Clergyman (see also Montpelier Road and Ship Street) |

Montpelier Villas

5	Ada Ellen Bayly (1857–1903), Novelist (writing as Edna Lyall)
17	Francis King (1923–2011), Novelist and critic
20	Gilbert Harding (1907–1960), Television personality

New Road

| 26 and 34 (26 is now the pub Mrs Fitzherbert's) | Mary Elizabeth Braddon (1835–1915), Author and actor |

New Church Road, Hove

| 8 Rutland Court | Sir George Robey (1869–1954), Comedian (see also Arundel Drive, Saltdean) |

Newlands Road, Rottingdean

| 24 | Fred Perry (1909–1995), Lawn tennis champion (see also Dean Court Road, Rottingdean and Little Crescent, Rottingdean) |

Nizells Avenue, Hove

| Flat 1, St Anne's Court 🅟 | Lord Alfred Douglas (1870–1945), Poet and lover of Oscar Wilde (see also Brunswick Square, Hove and Fourth Avenue) |

Norfolk Terrace

| 12 | Grace Eyre Woodhead (1864–1936), Philanthropist and social reformer (see also Compton Avenue) |

North Road

| 23 🅟 | Ken Fines (1923–2008), Planning officer (see also Northease Drive) |

North Street

| 20 (now the site of Huntingdon House) | Selina, Countess of Huntingdon (1707–1791), Religious reformer |
| 34 (gone) | Levy Emanuel Cohen (1796–1860), Newspaper editor and owner and social reformer (see also Clarence Square) |

Northease Drive

| 74 | Ken Fines (1923–2008), Planning officer |

Norton Road, Hove

59   George Augustus Sala (1828–1895), Journalist and writer (see also Eastern Terrace)

Old Steine

Royal Pavilion and Marlborough House   George IV (1762–1830), Monarch

Royal Pavilion and Royal York Hotel (nowYouth Hostel) **P**   William IV (1765–1837), Monarch (see also Marine Parade)

Royal Pavilion   Victoria (1819–1901), Monarch

Royal York Hotel, (now Youth Hostel)   William Makepeace Thackeray (1811–1863), Novelist (see also East Street and Kings Road)

Royal York Hotel (now Youth Hostel)   Arnold Bennett (1867–1931), Novelist

7   Walter Sickert (1860–1942), Painter (see also Bear Road and Lewes Crescent)

9 **P**   Charles-Maurice de Talleyrand-Périgord (1754–1838), Diplomat

20 **P**   Gideon Mantell (1790–1852), Surgeon and geologist

30 **P**   Sir Edward Marshall Hall (1858–1927), Barrister and MP

32 (gone) **P** (Royal Albion Hotel, Kings Road side)   Richard Russell (1687–1759), Physician

Royal Albion Hotel, 35   Graham Greene (1904–1991), Novelist (see also Kings Road)

55 **P** (now Youth Hostel)   Maria Fitzherbert (1756–1837), Morganatic wife of George IV (see also Bristol Road)

Oxford Street

15 **P**   John Saxby (1821–1913), Inventor and railway engineer (see also Brighton Railway Station and Buckingham Street)

Palmeira Avenue, Hove

13 **P**   Sir John Berry ('Jack') Hobbs (1882–1963), Surrey and England cricketer (see also Furze Hill, Hove)

Flat 1, 14 **P**   Victoria Lidiard (1889-1992), Suffragette

Park Crescent

4   Lewis Carroll (1832–1898), Writer, mathematician and photographer (see also Sussex Square)

7   Arnold Ruge (1802–1880), Writer and political thinker

Park Crescent Place

21   Chesney Allen (1893–1982), Comedian

Percival Terrace

3 **P**   Sir James Knowles (1831–1908), Architect and journal editor

5 **P**   Herbert Spencer (1820–1903), Philosopher, social theorist and sociologist

Pembroke Crescent, Hove
Redcliff   Edna Best (1900–1974), Actor (see also St Aubyns)

Preston Drove
Preston Manor   Sir Charles Thomas-Stanford (1858–1932), Politician

Preston Road
40   Magnus Volk (1851–1937), Electrical engineer and inventor (see also Western Road, Hove; Gloucester Place, Preston Street and Dyke Road)

Preston Street
51   Magnus Volk (1851–1937), Electrical engineer and inventor (see also Western Road, Hove; Gloucester Place, Preston Road and Dyke Road)

Prestonville Road
2   Eric Gill (1882–1940), Sculptor, typographer and wood engraver (see also Clifton Road, Hamilton Road and Highcroft Villas)
15   Sir Charles (CB) Cochran (1872–1951), Theatrical impresario

Queen's Road
104–109 (now site of Queensberry House) William Moon (1818–1894), Inventor of typography for blind people (see also Kensington Place)

Regency Square
2 **ⓟ**   Dr William King (1786–1865), Social reformer, Co-operative pioneer, physician and mathematician (see also Montpelier Road)
65–66 **ⓟ**   Sir Edwin Landseer (1802–1873), Animal painter and sculptor

Roman Crescent, Southwick
Laboratory Lodge (now The Cottage), 10   George Smith (1864–1959), Cinema pioneer and filmmaker (see also Caburn Road, Hove; Melville Road, Hove; and Chanctonbury Road, Hove)

Royal Crescent
4 **ⓟ**   Sir Laurence Olivier, later Baron Olivier (1907–1989), Actor and theatrical director
7   Sir John Clements (1910–1988), Actor and theatre manager, and Kay Hammond (1909–1980), Actor
12   Thomas Tanner (1824–1871), Doctor
13   Eddie Whaley (1877–1960), Comedian (see also Bear Road and Marine Parade)

Russell Square
36   Rev Richard Enraght (1837–1898), Clergyman and controversialist (see also Station Road, Portslade)

Sandgate Road

15 — Henry Salt (1851–1939), Social reformer, writer and classical scholar (see also Cleveland Road and Highdown Road)

Selbourne Road, Hove

27 — Sir C Aubrey Smith (1863–1948), Stage and film actor and Sussex and England cricketer (see also Albany Villas, Hove)

Ship Street

16 — Thomas Simpson (1825–1908), Architect (see also Connaught Road)

58 — Constance Garnett (1861–1946), Translator

Holy Trinity Church **P** — Rev Frederick Robertson (1816–1853), Clergyman (see also Montpelier Road and Montpelier Terrace)

Sillwood Road

11 **P** — John Constable (1776–1837), Painter

Station Road, Portslade

5 (formerly 5 Courtney Terrace) — Rev Richard Enraght (1837–1898), Clergyman and controversialist (see also Russell Square)

St Ann's Well Gardens

32 Furze Croft — Sir John Berry ('Jack') Hobbs (1882–1963), Surrey and England cricketer (see also Palmeira Avenue, Hove)

St Aubyns, Hove

2 (now Kingsway Hotel) — Edna Best (1900–1974), Actor (see also Pembroke Crescent)

St Nicholas Road

1 — Hector Bolitho (1897–1974), Writer

Steyning Road, Rottingdean

Half Way House — Maurice Baring (1874–1945), Novelist and poet

Surrenden Road

Varndean School for Boys (now Varndean School, Balfour Road) — Sir Paul Scofield (1922–2008), Actor

Sussex Square

11 **P** — Lewis Carroll (1832–1898), Writer, mathematician and photographer (see also Park Crescent)

13 — Sophia Jex-Blake (1840–1912), Doctor and campaigner for women's rights

14 **P** — Lord John Russell (1792–1878), Prime minister

18, Flat 3 — Gerald de Gaury MC (1897–1984), Diplomat, explorer, writer, soldier and Arabist

19–20	Frederick Hervey, 1st Marquess of Bristol and 5th Earl of Bristol (1768–1859), Politician and landowner and philanthropist
22 **P**	Thomas Read Kemp (1782–1844), Property speculator
35–37	Penelope Lawrence (1856–1932), Dorothy Lawrence (1860–1933), and Millicent Lawrence (1863–1925), Founders of Roedean School (see also Arundel Terrace, Chesham Road and Lewes Crescent)
39/40/40a	Vita Sackville-West (1892–1962), Writer and gardener and Lady Sackville (1862–1936), Aristocrat (see also The Cliff, Roedean)
46 **P**	Antony Dale (1912–1993), Historian and conservationist

Temple Gardens
The Old Vicarage **P**	Rev Henry Wagner (1792–1870), Clergyman and church builder and Rev Arthur Wagner (1824–1902), Clergyman and philanthropist
Belvedere (now site of Park Royal apartments, Montpelier Road **P**	Rev Arthur Wagner (1824–1902), Clergyman and philanthropist

The Cliff, Roedean
White Lodge, 40	Lady Sackville (1862–1936), Aristocrat (see also Sussex Square)

The Drive, Hove
20 **P**	Dame Ivy Compton-Burnett (1884–1969), Novelist

The Green, Rottingdean
The Elms **P**	Rudyard Kipling (1865–1936), Writer and poet
The Grange (now The Grange Museum and Art Gallery)	Rev Thomas Redman Hooker (1762–1838), Clergyman and headmaster
The Grange (now The Grange Museum and Art Gallery)	William Henry Fox Talbot (1800–1877), Pioneer of photography
The Grange (now The Grange Museum and Art Gallery)	Edward Bulwer-Lytton, later Baron Knebworth (1803–1873), Writer and politician
	Sir William Nicholson (1872–1949), Painter
North End House (now Aubrey House) **P**	Sir Edward Burne-Jones (1833–1898), Painter
North End House (now Aubrey House) **P**	Angela Thirkell (1890–1960), Novelist
North End House (now Aubrey House)	Sir William Nicholson (1872–1949), Painter
North End House (now Aubrey House) **P**	Enid Bagnold (1889–1981), Novelist and playwright

The Upper Drive, Hove
Convent of the Sacred Heart School (site now of Cardinal Newman School)	Clarissa Dickson Wright (1946–2014), Broadcaster, cook, barrister, writer and bookshop owner

Tisbury Road, Hove
78   Anthony Burgess (1917–1993), Novelist, critic and composer

Titchborne Street
🅿 on Guitar and Amp Shop,   Tom Sayers (1826–1865), English bare-knuckle champion boxer
79–80 North Road

Vernon Terrace
6 🅿   Eleanor Marx (1855–1898), Socialist revolutionary (see also
                                      Manchester Street)

Victoria Street
28   Alan Melville (1910–1983), Television and radio personality,
                                     writer and lyricist (see also Clifton Terrace)

Walsingham Terrace, Hove
10 (now site of Dorset Court,   Charles Stewart Parnell (1846–1891), Irish Nationalist leader
Kingsway) 🅿   (see also Medina Villas)

Warleigh Road
28 🅿   Maurice Tate (1895–1956), Sussex and England cricketer

Waterloo Place
11   CA Busby (1786–1834), Architect (see also Lansdowne Place,
                                     Hove)

Wellington Road, Portslade
163 (gone)   Edward Vaughan Kenealy (1818–1880), Barrister

Wentworth Street
10   Nancy Spain (1917–1964), Journalist, writer and television
                                     personality

West Street
77 🅿 (gone)   Samuel Johnson (1709–1784), Writer and lexicographer (see also
                                     Church Street)

77 🅿 (gone)   Hester Thrale (1741–1821), Writer

West Hill Road
19   Sir Herbert Carden (1867–1941), Local politician and mayor of
                                     Brighton (see Marine Parade)

West Hill Street
32   Jacqueline Nearne (1916–1982), Officer, Special Operations
                                     Executive

Western Road, Hove

Hampton Lodge (gone but was on land partly now the corner of Hampton Place and Western Road) — Henry Fauntleroy (1784–1824), Banker and forger

40 (now 35) — Magnus Volk (1851–1937), Electrical engineer and inventor (see also Preston Road, Preston Street, Gloucester Place and Dyke Road)

55 — James Williamson (1855–1933), Cinematic innovator, inventor and filmmaker (see also Cambridge Grove and Church Road)

140 **Ⓟ** — Sir Edward Codrington (1770–1851), Naval officer, commander of combined fleets at the Battle of Navarino and MP

Western Terrace, Hove

9 Western Pavilion **Ⓟ** — Amon Henry Wilds (baptised 1790–1857), Architect

Windlesham Road, Hove

Windlesham House (now site of York Mansions East) — Louisa Martindale (1872–1966), Gynaecologist and feminist (see also Adelaide Crescent, Hove and Lancaster Road)

Wish Road, Hove

45 **Ⓟ** — Dame Henrietta Barnett (1851–1936), Social reformer

Worcester Villas, Portslade

9 — William Friese-Greene (1855–1921), Developer of the cinematograph (see also Middle Street)

Wyndham Street

13 — Terence Morgan (1921–2005), Actor

York Place

York Place School (now Varndean School, Balfour Road) — Evelyn Laye (1900–1996), Actor and singer (see also Egremont Place)

Reading list

In researching this book, I have consulted or read a large number of books – from biographies and autobiographies to novels and guides – as well as the occasional newspaper and magazine article. Assisting much of this research has been the indispensable *Oxford Dictionary of National Biography*.

I have made use of the following:

Abbott, R, Brighton's Unofficial Queen, *The Tablet*, 1 September 2007

Ackroyd, P (2012), *Wilkie Collins*, London: Chatto & Windus

Alister, R (1949), *Friese-Greene: Close-Up of an Inventor*, New York: Marsland

Allen, DR (2005), *Sir Aubrey: A Biography of C. Aubrey Smith, England Cricketer, West End Actor, Hollywood Star*, Epsom: JW McKenzie

Andrews, M (2006), *Charles Dickens and His Reading Selves: Dickens and the Public Readings*, Oxford: Oxford University Press

Anonymous (2008), *Hilly Laine to Hanover: A Brighton Neighbourhood*, Brighton: Brighton Books Publishing

Arlott, J (1981), *Jack Hobbs: Profile of the Master*, London: John Murray/Davis-Poynter

Arnold, HJP (1977), *William Henry Fox Talbot: Pioneer of Photography and Man of Science*, London: Hutchinson Benham

Bagnold, E (1969), *Enid Bagnold's Autobiography*, London: Heinemann

Bakewell, M (1996), *Lewis Carroll: A Biography*, London: Heinemann

Barrow, K (1981), *Flora: An Appreciation of the Life and Work of Dame Flora Robson*, London: Heinemann

Bennett, A (1932), *The Journals of Arnold Bennett 1896–1910* (edited by Newman Flower), London: Cassell and Company

Bennett, A (1984), *The Journals* (selected and edited by Frank Swinnerton), London: Penguin Books

Bondfield, M (1948), *A Life's Work*, London: Hutchinson

Brady, LW and TP (1983), *O'Connor and the Liverpool Irish*, London: Royal Historical Society

Brodribb, G (1976), *Maurice Tate: A Biography*, London: London Magazine Editions Ltd.

Bresler, F (1999), *Napoleon III: A Life*, London: HarperCollins

Buczacki, S (2007), *Churchill and Chartwell: The Untold Story of Churchill's Houses and Gardens*, London: Frances Lincoln Ltd

Burgess, A (1987), *Little Wilson and Big God*, London: William Heinemann

Burgess, A (1990), *You've Had Your Time*, London: William Heinemann

Butler, Lord (1971), *The Art of the Possible*, London: Hamish Hamilton

Byng, D (1970), *As You Were*, London: Duckworth

Callow, S (2012), *Charles Dickens and the Great Theatre of the World*, London: Harper Press

Carder, T (1990), *The Encyclopaedia of Brighton*, Brighton: East Sussex County Record Office

Carpenter, E (1916), *My Days and Dreams*, London: George Allen & Unwin

Chambers, C (1997), *Peggy: The Life of Peggy Ramsay*, London: Nick Hern Books

Champneys, B (1915), *The Honourable Adelaide Drummond. Retrospect and Memoir*, London: Smith, Elder & Co

Chisholm, K (2011), *Wits & Wives. Dr Johnson in the Company of Women*, London: Chatto & Windus

Churchill, R (1966), *Winston S Churchill: Youth 1874–1900*, London: William Heinemann

Clifford, JL (1987), *Hester Lynch Piozzi (Mrs Thrale)*, Oxford: Oxford University Press

Coleman, T (2005), *Olivier*, London: Bloomsbury

Collis, R (1997), *A Trouser-Wearing Character: The Life and Times of Nancy Spain*, London: Cassell & Co.

Collis, R (2010), *The New Encyclopaedia of Brighton*, Brighton: Brighton and Hove Libraries

Collis, R, Peter Burton: Writer and Publisher who Championed Gay Literature for over 35 years, *The Independent*, 19 November, 2011

Cooper, D (2013), *Darling Monster. The Letters of Lady Diana Cooper to her Son, John Julius Norwich 1939–1952*, London: Chatto & Windus

Coppard, AE (1957), *It's Me, O Lord!*, York: Methuen and Co.

Copper, B (1971), *A Song for Every Season*, London: William Heinemann

Obituary: Nigel Nicolson, *The Daily Telegraph*, 24 September 2004

Dale, A (1947; 1987), *Fashionable Brighton 1820–1860*, London: Country Life; Oxford: Oriel Press

Dalyell, T, Obituary: Thomas Skeffington-Lodge, *The Independent*, 26 February, 1994

Darlow, M (2000), *Terence Rattigan: The Man and His Work*, London: Quartet Books

Dennison, M (2014), *Behind the Mask: The Secret Life of Vita Sackville-West*, London: William Collins

Dickson Wright, C (2007), *Spilling the Beans*, London: Hodder and Stoughton

Duncan, D (1908; 1996), *The Life and Letters of Herbert Spencer*, York: Methuen & Co; London: Routledge/Thoemmes Press

Drabble, M (1974), *Arnold Bennett*, London: Weidenfeld & Nicolson

Duran, L (1994), *Graham Greene, Friend and Brother*, London: HarperCollins

Eagle, D and Stephens, M (1992, 2nd edition), *The Oxford Illustrated Literary Guide to Great Britain and Ireland*, Oxford: Oxford University Press

Elleray, R (1987), *Brighton: A Pictorial History*, Stroud: Phillimore & Co.

Ellman, R (1984), *Oscar Wilde*, London: Hamish Hamilton

Faber, G (1933, 1974), *Oxford Apostles. A Character Study of the Oxford Movement*, London: Faber & Faber

Falk, Q (2000), *Travels in Greeneland. The Complete Guide to the Cinema of Graham Greene*, London: Reynolds & Hearn

Faulkenburg Thomas, M (2001), *Victorian Conscience: F.W. Robertson*, New York: Peter Lang Publishing

Fawkes, R (1979), *Dion Boucicault: A Biography*, London: Quartet Books

Fisher, D (2012), *Cinema-by-Sea. Film and Cinema in Brighton and Hove since 1896*, Brighton: Terra Media

Garnett, R (1991), *Constance Garnett. A Heroic Life*, London: Sinclair-Stevenson

Gilbert, Edmund M (1975), *Brighton: Old Ocean's Bauble*, Hassocks: Flare Books

Glendinning, V (1983), *Vita: The Life of V. Sackville-West*, London: Penguin Books

Granger, D, Obituary: Robert Flemyng, *The Independent*, 24 May 1995

Greene, G (1969), *Travels with My Aunt,* London: The Bodley Head

Greene, G (1971), *A Sort of Life*, London: The Bodley Head

Greene, G (1981), *Ways of Escape*, London: Penguin Books

Greenslade, R, Letters (Obituaries: Kay Dick), *The Guardian*, 25 October 2001

Greer, D (editor) (1978), *Hamilton Harty: His Life and Music*, Belfast: Blackstaff Press

Grenell, S (editor) (1961), *Gilbert Harding by his Friends*, London: Andre Deutsch

Hamilton, MA (1924), *Margaret Bondfield*, London: Leonard Parsons

Harding, J (1956), *Prime Minister of Mirth. The Biography of Sir George Robey CBE*, London: Odhams Press

Harding, J (1988), *Cochran*, York: Methuen &Co

Hastings, S (2009), *The Secret Lives of Somerset Maugham*, London: John Murray

Heater, D (1993), *The Remarkable History of Rottingdean*, Brighton: Dyke Publications

Henderson, J (2009), *The Last Champion. The Life of Fred Perry*, London: Yellow Jersey Press

Hey, C (1989), *Rowland Hill: Victorian Genius and Benefactor*, Shrewsbury: Quiller Press

Hibbert, C (1976), *Edward VII*, London: Allen Lane,

Hinde, W (1973), *George Canning*, London: Collins

Holmes, R (2014), *Eleanor Marx. A Life*, London: Bloomsbury

Hordern, M, with England, P (1993), *A World Elsewhere*, London: Michael O'Mara Books

Howard, A (1987), *RAB. The Life of R.A. Butler*, London: Jonathan Cape

Hunt, K, Bob Copper (obituary), *The Independent*, 1 April 2004

Jackson, S (2012), *Death by Chocolate. The Serial Poisoning of Victorian Brighton*, Stroud: Fonthill Media

Jenkins, R (2002), *Gladstone*, London: Pan Books

de Joinville, Prince (1894), *Vieux Souvenirs*, London: Macmillan and Co.

Jones, N (1991), *Through A Glass Darkly. The Life of Patrick Hamilton*, London: Abacus

Kapp, Y (1972), *Eleanor Marx. Volume 1: Family Life (1855–1883)*, London: Lawrence and Wishart

Kee, R (1993), *The Laurel and the Ivy: The Story of Charles Stewart Parnell and Irish Nationalism*, London: Hamish Hamilton

Ker, I (2009), *John Henry Newman: A Biography*, Oxford: Oxford University Press

King, F (1993), *Yesterday Came Suddenly. An Autobiography*, London: Constable

Kipling, R (2008), *Something of Myself*, Ware: Wordsworth Editions

Kripalani, K (1971), *Tagore: A Life*, Self-published

Langfield, V (2002), *Roger Quilter: His Life and Music*, Martelsham: The Boydell Press

Lawday, D (2006), *Napoleon's Master: A Life of Prince Talleyrand*, London: Jonathan Cape

Lester Browne, V (2004), *Phiz: The Man Who Drew Dickens*, London: Chatto & Windus

Letley, E (1991), *Maurice Baring. A Citizen of Europe*, London: Constable

Longford, E (1964), *Victoria RI*, London: Weidenfeld & Nicolson

Mackenzie, J (editor), *Letters of George Augustus Sala to Edmund Yale*, Brisbane: Department of English, University of Queensland

Magus, P (1964), *King Edward the Seventh*, London: John Murray

Maitland, S (1988), *Vesta Tilley*, London: Virago Press

Marjoribanks, E (1972; 1929), *The Life of Sir Edward Marshall Hall*, Bath: Cedric Chivers; London: Gollancz

Martindale, H (1944), *From One Generation to Another, 1839–1944. A Book of Memories*, London: G Allen & Unwin

Martindale, L (1951), *A Woman Surgeon*, London: Gollancz

McCabe, J (1908), *Life and Letters of George Jacob Holyoake. Volume 11*, London: Watts & Co

McCarthy, F (1989), *Eric Gill*, London: Faber & Faber

Meyer Grosvenor, M, Bob Copper (obituary), *The Guardian*, 3 April 2004

Middleton, J (2001), *Encyclopaedia of Hove and Portslade, Volume 1*, Self-published

Miller, MA (1976), *Kropotkin*, Chicago: University of Chicago Press

Moss, R (2010), Tracing the Brighton line, *The Tablet*, 11 September 2010

Murray, D (2000), *Bosie: A Biography of Lord Alfred Douglas*, London: Hodder & Stoughton

Musgrave, C (1970), *Life in Brighton*, London: Faber and Faber

Nelson, JG (1966), *Sir William Watson*, Woodbridge: Twayne Publishers

Neumann Rayford, B (1978), *Robert Smith Surtees*, Woodbridge: Twayne Publishers

Nicholl, C, The Scholar tramp, *Guardian Review*, 12 April 2014

Nicolson, H (edited by Nicolson, N) (1966), *Diaries and Letters 1930–1939*, London: Collins

Nicolson, N (1974), *Portrait of a Marriage*, Leander: Futura Publishing

Nicolson, N (1997), *A Long Life*, London: Weidenfeld & Nicolson

Nokes, D (2009), *Samuel Johnson. A Life*, London: Faber & Faber

Oakensen, DJ (1994), *The Origins and Development of Policing in Brighton and Hove, 1830–1900*, Unpublished PhD thesis: University of Brighton

Palmer, A (1972), *Metternich*, London: Weidenfeld & Nicolson

Paprocki Beck, S (2010), *Anita Roddick*, New York: Chelsea House Publishers

Perry, F (1984), *An Autobiography*, London: Hutchinson

Powell, WR (2001), *John Horace Round. Historian and Gentleman of Essex*, Chelmsford: Essex Record Office

Pulsifer, G, Peter Burton: Writer and pioneer of gay journalism (obituary), *The Guardian*, 8 November 2011

Ratcliffe, M, Letters (Obituaries: Kay Dick), *The Guardian*, 25 October 2001

Reyburn, W (1978), *Gilbert Harding: A Candid Portrait*, Sydney: Angus & Robertson

Ridley, J (1979), *Napoleon III and Eugenie*, London: Constable

Roberts, S (1993), *Sophia Jex-Blake. A Woman Pioneer in Nineteenth Century Medical Reform*, London: Routledge

Sala, GA, *The Life and Adventures of George Augustus Sala*, London: Cassell & Company

Schlicke, P (editor) (2011), *The Oxford Companion to Charles Dickens*, Oxford: Oxford University Press

Sebba, A (1986), *Enid Bagnold. The Authorised Biography*, London: Weidenfeld & Nicolson

Shannon, R (1999), *Gladstone: Peel's Inheritor 1809–1865*, London: Penguin Books

Shannon R (1999), *Gladstone: Heroic Minister 1865–1898*, London: Allen Lane, The Penguin Press

Shelden, M (1994), *Graham Greene: The Man Within*, London: Heinemann

Sherry, N (2004), *The Life of Graham Greene. Volume Three: 1955–1991*, London: Jonathan Cape

Slater, M (2011), *Charles Dickens*, Yale: Yale University Press

Somerset, A (1980), *The Life and Times of William IV*, London: Weidenfeld & Nicolson

Speaight, R (1966), *The Life of Eric Gill*, York: Methuen

Spurling, H (1995), *The Life of I. Compton-Burnett*, London: Richard Cohen Books

Stansfield, S, The Dodgson sisters, *The Carrollian* (journal of the Lewis Carroll Society), No 2, Autumn, 1998

Stenlake, F (1999), *From Cuckfield to Camden Town: The Story of the Artist Robert Bevan*, Cuckfield: Cuckfield Museum

Storey, G and Fielding, KJ (editors) (1981), *The Letters of Charles Dickens. Volume Five 1847–1849*, Oxford: Clarendon Press

Storey, G, Tillotson, K and Briggs, N (editors) (1988), *The Letters of Charles Dickens. Volume Six 1850–1852*, Oxford: Clarendon Press

Storey, G, Tillotson, K and Easson, A, (editors) (1993), *The Letters of Charles Dickens Volume Seven 1853–1855*, Oxford: Clarendon Press

Sturgis, M (1998), *Aubrey Beardsley: A Biography,* London: Harper Collins

Sturgis, M (2005), *Walter Sickert: A Life*, London: Harper Perennial

Summerscale, K (2008), *The Suspicions of Mr Witcher*, London: Bloomsbury

Taylor, DJ (1999), *Thackeray*, London: Chatto & Windus

Taylor, DJ, Francis King: Novelist and Man of Letters who specialised in depicting characters thrown together, but who longed to break free, *The Independent*, 26 July 2011

Thesiger, W (1987), *The Life of My Choice*, London: Collins

Thirkell, A (1931; 1970), *Three Houses*, Oxford: Oxford University Press; Leeds: Morley Baker

Thomas, D (1974), *Cardigan: The Hero of Balaklava*, London: Routledge & Kegan Paul

Thomas, M (2008), *The Diary: Sex, Death, and God in the Affairs of a Victorian Cleric*, Bloomington, Ind: Authorhouse

Thornton, M, Edith Bagnold: The Fascinating First Lady of a Gilded Dynasty, *The Daily Telegraph*, 27 April 2012

Todd, M (1918), *The Life of Sophia Jex-Blake*, London: Macmillan & Co

Toibin, C (2010), *Love in a Dark Time: Gay Lives from Wilde to Almodovar*, London: Picador

Tomalin, C (2011), *Charles Dickens: A Life*, London: Viking

Tsuzuki, C (1967), *The Life of Eleanor Marx 1855–1898. A Socialist Tragedy*, Oxford: Clarendon Press

Volk, C (1971), *Magnus Volk of Brighton*, Stroud: Phillimore

Weintraub, S (1967), *Beardsley: A Biography*, London: W.H. Allen

Westwood, L (2007), Care in the Community for the Mentally Disordered: The case of the Guardianship Society 1900–1939, *Social History of Medicine*, Vol 20, No 1, pp 57–72

Wheen, F (1999), *Karl Marx*, London: Fourth Estate

Wilcox, H (1967), *Twenty Five Thousand Sunsets*, London: The Bodley Head

Wilson Moorcroft, J (1981), *I Was an English Poet: A Critical Biography of Sir William Watson (1858–1936)*, London: Cecil Woolf

Wolff Lee, R (1979), *Sensational Victorian: The Life and Fiction of Mary Elizabeth Braddon*, New York: Garland Publishing

Woodcock, G and Avakumovit, I (1950), *The Anarchist Prince. A Biographical Study of Peter Kropotkin*, TW Boardman & Co

Woodham-Smith, C (1972), *Queen Victoria: Her Life and Times, 1819–1861*, London: Hamish Hamilton

Woolf, J (2010), *The Mystery of Lewis Carroll. Understanding the Author of Alice in Wonderland,* London: Haus

Ziegler, P (1971), *King William IV*, London: Cassell Publishers

Ziegler, P (2013), *Olivier*, London: Maclehose Press

The following websites have also proven helpful:

The Bioscope (www.thebioscope.net)

www.brightonfilm.com

Brighton and Hove Black History Society (www.black-history.org.uk)

www.brightonourstory.co.uk

www.openplaques.org

www.mybrightonandhove.org.uk

The Regency Society (www.regencysociety.org)

www.visitbrighton.com

www.brightonhistory.org.uk

MercureBrighton Seafront

A unique 4 star hotel set on Brighton's elegant regency seafront overlooking the promenade, this impresive hotel has a wide range of facilities.

With 116 en suite bedrooms and 6 meeting rooms the hotel is ideal for both leisure and corporate needs. With a stunning regency insipred ballroom the hotel also makes a superb Wedding venue.

Mercure Brighton Seafront Hotel
0844 815 9061
sales.mercurebrightonseafront@jupiterhotels.co.uk

www.mercurebrighton.co.uk

Mercure
HOTELS